NEW CENTURY BIBLE COMMENTARY

Based on the Revised Standard Version

The Johannine Epistles

KENNETH GRAYSTON

Emeritus Professor of Theology
University of Bristol

WM. B. EERDMANS PUBL. CO., GRAND RAPIDS

MARSHALL, MORGAN & SCOTT PUBL. LTD., LONDON

P9-BJA-145

Grayston, Kenneth.

BS
2805.3   The Johannine E-
.G76   pistles
1984

56, 366

© Marshall Morgan & Scott 1984
First published 1984

All rights reserved

Printed in the United States of America
for
Wm. B. Eerdmans Publishing Company
255 Jefferson Ave. S.E., Grand Rapids, Mich. 49503
and
Marshall Morgan & Scott
3 Beggarwood Lane, Basingstoke, Hants, UK.
ISBN 0 551 01089 4

Library of Congress Cataloging in Publication Data

Grayston, Kenneth.
The Johannine Epistles.

(New Century Bible commentary)
Bibliography: p. xiii
Includes indexes.
1. Bible. N.T. Epistles of John — Commentaries.
I. Title. II. Series.
BS2805.3.G76   1984   227'.9407   83-16291

ISBN 0-8028-1981-8

The Bible text in this publication is from the Revised Standard Version of the Bible, copyrighted 1946 and 1953 by the Division of Christian Education, National Council of the Churches of Christ, and used by permission.

NEW CENTURY BIBLE
COMMENTARY

General Editors

RONALD E. CLEMENTS   MATTHEW BLACK
(Old Testament)   (New Testament)

The Johannine
Epistles

THE NEW CENTURY BIBLE COMMENTARIES

CONTENTS

CAMROSE LUTHERAN COLLEGE
LIBRARY

PREFACE

At the present time, Johannine scholarship is very fruitful but to some extent it relies on commonly accepted results which need re-examination. In the course of attempting an exegesis of the Johannine epistles I have been led to reformulate some agreed views in this field, but never without respect for other commentators with whom I have come to disagree. From their scholarship and judgments I have constantly received profit. In writing out my exegesis I have not assumed that most readers will know Greek, but that some will, and so I have included references to transliterated Greek and to grammatical points. I have not reserved these matters for separate notes because readers ought to realise that what they are trying to understand depends on the meaning of language, grammar, and the significance of words. I have often written out quotations in some fullness—from elsewhere in the Bible and from other primary sources—because readers seldom look up references and often cannot consult non-biblical texts. If quotations are worth making at all, they ought to be easily present to the reader's eye. Commentaries have various uses: some to provide information, some to survey existing studies, some to give critical support to a confessional position, and so on. The aim of this commentary is, if possible, to involve the reader in the effort of trying to understand some New Testament writings in their appropriate cultural situation. There are doubtless theological judgments which follow as a consequence and have a bearing on the religious convictions of the readers of the commentary. But the commentator need not be a preacher or a moralist: if he has done his work adequately, his readers will themselves perceive questions of faith and morals. I have written an introduction because it is expected, and because the reader deserves to know whether the commentator has been able to make up his mind about questions raised by the text. But, of course, Charles Cranfield is entirely right when, on the first page of his commentary on Romans, he indicates that the correct place for an author's opinions is at the end. At least I may claim that the introduction cannot be separated from the exegesis which I hope justifies it.

ACKNOWLEDGMENTS

I acknowledge with gratitude the patience and encouragement of the New Testament Editor who invited me to write this contribution to the series; the skill and care of Mrs Ann Cade's typing; and my wife's invaluable help in reading the proofs and in compiling and checking the indexes.

LISTS OF ABBREVIATIONS

BIBLICAL

OLD TESTAMENT (*OT*)

Gen.	Jg.	1 Chr.	Ps.	Lam.	Ob.	Hag.
Exod.	Ru.	2 Chr.	Prov.	Ezek.	Jon.	Zech.
Lev.	1 Sam.	Ezr.	Ec.	Dan.	Mic.	Mal.
Num.	2 Sam.	Neh.	Ca.	Hos.	Nah.	
Dt.	1 Kg.	Est.	Isa.	Jl	Hab.	
Jos.	2 Kg.	Job	Jer.	Am.	Zeph.	

APOCRYPHA (*Apoc.*)

1 Esd.	Tob.	Ad. Est.	Sir.	S 3 Ch.	Bel	1 Mac.
2 Esd.	Jdt.	Wis.	Bar.	Sus.	Man.	2 Mac.
			Ep. Jer.			

NEW TESTAMENT (*NT*)

Mt.	Ac.	Gal.	1 Th.	Tit.	1 Pet.	3 Jn
Mk	Rom.	Eph.	2 Th.	Phm.	2 Pet.	Jude
Lk.	1 C.	Phil.	1 Tim.	Heb.	1 Jn	Rev.
Jn	2 C.	Col.	2 Tim.	Jas.	2 Jn	

DEAD SEA SCROLLS (*DSS*)

CD	Fragments of a Zadokite Work (Damascus Document)
1QH	Hymns of Thanksgiving
1QS	Rule of the Community (Manual of Discipline)

OTHER JEWISH WRITINGS

Aboth	Tractate of the Mishnah
Apoc. Mos.	*Apocalypse of Moses*, in K. von Tischendorf, *Apocalypses Apocryphae* (Hildesheim, 1866, rp 1966)
b *Tem.*	Tractate *Temurah* in Babylonian Talmud
1 En.	*1 Enoch*, in R. H. Charles, *The Apocrypha and Pseudepigrapha of the Old Testament*, Vol. II (Oxford, 1913)
Jos. *Ant.*	Josephus, *Antiquities*—*see* Bibliography
Jub.	*Jubilees*, in Charles (as above)

Ps. Sol.	*Psalms of Solomon*, in H. R. Ryle and M. R. James, *Psalmoi Solomontos* (Cambridge, 1891)
Rabb. Anth.	*Rabbinic Anthology*—see Bibliography
Test.	*Testaments of the Twelve Patriarchs*, in Charles (as above)
Zadokite Documents	*see* Rabin in the Bibliography

GENERAL

AGB	*A Greek-English Lexicon of the New Testament.* ed. by W. F. Arndt and F. W. Gingrich, from W. Bauer's *Wörterbuch* (Chicago and Cambridge, 1957)
Apost. Trad.	Hippolytus, *Apostolic Traditions*
AV	*Authorised (King James') Version*
BDF	*A Greek Grammar of the New Testament*, a revision of Blass-Debrunner, ed. by R. W. Funk (Cambridge and Chicago, 1961)
CE, BCE	Common Era, Before the Common Era: used for dating Jewish writings in preference to the Christian conventions AD and BC
CH	*Corpus Hermeticum*
ET	*English Translation*
Eusebius, *H.E.*	*Ecclesiastical History*
EV	*Gospel of Truth*
Exc. Theod.	Clement of Alexandria, *Excerpta ex Theodoto*
ExpT	*Expository Times*
GCS	*Griechische Christliche Schriftsteller*
GNB	*Good News Bible* (The Bible Societies and Collins, 1976)
Ign. *Eph.*	Ignatius, *Letter to the Ephesians*
Mag.	*Letter to the Magnesians*
Philad.	*Letter to the Philadelphians*
Smyr.	*Letter to the Symrnaeans*
Trall.	*Letter to the Trallians*
Irenaeus, *A.H.*	*Against the Heresies*
JB	*Jerusalem Bible* (London, 1966)
JSNT	*Journal for the Study of the New Testament*
JTS	*Journal of Theological Studies*
Knox	*The New Testament . . . translated from the Vulgate Latin*, by R. A. Knox (London, 1945).
Mart. Polyc.	*Martyrdom of Polycarp.*
Metzger	*A Textual Commentary on the Greek New Testament*, by B. M. Metzger (United Bible Societies, 1971)

MHT	*A Grammar of New Testament Greek* (Edinburgh)
	Vol. 1 by J. H. Moulton (^{3}1919)
	Vol. 2 by J. H. Moulton and W. F. Howard (1929)
	Vols 3 and 4 by N. Turner (1963, 1976)
MM	*Vocabulary of the Greek New Testament . . . from the Papyri*, by J. H. Moulton and G. Milligan (London, 1930)
MTZ	*Münchener Theologische Zeitschrift*
NEB	*New English Bible*, New Testament (Oxford and Cambridge, ^{2}1970)
Nestle-Aland	*Novum Testamentum Graece* (Stuttgart, ^{26}1979)
NIV	*Holy Bible: New International Version* (London, 1978)
NTAF	*The New Testament in the Apostolic Fathers*, (Committee of the Oxford Society of Historical Theology, Oxford, 1905)
NTS	*New Testament Studies*
ODCC	*Oxford Dictionary of the Christian Church*, ed. F. L. Cross and E. A. Livingstone (Oxford, ^{2}1974)
PGL	*Patristic Greek Lexicon*, by G. W. H. Lampe (Oxford, 1961–68)
Or.	Gregory of Nazianzus, *Five Theological Orations*
RSV	*Holy Bible: Revised Standard Version* (New York and Glasgow, 1973)
SB	*Kommentar zum Neuen Testament aus Talmud und Midrasch*, by H. L. Strack and P. Billerbeck, 6 vols (Munich, 1922–63)
SOED	*Shorter Oxford English Dictionary*
Strom.	Clement of Alexandria, *Stromateis*
s.v.	sub voce, i.e. under the appropriate word
TU	*Texte und Untersuchungen*
TWNT	*Theologisches Wörterbuch zum Neuen Testament*, ed. G. Kittel and G. Friedrich, 10 vols (Stuttgart, 1933–79). Those who use the ET by G. W. Bromiley (*Theological Dictionary of the New Testament*, Grand Rapids, 1964–76) will have little difficulty in finding the corresponding references.
UBS	*The Greek Testament* (United Bible Societies, ^{3}1975)
ZTK	*Zeitschrift für Theologie und Kirche*

SELECT BIBLIOGRAPHY

COMMENTARIES

The transition from the older to the modern phase of commentaries on the Epistles of John was marked by Dodd's commentary in 1946. It is very readable, and deserves to be read for its civilised presentation of the thought of the epistles in their hellenistic culture. Behind all more recent exegesis, however, lies Schnackenburg's immensely learned and thorough German commentary (^{3}1965), though it now needs to be studied in relation to his developing thought about the Gospel. Bruce's commentary (1970), intended for the general reader, contains careful judgments based on unobtrusive scholarship. Bultmann's commentary (which demands knowledge of Greek in its readers) appeared in English translation in 1973; it is essential reading in any serious study of thought, structure, and religious affiliations. In the same year appeared Houlden's concise and firmly argued commentary which is notable, on the British scene, for relating the Epistles to a conjectured history of the Johannine community. Marshall's commentary (1978) is a very careful survey of recent scholarly work and how it may be assessed. It contains what every serious student needs to know and, in the main text, does not require knowledge of Greek. Brown's massive commentary (1983), running to more than eight hundred pages, offers the fullest discussion relating to the Johannine Epistles and a full expansion of the views put forward in his smaller study of the Johannine community. The present writer, however, does not cede the position taken up in this commentary.

SELECT BIBLIOGRAPHY

References in the text may be identified by the author's surname and, if necessary, by the year of publication of his work.

Barret, C. K. *The Gospel according to St John* (London, ²1978)
  Essays on John (London, 1982) 'Jews and Judaizers in the Epistles of Ignatius', in *Jews, Greeks and Christians*, ed. R. Hamerton-Kelly and R. Suggs (Leiden, 1976).
Bauer, W. *Orthodoxy and Heresy in Earliest Christianity* (London, 1972; ET of 2nd German edition of 1964)
Becker, J. 'Die Abschiedsreden Jesu in Johannes-evangelium', *ZNW* 61 (1970), pp. 215–46
Betz, H. D. *Plutarch's Ethical Writings and Early Christian Literature* (Studia ad Corpus Hellensticium Novi Testamenti, Vol. IV) (Leiden, 1978)
Black, M. *The Scrolls and Christian Origins* (Edinburgh, 1961)
Bogart, J. *Orthodox and Heretical Perfectionism in the Johannine Community as evident in the First Epistle of John*, SBL Dissertation Series 33 (Missoula, 1977)
Boismard, M.-E. 'The First Epistle of John and the Writings of Qumran', pp. 156–65 in *John and Qumran*, ed. J. H. Charlesworth (London, 1972).
Boulay, J. du *Portrait of a Greek Mountain Village* (Oxford, 1974)
Braun, H. 'Literaranalyse und theologische Schichtung im ersten Johannesbrief', *ZTK* 48 (1951), pp. 262–92
Brooke, A. E. *A Critical and Exegetical Commentary on the Johannine Epistles* (Edinburgh, 1912)
Brown, R. E. *The Gospel according to John I-XII* (New York, 1966); *XIII-XXI* (London, 1971)
  The Community of the Beloved Disciple (London, 1979)
  The Epistles of John (London, 1983)
Bruce, F. F. *The Epistles of John* (London, 1970)
Bultmann, R. *The Johannine Epistles* (Philadelphia, 1973; ET of German 2nd edition, 1967)
Chadwick, H. *The Sentences of Sextus* (Cambridge, 1959)
Conzelmann, H. 'Was von Anfang war', *Neutestamentliche Studien für R. Bultmann* (Berlin, 1954)
Danby, H. *The Mishnah* (Oxford, 1933)
Davies, W. D. *Christian Origins and Judaism* (London, 1962)

Derrett, J. D. M. *Law in the New Testament* (London, 1970)
    Jesus's Audience (London, 1973)
Didache *Ancient Christian Writers*, No. 6, ed. J. A. Kleist (Maryland and London, 1948)
Dix, G. *The Treatise on the Apostolic Tradition of St Hippolytus of Rome* (London, 1937)
Dodd, C. H. *The Bible and the Greeks* (London, 1935)
    The Johannine Epistles (London, 1946)
Ehrhardt, A. *The Beginning* (Manchester, 1968)
Feuillet, A 'Les Épîtres Johanniques', in *Introduction a la Bible* II ed. A. Robert et A. Feuillet (Tournai, 1959)
Fitzmyer, J. A. *Essays on the Semitic Background of the New Testament* (London, 1971)
Foerster, W. *Gnosis* I and II (Oxford, 1972 and 1974), ET ed. R. McL. Wilson
Gaster, T. H. *The Scriptures of the Dead Sea Sect* (London, 1957)
Gerhardsson, B. *Memory and Manuscript* (Lund, 1961)
Goodenough, E. R. *By Light, Light* (Newhaven, 1935; rp Amsterdam, 1969)
    An Introduction to Philo (Oxford, ²1962)
Grayston, K. 'The Meaning of PARAKLĒTOS', *JSNT* 13 (1981), pp. 67–82
    'ΙΛΑΣΚΕΣΘΑΙ and related words in LXX', *NTS* 27 (1981), pp. 640–56
Grese, W. C. *Corpus Hermeticum XIII and Early Christian Literature*, Studia ad Corpus Hellenisticum Novi Testamenti, Vol. 5 (Leiden, 1979)
Hackforth, R. *Plato's Phaedrus* (Cambridge, 1952)
Harnack, A. von 'Über den dritten Johannesbrief', *TU* 15.3 (Leipzig, 1897)
Harvey, A. E. *Jesus on Trial* (London, 1976)
    Jesus and the Constraints of History (London, 1982)
Hengel, M. *The Atonement* (London, 1981)
Hennecke, E. *New Testament Apocrypha* I and II (London, 1963, 1965) ed. W. Schneemelcher; ET ed. R. McL. Wilson
Hill, D. *Greek Words and Hebrew Meanings* (Cambridge, 1967)
    New Testament Prophecy (London, 1979)
Houlden, J. L. *A Commentary on the Johannine Epistles* (London, 1973)
Howard, W. F. *The Fourth Gospel in Recent Criticism and Interpretation*, rev. by C. K. Barrett (London, 1955)
Jones, P. R. 'A Structural Analysis of 1 John', *Review & Expositor* 57 (1970), pp. 433–44
Jonge, M. de 'The Use of the Word ΧΡΙΣΤΟΣ in the Johannine

Epistles', in *Studies in John*, Sevenster *Festschrift*, *Supplement to Novum Testamentum* (Leiden, 1970)

Jonge, M. de, and Woude, A. S. von der '11Q Melchizedek and the New Testament', *NTS* 12 (1965–6), pp. 301–26

Josephus Loeb Edition (London and Cambridge, Mass., 1930–43 and reprints)

Käsemann, E. 'Ketzer und Zeuge: zum johanneischen Verfasserproblem', *ZTK* 48 (1957), pp. 292–311, reprinted in *Exegetische Versuche und Besinnungen I* (Göttingen, 1960), with some modifications in *II* (Göttingen, 1964), p. 133, n. 1
The Testament of Jesus (London, 1968)

Kelly, J. N. D. *A Commentary on the Epistles of Peter and Jude* (London, 1969)

Kilpatrick, G. D. 'What John tells us about John', in *Studies in John*, Sevenster *Festschrift*, *Supplement to Novum Testamentum* (Leiden, 1970)

Klein, G. 'Das wahre Licht scheint schon. Beobachtungen zur Zeit- und Geschichtserfahrung einer urchristlichen Schule', *ZTK* 68 (1971), pp. 231–326.

Knox, R. A. *The New Testament . . . newly translated from the Vulgate Latin* (London, 1945)

Kümmel, W. G. *Introduction to the New Testament* Revised edition (London, 1975), ET of 17th German edition 1973.

Lampe, G. W. H. *The Seal of the Spirit* (London, ²1967)

Law, R. *The Tests of Life* (Edinburgh, 1909)

Leaney, A. R. C. *The Rule of Qumran and its Meaning* (London, 1966)

Lightfoot, J. B. *The Apostolic Fathers II: Ignatius and Polycarp*, (London, 1889)

Lindars, B. *The Gospel of John* (London, 1972)

Lohse, E. *Colossians and Philemon* (Philadelphia, 1971) ET of German edition 1968

Malatesta, E. *Interiority and Covenant: A study of* einai en *and* menein en *in the First Letter of Saint John* (Rome, 1978)

Manson, T. W. 'Entry into Membership of the Early Church', *JTS* 48 (1947), pp. 25ff.

Marshall, I. H. *The Epistles of John* (Grand Rapids, 1978)

Martin, R. P. *Colossians* (Exeter, 1972)

Ménard, J.-E. *L'Évangile selon Philippe* (Strasbourg, 1967)
L'Évangile selon Thomas (Leiden, 1975)
L'Authentikos Logos (Quebec, 1977)

Metzger, B. M. *A Textual Commentary on the Greek New Testament* (London and New York, 1971)

Meyer, M. W. (Ed.) *The Nag Hammadi Library in English* (Leiden, 1971)

Mitchell, L. L. *Baptismal Anointing* (London, 1966)

Moffatt, J. *The New Testament—a New Translation* New edition revised (London, 1934)

Moule, C. F. D. *The Origin of Christology* (Cambridge, 1977)

Nauck, W. *Die Tradition und der Character des ersten Johannesbriefes* (Tübingen, 1957)

O'Neill, J. C. *The Puzzle of I John* (London, 1966)

Philo Loeb Edition (London and Cambridge, Mass., 1929–43, and reprints)

Philonenko, M. *Joseph et Asénath*. Studia Post-biblica XIII (Leiden, 1968)

Pratscher, W. 'Gott ist grösser als unser Herz', *TZ* 32 (1976), pp. 272–81

Price, J. L. 'Light from Qumran on Some Aspects of Johannine Theology', in *John and Qumran*, ed. J. H. Charlesworth (London, 1972)

Rabbinic Anthology ed. C. G. Montefiore and H. Loewe (London, 1938; reprinted New York, Philadelphia, 1960).

Rabin, C. *The Zadokite Documents* (Oxford, ²1958)

Riches, J. *Jesus and the Transformation of Judaism* (London, 1980)

Richter, G. 'Die Fusswaschung Joh 13:1–20', *MTZ* 16 (1965), pp. 13–26

Rigaux, B. *L'Antéchrist et l'opposition au Royaume Messianique dans l'Ancient et le Nouveau Testament* (Gembloux, 1932)

Robertson, A. T. *A Grammar of the Greek New Testament in the Light of Historical Research* (London, ³1919)

Robinson, J. A. T. 'The Destination and Purpose of the Johannine Epistles', *NTS* 7 (1960–1), pp. 55–65; reprinted in *Twelve New Testament Studies* (London, 1962)

Sanders, E. P. *Paul and Palestinian Judaism* (London, 1977)

Schnackenburg, R. *Die Johannesbriefe* (Freiburg, ³1963)
 Das Johannesevangelium III (Freiburg, 1975) ET London 1982

Schweizer, E. 'Der Kirchenbegrift im Evangelium und den Briefen des Johannes', *Neotestamentica*, pp. 254–71 (Zurich, 1963)

Segovia, F. F. *AGAPE/AGAPAN in I John and in the Fourth Gospel*, Dissertation, 1978 (University Microfilms International, 1981)

Smith, D. Moody 'Johannine Christianity: Some Reflections on its Character and Delineation', *NTS 21* (1974–5), pp. 222–48

Thyen, H. 'Johannes 13 und die Kirchliche Redaktion des vierten Evangeliums', in *Tradition und Glaube: Festgabe für K. G. Kuhn*, pp. 343–56 (Göttingen, 1971)

Trevett, C. 'The Much-maligned Ignatius', *ExpT* 93 (1981–2), pp. 299–302

Trites, A. A. *The New Testament Concept of Witness* (Cambridge, 1977)

Vermes, G. *The Dead Sea Scrolls in English* (Harmondsworth, [2]1975) *The Gospel of Jesus the Jew* (Newcastle 1981)

Vögtle, A. *Das Neue Testament und der Zukunft des Kosmos* (Düsseldorf, 1970)

Weiser, A. *The Psalms* (London, 1962) ET of 5th German edition, 1959

Weiss, K. 'Die "Gnosis" im Hintergrund und im Spiegel der Johannesbriefe', in K.-W. Tröger (ed.) *Gnosis und Neues Testament* (Gütersluh, 1973)

Wengst, K. *Häresie und Orthodoxie im Spiegel des ersten Johannesbriefes* (Gütersloh, 1976)

Westcott, B. F. *The Epistles of St John* (London, [4]1902)

Westermann, C. *Isaiah 40–66* (London, 1969), ET of 5th German edition 1966

Wilson, R. McL. *The Gospel of Philip* (London, 1962)

Wilson, W. G. 'An Examination of the Linguistic Evidence adduced against the Unity of the First Epistle of John and the Fourth Gospel', *JTS* 49 (1948), pp. 147–56

Windisch, H. *Die Katholischen Briefe*, revised by H. Preisker (Tübingen, [3]1951)

Woll, D. B. *Johannine Christianity in Conflict: Authority, Rank and Succession in the First Farewell Discourse*. SBL Dissertation Series 60 (Chico, Calif., 1981)

INTRODUCTION

to

The Johannine Epistles

I. FORM OF THE FIRST EPISTLE

I John is a written communication (see on 1:1–4), deliberately composed for a particular Christian group in some way related to the wider Johannine community. Yet, as everyone says, it is not an epistle: it lacks the standard form of opening greeting and final salutation, such as are present in the communal epistle 2 John and in the individual epistle 3 John.

In the opening section, a group of people who sound like guardians and interpreters of the tradition, address another group and invite them into fellowship with themselves. Their appeal rests upon a carefully formulated understanding of the tradition, which chiefly refers to keeping the commandments of love and to the model of Jesus as guide to our actions and his death as remedy for our faults. This may well have been an agreed statement, available for use in a variety of circumstances. It is interpolated at two points (2:1–2, 7–8) by a single writer who addresses the readers with pastoral care, and then, after an elaborate transition (2:12–14), writes at length on the two chief themes of the first section. It soon becomes clear that what he writes is a defence of the tradition against the views of a dissident group which had left the community. The defence is not straightforward, partly because the writer himself is drawn to some aspects of the dissidents' convictions, and partly because he has limited himself to two essential convictions of his own which are made to serve at every turn. Those two are the confession of Jesus as Son of God and the practice of love within the community, and may correspond to the chief themes of the agreed statement.

The writer does not argue his case; he relies on assertion. As he himself says, 'I write to you, not because you do not know the truth, but because you know it, and know that no lie is of the truth' (2:21). He reminds his hearers of the tradition they already know, shows them how to adapt that tradition when their situation has been radically changed, and helps them to identify false views that negate the tradition. The repetitions which every reader notices are deliberate. Nothing is acceptable until it has been said, and repeated, and confirmed. Once a point has been gained, it is characteristically formulated according to a stock pattern, often first in positive form and then in the corresponding negative (see on 2:10, and below, p. 23–4). This is obviously a teaching device put at the disposal of those who must strengthen a community perplexed by dissensions. The writer does not expect his readers to discuss and evaluate what he says, but to recognise it as true. They have no need of anyone to teach them; their own anointing teaches them about everything and enables them to recognise the truth (2:27). Consequently I John is neither epistle nor treatise but an enchiridion, an instruction booklet for applying the tradition in disturbing circumstances.

2. STRUCTURE

Both the purpose of the Epistle and the writer's method of composition cause some difficulty to a reader who tries to follow the train of thought. Many suggestions have been made for displaying the Epistle's structure (tabular summary of eleven in Segovia, pp. 69–70), and some kind of spiral arrangement (suggested by Law, p. 5, in 1909) is, for good reason, often favoured. Despite the common agreement that the Epistle lacks a discernible structure or logical progression of thought, even the most pessimistic critics attempt an analysis (Kümmel, pp. 435f.; Feuillet, pp. 687ff.).

It is not too difficult to discern a general pattern depending on emphases rather than on subject matter. The following is proposed:

(1) **1:1–2:11** a statement agreed by a group of leaders.

    1:1–4 lightly sketches the tradition and the disclosure of life in the Son.

    1:5–2:11 is chiefly concerned with the moral consequences. At two points the writer interposes his own supplementary comments. At 2:1–2 he qualifies what the statement has said about sin in the community, and introduces the first reference to the *kosmos*. At 2:7–8 he introduces his paradox of the old commandment which is also new, because the darkness is passing away and the true light is already shining. This indicates the general trend of what he intends to write by way of expanding the agreed statement.

(2) **2:12–14** is a transition from the statement to the writer's development of it.

(3) **2:15–3:10** deals with the ending of the old *kosmos*.

    2:15–17 the attraction of the *kosmos* which is passing away.

    2:18–25 the final hour marked by denial of the Son, the Anointed One.

    2:26–27 the anointing possessed by the community.

    2:28–3:3 members of the community are already children of God.

3:4–10 the distinction between children of God and children of the devil.

This section is built round a major attack (in 2:18–25) on the dissident group.

(4) **3:11–4:21** turns to the old commandment in the new *kosmos*.

3:11–18 opens by stating the message heard from the beginning and then displaying its relation to the death of Christ.

3:19–24 formally relates the commandment of community-love to the commandment requiring faith in the Son. Verse 23 contains A, 'believe in the Son', and B, 'love one another'. Verse 24 adds X, the characteristic Johannine theme of indwelling, and then suddenly mentions the Spirit.

4:1–6   considers the spirits of truth and error in relation to A.

4:7–12 returns to B and A.

4:13–16 summarises, and repeats the themes of 3:19–24, namely, X, the Spirit, A and B. Hence these two sections form an *inclusio*, and are built round the second major attack on the dissident group. Everything is held together by the community's distinction from the *kosmos* (3:13, 17; 4:1, 3, 4, 5, 9, 14).

4:17–21 with another reference to the *kosmos*, provides a restatement of theme B, namely, the message heard from the beginning, in 3:11–18.

(5) **5:1–13** deals with the testimony of the Spirit and faith in the Son.

5:1–5   is yet another variant of themes A and B, by which the writer cautiously approaches his final subject.

5:6–13 at last manages to say, allusively indeed but sufficiently firmly, that experience of the Spirit cannot dispense with faith in the Son. It appears to be another, though less confident, attack on the dissidents. And there the matter ends, with eternal life dependent on the Son, much as the Gospel ends in Jn 20:31.

(6) **5:14–17** is a postscript (just as the Gospel has a postscript in Jn 21) dealing with a matter of casuistry.

5:18–21 is a thematic summary and rhetorical ending, the world being consigned to the evil one and the dissidents to their idolatry. If any suspicion were aroused about additions to the Epistle, this final section would be a candidate for sacrifice (Kümmel, p. 440).

3. THE SECOND AND THIRD EPISTLES

The problems of 2 and 3 Jn are less troublesome. Both are close to standard hellenistic letter forms, though the writer conceals his name. Moreover, he addresses 2 Jn to 'the elect lady and her children', and in turn offers greetings from 'the children of her elect sister'; and in 3 Jn he addresses 'the beloved Gaius', but neglects to add the expected initial greeting. Hence these Epistles too are different from conventional letters, and rather different from other *NT* epistles.

2 Jn has the appearance of a letter which could be sent to any community where 'the elder' was known and his message was pertinent.

1–3   provide a formal address from 'the elder' and 'all who know the truth' to the elect lady.

4–7   are directed, in language echoing 1 Jn, against 'many deceivers' who neglect the commandment of love and refuse to 'acknowledge the coming of Jesus Christ in the flesh'.

8–11 urge that such persons and their views should not be received.

12–13 add a formal ending.

3 Jn has the appearance of a personal letter, but is much more like a formal testimonial favouring one party and repudiating the other party in a struggle within the community.

1   is the address to Gaius.

2–4 certify that Gaius belongs to the truth.

5–8 approve the actions of Gaius.

9–11 disapprove the actions of Diotrephes.

12 commends Demetrius.

13–15 are a formal ending, close in part to the ending of 2 Jn.

4. DIVERSITY OF AUTHORSHIP

Thus all three Epistles are samples of written communications passing between sections of the wider Johannine community at a time when disruption was threatening both convictions and fellowship. They are written much in the same style as the Gospel, use similar turns of language for expressing characteristic ideas, and share a common set of theological convictions (except perhaps for 3 Jn, which is rather barren). Even if they bear a Johannine stamp, however, they are not uniformly the same. The elder of 2 Jn (who doubtless also wrote 3 Jn) is less apt as a writer than the author of 1 Jn, and prefers speaking to writing. He repeats what he has read or been taught, repudiates any divergence, and avoids discussion. It could perhaps be suggested that 2 Jn contains a first hasty response to the disturbance within the community, and that 1 Jn presents a fuller treatment, when it has become plain that the challenge is more complex than at first it seemed. Even so, two writers were involved, not one. But, since 2 Jn gives the impression of secondary writing, it is more likely that it followed 1 Jn; and that the writer was trying to convey the main thrust of 1 Jn in his own more limited way. The fact that he writes more confidently (though not necessarily more sensibly) about the management of people than about the significance of ideas, tells us about his temperament. It does not necessarily imply that the Johannine community had passed from a theologically innovative phase to an institutional phase. Innovation and institution are seldom far apart. Although 2 Jn is secondary, the two Epistles were probably more or less contemporary responses to the same disturbance.

5. THE FIRST EPISTLE AND THE GOSPEL

What then of the relation of 1 Jn to the Gospel of John? (cf. Segovia, pp. 20–32). During the last forty-five years, since the publication of an article by C. H. Dodd which started the modern discussion, it has been more or less taken for granted that both Epistle and Gospel could be ascribed to authors, and that the Epistle was written later than the Gospel.

These two assumptions need to be questioned, and will indeed be considered later; but first we may note how the relation between Epistle and Gospel was treated when it was put in the form: Did the two writings have the same author or different authors?

(i) First, the style and language of the two were compared. It is universally admitted that they are remarkably similar (Brooke, pp. iiff.), although the Gospel shows 'a richness, a subtlety, a penetrating quality of style to which the Epistle cannot pretend' (Dodd, p. xlix). This general impression can be substantiated by detailed examination of stylistic features and grammatical forms. But the results are inconclusive, especially when account is taken of differences which are likely to arise in writing such diverse documents as an epistle (in this case an instruction booklet) and a narrative gospel. The similarity of style with divergences could suggest a single author for the two documents, or one author imitating another, or the existence of a common 'house style' within a closed religious group.

(ii) It is not so easy, however, to set aside differences of wording

and substance. Since the Gospel is a much longer document than
the Epistle, it is not surprising that its vocabulary is larger; but it
is surprising that some words characteristic of the Gospel are missing
from the Epistle. For example, 'glory' (18 times) and 'glorify' (22
times) are widely distributed through the Gospel, but occur nowhere
in the Epistle (other examples are less striking). On the other side,
two remarkable words, 'seed' (*sperma*) and 'anointing' (*chrisma*),
turn up in the Epistle, but play no part in the Gospel. Such differences, however, may merely indicate the kind of words that happened to be necessary or dispensable in the particular conflict which
engaged the attention of whoever wrote the Epistle.

To go beyond words to themes, it is rightly said that the Epistle
gives voice to certain convictions in a primitive Christian and rela-
tively undeveloped form: the nearness of the last hour and the day
of judgment (2:18; 4:17), the power of Jesus' blood to cleanse from
sin and effect expiation (1:7; 2:2; 4:10); and the presence of the
spirit of truth as a rival to the spirit of error (4:6). It may be agreed
that the Gospel shows awareness of these convictions, but by transforming them, not by reproducing them in this primitive form. The
Gospel's statements about the Spirit, some distributed through the
first twelve chapters, the others gathered in the Farewell Discourses,
are themselves not of one kind; but all are far richer than the
minimal references in the Epistle. The Gospel's concern with the
death of Christ reaches back before the Passion narrative into the
earlier discourses and dialogues, but its exploration of the theme is
not illuminated by sacrificial, atonement language (it really will not
do to rely on John Baptist's testimony to the Lamb of God, Jn
1:29). And of the Gospel's subtle, though infrequent, use of eschatological language there is scarcely a hint in the Epistle. Is all this
the work of one and the same author, or of an imitator, or of
someone else who shares the 'house style' of writing but has a less
creative grasp of the tradition?

(iii) It is not, however, entirely satisfactory to compare two documents by noting what is present in one and absent in the other.
It is perhaps more illuminating to consider expressions that occur
in both and to look for shifts of meaning. For example, both Gospel
and Epistle use the contrast of light and darkness: in the Gospel
they are opposing powers which are perceived, in past, present and
future, as opening up the possibility of existential decisions. But in
1 Jn 2:8 they are chronologically distinguished in that darkness
passes away and is succeeded by light. Hence the contrast between
light and darkness has ceased to be existential and has become
historical. This and other transformations imply that the writer of
1 Jn regarded the Gospel as a fixed authority but adapted its teaching

to his own concerns: and, since what is historical is destructive of what is existential, he thereby degraded it. Or so it may be said.

The stylistic arguments were presented by Dodd and contested by Howard, pp. 276–96, and Wilson. Howard also set aside the arguments from differences of subject-matter, but others have affirmed them: Conzelmann, Schweizer, and (in the existential vein) Klein. Cf. Marshall, pp. 31–42; Segovia, pp. 20–31.

6. AUTHORS AND COMMUNITY

The result of these enquiries is to give detailed proof of what is obvious to any thoughtful reading of the two writings: the Epistle is written well below the level of the Gospel. Separate authorship is a reasonable supposition; but if not, then the common author partly changed his mind and his style and was constrained to work within different ranges of ability. In that case deciding questions of authorship is less important than discerning varieties of perception, and discovering whether they diverge or converge. We are no longer required to give proof of authorship as a means of deciding a document's authority, though enquiries about authorship may play some part in discovering the processes of change and development within a Christian community.

At this point it is relevant to ask whether either the Gospel or the Epistle can properly be ascribed to one author, as 2 John and 3 John can. On the view taken in this commentary, the Epistle had more than a single author, namely, those who composed the initial agreed statement and the main writer who used the statement and expanded it. The Gospel had an authorising group who showed their presence by the first person plural (Jn 1:14, 16 and 21:24), and a writer who added Chapter 21, and perhaps more than one contributor to the main part of the work (cf. Barrett (1982), p. 127: 'There is in truth no reason why a number of authors should not be involved: one for John 1–20, another for John 21, a third for the first Epistle and a fourth for 2 and 3 John. Those who venture on a more extensive analysis of the Gospel may of course find a larger number of distinct authors and editors.').

The suggestion that the Gospel reached its present form only after several stages of drafting, rearrangement and the incorporation of fresh material (Brown I (1966), pp. xxxii–xxxix, Lindars, pp. 46–54) has given a new complexion to the question of authorship. It need not lead to the denial of a single mind prompting the growth of the Gospel and overseeing its completion; but it does make room for the incorporation of material originating from a variety of persons. Hence the relation of the Epistle to the Gospel is no longer helpfully discussed in terms of 'the same author or different authors?' The question has become 'where does the material of the Epistle stand in relation to the process by which the Gospel came into being and exercised its influence?' The answer to that question lies within an investigation of the origins, growth and development of the Johannine community. That investigation is now a thriving industry, deservedly providing employment for many scholars (Brown (1979) reviews the proposals of Martyn, Richter, Cullmann, Boismard and Langbrandter, and offers his own strikingly complex suggestions; Segovia adds Meeks, Moody Smith, Culpepper and Bogart on the Johannine community).

It is too soon for a consensus to have formed, but there is considerable agreement on the method to be followed. (i) The Gospel as it stands shows how Jesus was thought of in a Christian community living in the last part of the first century. Indirectly this presentation gives some information about the life of the community when the Gospel was composed. (ii) If the Gospel is separated into its component materials, something may be discovered about the earlier history of the christological views it contains. If the component materials belonged to the community's tradition (rather than being imported from outside), this analysis indirectly may provide clues to the history of the community earlier in the century (based on Brown (1979), pp. 17f.). So, for example, divergent statements about christology may derive from particular groups that joined the community in its earlier stages; and strongly polemical statements in the Gospel may indicate conflicts not only between the community and its opponents but also within the community itself. Particular reconstructions of the community's history need not, for present purposes, be described; it is sufficient to note that the way is open for a more flexible assessment of the chronological relation between Epistle and Gospel.

When the Gospel was simplistically attributed to 'an author' it was sensible to ask whether the Epistle was written before the Gospel or after (especially when the two were attributed to the same author). But if the composition of the Gospel was the work of several hands it is possible to ask whether questions debated in the Epistle made some contribution to the Gospel in one of its stages of formation. This possibility was rejected by Dodd (pp. lvf.) because the tide of criticism seemed to be setting against separatist theories and the Gospel bore the stamp of a single mind. But more recently some have gone so far as to discover the author of 1 Jn as the redactor at least of Jn 13–17 (Richter, pp. 35f.; Thyen, p. 350; Segovia, pp. 29–31, 382–91). The proposal may be more cautiously stated in the form that elements of the Farewell Discourses derived from a situation like that of 1 Jn (Becker, p. 233; Schnackenburg III, pp. 101–6, 140–3). Indeed it becomes necessary to consider the possibility that one of the stages of revision was promoted by the need to deal more adequately with questions half perceived and certainly not fully solved by 1 Jn.

If, of course, it can be shown that the Epistle was written after the Gospel (as is commonly taken for granted) that proposal is excluded; but anything like satisfactory proof is hard to find. Dodd (pp. lv) thought it 'difficult to set aside the impression, which is confirmed by a wide consensus of scholars, that the Gospel is the earlier work and is presupposed in the Epistle', and he thought that Brooke was conclusive on this point. But Brooke's treatment (pp. xix–xxvii) was confused and indecisive: most of his arguments, as he himself admitted, could tell either way. In the end he relied on 'the general impression gained from studying the two writings', namely, that the Epistle 'was written to help and warn those for whom the Gospel, or "a body of teaching like" it, had not accomplished all that the writer hoped.' The argument is frail; the conclusion feeble.

It cannot be denied that many passages in the Epistle have close parallels in the Gospel, and can be understood somewhat better in their context in the Gospel. But did the writer of the Epistle draw them from the Gospel he already knew, or did the Gospel writer incorporate them lucidly in his more extensive work? An answer can be reached only by fitting the Epistle here and there and seeing where it fits best.

The impression, widely held, that the Epistle must be fitted in *after* the Gospel probably arises from three considerations: that a Gospel is a foundation document, and an Epistle must be a successor document (Robinson, p. 57); that the christological views opposed in the Epistle are of such an advanced gnostic kind that they could have developed only after the Gospel's christology had been worked out; and that the Epistle shows an interest in ecclesiastical matters that was not evident in the Gospel.

The primacy of Gospel over Epistle would, of course, be quickly rejected by anyone who holds modern critical views about the historicity of the Gospel. Nevertheless, the Epistle stands in the shadow of the Gospel which towers like a mountain over its foothills: there is intellectual and spiritual pressure to approach the Epistle after experiencing the Gospel. In fact the Epistle may be the most sensible approach to the top.

As for the advanced gnostic christology of the dissident group, the identification seems to be wrong. The problem was not whether the Christ was to be protected from contact with Jesus by a high supernaturalist christology, but whether it was necessary to attach any christology to Jesus at all. And that was a problem to be settled earlier, not later, in the community's history.

Nor can it be presumed that the early stages of that history were free from problems that can be called ecclesiastical. Every group has its own structure, increases its own consciousness as a group by handling structural problems, and often develops by conflict about them. The Epistle presents us with the third stage (first dispute, second secession, third realignment) of an episode within the community which seeks to reassure itself by maximising its separation from the world and by drawing a boundary between what is acceptable (*dikaiosynē*) within the community and what is unacceptable (*hamartia*). The boundary is not a sharply-defined line but a narrow area of no-man's-land into which it is possible to stray without being finally alienated, but which cannot be crossed without leaving the community. There are no precise rules for recognising the extent of this borderland: only the traditional teaching guarded by the community's leadership, and the guidance provided by the pastor who writes the Epistle, and the anointing which his readers possess.

It is not to be expected that a Gospel would deal with such problems in the same way; but given the appropriate change of format, does not Jn 13–17 deal with the internal problems of the community and its relation to the world? Has the Epistle adapted the teaching of the Farewell Discourses to solve an ecclesiastical problem? Or has the Gospel, at a more creative theological level, incorporated the stress and distress of the community?

7. PRIORITY OF THE FIRST EPISTLE

When the Epistle is placed after the Gospel, it is necessary to explain why so much in the Epistle seems to reproduce ideas that belong to an earlier phase of Christian awareness. For example, Houlden, p. 14, admits that the general christology of the Epistle is less advanced, more traditional and simple than that of the Gospel. He accounts for it by suggesting an attempt, under conservative pressure, to draw back from tendencies of a gnostic type towards the teaching of the main body of the Church. It would be easier to suppose that the christology of the Epistle had not yet reached the level of christology in the Gospel. Indeed, the Epistle's christology, far from being a withdrawal, is an attempt to hold the line. Further, references in the Epistle to the atoning efficacy of the death of Christ and to the older futuristic eschatology have some analogues in the

Gospel and are perhaps to be explained as anti-gnostic modifications
of the Johannine scheme to bring it within the main stream. But is
it not easier to suppose that these features, which play a considerable
part in the Epistle, were given some recognition in the Gospel and
made part of a richer understanding of the death of Christ and the
significance of eschatology?

Brown (1979), pp. 96f., admits that there are both early and
Jewish motifs in 1 Jn but regards that only as evidence that the
Johannine tradition had earlier forms and arose among Jewish
Christians. He further admits that 1 Jn ignores some of the higher
christological stresses of the Gospel and plays down the role of the
Spirit-Paraclete—not because he did not know them but because
the dissidents were defending their exaggerated version of the Gospel's high christology by appealing to their possession of the teaching
Spirit. Perhaps so, but it would have been singularly ineffective to
ignore the strongest arguments which (in Brown's view) the dissidents could offer. He thinks that the dating is decided by the fact
that the Gospel displays conflict with outsiders, the Epistle with
insiders. 'If the Epistles were written before the Gospel, it would
have been an already divided and decimated community that was
struggling with the outsiders; and we get no indication of that'. But
we do in Jn 13–17; and if Brown can detect in the community no
less than seven groups of believers, near-believers, and non-believ-
ers, one more would scarcely be out of place.

In Brown's view the dissidents disagreed with the author of 1
John on christology, ethics, eschatology and pneumatology because
they adopted interpretations which were unsatisfactory but had
some warrant in the Gospel. They 'believed that the human existence of Jesus, while real, was not salvifically significant'. They so
stressed the divine principle in Jesus that the earthly career of the
divine principle was neglected. That they gave small value to the
earthly career is surely true; that they attached excessive value, or
indeed any value, to the divine principle lacks evidence. It is no
more than an assumption by those who read the dissidents as advanced gnostics.

When Brown comes to the Epistle's references to the Spirit, he
is acutely embarrassed: the references are few, indirect, and not
authoritative. The writer mentions the Paraclete, but only to attach
that name to Jesus. If he had known (as Brown thinks he did) the
Paraclete sayings in Jn 13–17, which repeatedly stress the dependence of the Spirit on Jesus and the Spirit's function to bring to mind
what Jesus had said in his human existence, how could he possibly
have failed to use them? It is much more likely that he did not know
them, indeed that they did not exist in the community's tradition

until 1 Jn raised the questions they were designed to answer. The composer of Jn 13–17 took more seriously than 1 Jn the experience of the Spirit to which the dissidents bore testimony, but made sure that whole-hearted acceptance of the Spirit could never undermine the human existence of Jesus but always reinforced it. Earlier in the Gospel statements about the Spirit, which may well have originated in a group obsessed by their experience of the Spirit, are carefully neutralised by being attached to Jesus' actions and words, and to the descent and ascent of the Son.

If the Epistle is placed after the composition of the Gospel, somewhat elaborate theories are required to justify its presence. If the Epistle finds a place during the composition of the Gospel, it throws light on parts of the Gospel which have long puzzled exegetes. In this commentary it is argued that passages in the Epistle often look like first attempts at material which later appears in the Gospel, where its presence can be justified if it began from the situation for which the Epistle was the earlier written response. Attention may be drawn to the following sections of the exegesis: (a) on 1:1–4, which seems to be the basis of the prologue to the Gospel; (b) on 2:20, 25 and 3:22, where teaching about the Spirit is considered; (c) on 3:12–13, in relation to Judas; (d) on 3:18, where speech is depreciated; (e) on 3:23, in relation to believing; (f) on 4:14, as regards the world; (g) on 4:17, concerning judgment; (h) on 5:14–17, where readers are encouraged to ask anything of Christ; and on 5:20–21, where christologies are compared. On those points at least, the Epistle can help any attempt to discover how the Gospel came to be what it is.

8. THE DISSIDENTS AND THEIR VIEWS

In that case, what was the situation which called forth the Epistle? Irenaeus (*A.H.* 3.11.1) says that John the disciple of the Lord was intent on removing the error spread by Cerinthus and others and so directed the opening instruction of his Gospel to that end. This is the famous bold manoeuvre by which Irenaeus planned to recover John's Gospel from its ample use by the Valentinian gnostics and to refute their views from the Gospel itself (*A.H.* 3.11.7). The erroneous views were the affirmation of the creator as one person and the Father of the Lord another; a difference of persons between the son of the creator and the Christ from the higher Aeons who remained impassible, who descended on Jesus the son of the creator, and glided back again to his own pleroma; and that the created system to which we belong, brought into being by some lowly power, is cut off from communion in the things which are beyond sight and name. Irenaeus has little difficulty in setting the prologue against such views; but that was not the whole story, as an earlier reference to Cerinthus shows (*A.H.* 1.26.1). A certain Cerinthus in Asia taught the following propositions:

(i)   the world was not made by the first God but by a power widely separated and remote from the supreme power which is above all;

(ii)   that subordinate power did not know the God who is over all things;

(iii)   Jesus was not born of a virgin but was the son of Joseph and Mary;

(iv)   Jesus was far beyond the rest of men in justice and prudence and wisdom;

(v)   after the baptism of Jesus, Christ descended upon him in the form of a dove, from the power that is over all things;

(vi)   he then proclaimed the unknown Father and accomplished miracles;

(vii)   at the end Christ separated again from Jesus who suffered and was raised again, but Christ remained impassible because he was spiritual.

(See the translation in Foerster, I, pp. 35f., where the final word is rendered 'pneumatic'.)

In this fuller account of Cerinthus, items (i), (ii), (v) and (vii) are more or less the same as those views which the Gospel prologue was intended to refute; but the rest of the Gospel would have been little help in removing the other statements. The Gospel agrees with items (iv) and (vi), and does nothing to repudiate (iii). Outside the prologue it is not always confident about the status of the world; it allows John Baptist to refer in passing to the descent of the Spirit as a dove; and it would not be difficult to read most references to the death of Jesus as spiritual rather than physical. Irenaeus means no more than this, that the prologue was a valuable counter-statement against certain gnostic views. He implies nothing about the composition of John's Gospel as a whole, from which, by the way, he draws considerably fewer quotations than he does from Luke and far fewer than from Matthew. He has, of course, the well-known bit of ecclesiastical gossip, attributed to Papias, that John, the Lord's disciple, fled from the public baths at Ephesus when he encountered there Cerinthus, the enemy of the truth (*A.H.* 3.1.4). By the time of Epiphanius in the fourth century Cerinthus had become an all-purpose heretic to whom any religious unpleasantness could be attributed; indeed, Eusebius (*H.E.* 3.28) at second hand credited him with gross millenarian predictions. Despite the pathetic malice of the ancient fathers, it seems possible that Irenaeus' earlier report contains some genuine information about Cerinthus who may have had contacts with the entourage of Ignatius.

Did Cerinthus have genuine contacts with the Johannine community? If we put together the spirit which does not confess that Jesus Christ has come in the flesh (1 Jn 4:2) and the attitude which admits that Jesus came by water but not by blood (1 Jn 5:6), it is possible to conjecture (as many do) that Cerinthus is behind the dissidents' views. In the opinion of Wengst (p. 25) 'the similarity to Cerinthus is so striking that no writer who turns his attention even casually to the opponents in 1 John can forbear quoting or at least mentioning him'.

Yet it is certain that, once we are beyond a casual glance, reservations have to be made; and Wengst (who provides a convenient summary of information about Cerinthus) himself makes them. His three conclusions are that (a) the dissidents are Johannine Christians who most probably based their christological views on the Gospel; (b) those views agreed with the christology of Cerinthus; and (c) Cerinthus probably used the Gospel and relied on its authority. Yet since the dissidents lacked the cosmology of Cerinthus, it is best to regard the dissidents as belonging to a development that led to Cerinthus (Wengst, p. 34). So at the last moment, Cerinthus is not a model for the dissidents, but they are his forerunners. If the view taken in this commentary is correct, namely, that the Epistle did not follow the Gospel but contributed to its composition, Wengst's conclusion (a) must be rephrased. Even more important, it must be observed that Wengst approaches the dissidents with a pre-understanding of what their christology must be. The dissidents' belief in a bringer of salvation, who came by water but came not in the flesh and so is to be distinguished from the earthly Jesus and identified with the Spirit, is constructed by reading statements about the dissidents through a grid provided by Cerinthus. If we turn back once again to the seven items of Cerinthus' teaching, we find in references to the dissidents no evidence for items (i), (ii), (iii) and (v); evidence that they would have repudiated item (iv) and possibly item (vi); and only conjecture for item (vii). They were not far on the way to Cerinthus.

Their beliefs can more satisfactorily be discovered by noticing where the emphases fall in the Epistle, and by asking what views the writer is contesting. The chief indications are the following:

1:3   'Our fellowship is with the Father and with his son Jesus Christ': against those who claim fellowship with the Father but not with the Son.

1:6   'If we say we have fellowship with him', i.e., as the dis-
           sidents do.

1:8, 10   'If we say we have no sin', as some do, who therefore feel
           no need for the cleansing effect of Christ's blood.

2:3–4   'We may be sure that we know him', i.e., we as well as
           others who say 'I know him' but disobey his command-
           ments (remembering that obedience is a characteristic Jew-
           ish way of 'knowing' God).

2:6   'He who says he abides in him (i.e., God) ought to walk
           in the same way in which he (i.e., Jesus) walked': against
           those who used the language of abiding in God and dis-
           missed any need for the example of Jesus.

2:9   'He who says he is in the light and hates his brother'
           presumably refers to those who regard themselves as pos-
           sessing illumination and disregard fellow members of the
           community who are uninstructed.

2:18, 22   The dissidents are antichrists, that is, they deny that Jesus
           is the Christ, the Anointed One.

2:19   They have left the community, thus showing that they
           never really belonged to it.

2:20   'We have been anointed by the Holy One': against the
           claim that others possess the real anointing.

2:23   'No one who denies the Son has the Father': against those
           who, as in 1:3, deny the Son while claiming fellowship
           with the Father.

2:28   'If he appears (see commentary) we may have confidence
           and not shrink from him in shame at his coming': a some-
           what doubting response to an assertion that the divine
           person will himself appear, when only the illuminated will
           be confident and without shame in his presence.

3:2   'We are God's children now': to counter the implication
           that they are not.

3:9–10   'No one born of God commits sin': asserting what the
           dissidents assert for themselves and condemning them for
           their behaviour.

3:17   'If anyone has the world's goods and sees his brother in
           need, yet closes his heart against him': probably directed
           against some well-to-do members who have withdrawn
           financial support from the community.

4:1   'The spirits' and 'many false prophets' are indications that
           the dissidents – not simply two or three but many of them
           – claimed possession by the Spirit; and had 'gone out into
           the world', perhaps with the aim of saving it.

4:2–3   They did not confess Jesus as Christ, the Anointed One, come in the flesh, no doubt because they relied on their own anointing with the Spirit (cf. 2:18, 22).

4:5   'The world listens to them': showing some resentment of their success by classing them with the world.

4:12   'No man has ever seen God': implying that the dissidents claim to have seen him.

4:14   'The Father has sent his Son as the Saviour of the world': against those who think that they, possessed by the Spirit, are the intended saviours of the world.

4:17   'We may have confidence for the day of judgment, because as he (Jesus) is so are we in this world': a further reference (see 2:28) to the confidence which the dissidents claimed for themselves but denied to others.

5:6f.   'He who came by water and blood, Jesus Christ, not with the water only but with the water and the blood': clearly implying that the dissidents in some way rejected the blood of Christ because they believed that the Spirit was the truth. 'The testimony of God that he has borne witness to his Son': indicating that this testimony, which the community possessed in its tradition and continuing interpretation, was rejected by the dissidents who believed that their experience of the Spirit was sufficient proof of divine testimony.

We cannot be sure that all these contrary views were held by the dissidents, but at least we can ask whether as a whole they make a coherent impression. Nor can we take them without question as a fair description, since the writer who opposes the dissidents is necessarily partisan. If we attempt to present them a little more impartially, the picture looks like this:

A rather numerous group of well-to-do members have withdrawn themselves and their support from other members of the community. They regard those who have not followed them with disapproval and try to persuade them with religious threats, saying that the community will lack confidence when God appears and shrink from him in shame. The dissident group dislikes the separation from the world which the writer of the Epistle urges (2:15–17), and they think the world worth saving. They have gone out into the world exercising prophetic gifts and have met with a responsive hearing. They claim to be motivated by the Spirit, to be born of God and therefore to be sharers of the divine nature (for 'God is spirit', Jn 4:24, and the non-Johannine word 'fellowship' in 1:3 signifies participation). Hence they are in the

light and possess direct access to the Father; they know him and
have seen him (cf. perhaps the throne vision of Rev. 4, not
inappropriate to prophetically-inspired persons), and in what they
do they are anticipating his *parousia* (2:28). Since all they do is
prompted by the Spirit, they are naturally without sin: their
actions in themselves are a demonstration of what is right. Hence
they have no need of the commandments or of the example of
Jesus. It is inappropriate to call Jesus the Christ, *the* Anointed
One, as if he alone could provide access to the Father; for they
themselves have an anointing by the Spirit which gives them
unmediated access to God. 'We are Christians', they might have
said, 'not because Jesus was anointed, but because we all are'.
They accepted baptism as cleansing with water which admits to
the first stage of community life, and then anointing with the
spirit (or perhaps it should be written Spirit) which admits to the
stage of full maturity (contrast the Epistle's suggestion that maturity is demonstrated by loving 2:5; 4:12, 17, 18). Hence the
dissidents can give a half-recognition to Jesus as one who, after
the baptising work of John 'baptises with Holy Spirit' (Jn 1:33);
but they cannot recognise any benefits of his death, which was
shocking and perverse as Ignatius knew (Ign. *Eph.* 18:1).

That picture is not implausible (cf. Weiss for a somewhat similar
description). It would, of course, have to be rejected if the community for which the Epistle was written were already at a stage
beyond the Gospel; or if it were thought that all members of a
primitive Christian community must possess a christology in the
sense of ascribing recognised titles to Jesus. But if 'Christ' signified
the function of one who is prophetically anointed with the Spirit
(as is argued by Harvey (1982), pp. 140ff.), and if 'Son of God' was
intended to refer to the agent who acts for God, it would not be
surprising if some members of the community, who had been first
attracted by the Baptist's promise of divine spirit, behaved as that
description says they did. In the judgment of Woll (p. 128) 'the
occasion for the writing of the Gospel is a situation in which claims
to direct, independent access to the divine authority have, in the
author's eyes, gotten out of control by becoming a threat to the
primacy of the Son'. If members of the dissident group had in the
first place been attracted by the Baptist's promise of the Spirit, it
would not be surprising if they claimed to be anointed by the Spirit,
to exercise prophetic functions by speaking to the world and spontaneously practising such right actions as are approved by God, to
have received visions of God in anticipation of his parousia. To the
writer of the Epistle all these features were a threat to the community

and its tradition, so much so that he can scarcely perceive the importance of an experience of the Spirit.

In the Gospel things are different. Not only are there Paraclete sayings carefully tied to the primacy of Jesus, but the first major division of the Gospel includes teaching about the Spirit which would admirably fit the views of the dissident group. For example, 'it is the Spirit that gives life, the flesh is of no avail' would commend itself to those who refuse to acknowledge Jesus as the Anointed One come in the flesh. (It is neutralised in the Gospel by being interpreted as a reference to the *words* of Jesus, Jn 6:63.) Again 'God is spirit' might well be a dissident rallying cry, though in the Gospel it is boldly attributed to Jesus, and confined to worship (Jn 4:24). In the conversation with Nicodemus, Jesus speaks of being born of water and spirit (as the dissidents must have done), roundly asserts that 'that which is born of the flesh is flesh, and that which is born of the Spirit is spirit' (where flesh and spirit appear to be two contrary realms), and finally proclaims the uncontrollable spontaneity of Spirit and all who are born of it (Jn 3:5–8). This leaves no room for Jewish or early Christian tradition and, of course, says nothing about the death of Christ. It looks like the exact position of the dissidents, tempered by being placed on the lips of Jesus and moderated by the claim in Jn 3:13 that the heavenly ascent to God is possible only by means of the Son of man who descended – which is a subtle displacement of emphasis from spirit to Jesus. Once more, in a passage which may be intended to convey the teaching of John Baptist, it is said that 'He who comes from above is above all; he who is of the earth belongs to the earth, and of the earth he speaks' (Jn 3:31). This radical separation is supplemented by a reproach that no one receives this testimony which is based on the prophetic sending of God 'for it is not by measure that he gives the Spirit'. If that is the dissident voice being allowed to speak, its assertions are promptly corrected by a standard Johannine association of Father and Son, by attaching eternal life strictly to the Son (as in the Epistle), and by invoking, for the only time in John, the wrath of God (Jn 3:36).

It would be very difficult to argue that the dissidents had read the Gospel, seized on these passages and the Paraclete sayings, divested them of their association with Jesus, and constructed their own spirit theology; just as difficult as arguing that the writer of the Epistle had read the Gospel and almost entirely forgotten its teaching when he wrote of the Spirit. It is much more likely that these passages and sayings were a reconciling attempt to take account of that experience of the Spirit which the dissidents felt so strongly without allowing them to ignore thereby the centrality of Jesus.

These considerations allow us to dispose of one more suggestion for identifying the dissidents, namely, with the opponents of Ignatius at the beginning of the second century. In the course of his journey from Antioch towards an expected and desired martyrdom at Rome, Ignatius arrived at Smyrna and wrote four letters. One, addressed to Rome, was entirely concerned with his own future and said nothing about religious opponents. Three were sent to churches which he would not be able to visit: Ephesus, Magnesia and Tralles. Each church is praised for its theological soundness and order. At Ephesus 'no sect has any lodging among you' (Ign. *Eph.* 6.2), yet the writer sets out his theological convictions at some length in obviously credal terms. He finds the Magnesians well disciplined in godly love (*Mag.* 1.1), but thinks fit to warn them against strange doctrines and old fables and the continuation of Jewish practices— not that he has any evidence that the church is following such tendencies (*Mag.* 11.1). The Trallians 'have a disposition that is faultless' and nothing is known against the church (*Trall.* 1.1 and 8.2), but he tells them to stop their ears when any one speaks to them apart from Jesus Christ, especially anyone who says that 'he suffered only in semblance' (*to dokein peponthenai*, *Trall.* 9.1 and 10; the adjective 'docetic' derives from the verb *dokein*). So in these three letters Ignatius takes the opportunity of establishing his orthodoxy (or what he thinks is orthodox) to three churches of good reputation, and of attacking two forms of error. (Whether they were two different errors or two sides of one error is much disputed: see Barrett (1976) for the view that there was a single error; for other views, see Trevett.)

Ignatius left Smyrna and travelled on to Troas where he wrote three more letters: to the churches at Philadelphia and Smyrna (which he had visited), and to Polycarp, the bishop of Smyrna. At Philadelphia he had detected some kind of schism and someone had tried to lead him astray in matters, it would seem, of church government (*Philad.* 3.1–3 and 7.1); but his warning is directed against anyone who expounds Judaism to them and refuses to credit anything to the gospel unless he finds it in the charters, presumably the Old Testament records (*Philad.* 6.1 and 8.2). He does not say that the Philadelphians were in fact troubled by these errors. To the Smyrneans he reasserts his orthodoxy (were they still unconvinced?) against some unbelievers who say that Jesus suffered seemingly, who were unconvinced by the prophecies, or by the Law of Moses, or by the gospel, or by Ignatius' sufferings. Yet there is no evidence that the Smyrneans were heretical—they had a fixed and unshakable faith (*Smyr.* 1.1). He was but warning them in advance, and the names of the heretics he refuses to write down (*Smyr.* 4.1

and 5.3). When he writes to their bishop there is no mention of heresy. From this it must be concluded that Ignatius was less attacking Asian heretics than fighting his own battles, deriving no doubt from the conflict that had been provoked in his own church at Antioch. Perhaps in that church there were some who taught that Christ suffered only in semblance; if so, were they prophets and adherents of the Spirit? If they were, Ignatius has not mentioned it. For him 'flesh and spirit' is a common phrase signifying the Christian version of human and divine qualities, and the prophetic spirit appears only in one anecdotal reference (*Philad.* 7.1–2). There is no mention of the experience of the Spirit. There are three references to the Holy Spirit: as responsible for the Virgin Mary's conception, as establishing the threefold ministry in office, and as being compared to a rope used on a machine (the cross of Christ) to hoist up the living stones which make the temple of God (*Eph.* 18.2; *Philad.* Int.; *Eph.* 9.1). By the time Ignatius was writing, belief in the Spirit had become so formal that experience of the Spirit was (in orthodox circles) virtually excluded. This is all far removed from the live questions of 1 John. The dissidents must therefore be allowed their own independent existence.

9. THE TEACHING OF THE FIRST EPISTLE

Their views must now stand comparison with the views put forward by the community leaders and the writer of the Epistle. Some of his statements have an air of being uttered chiefly to controvert a conviction of the dissidents; they belong perhaps to his apologetic rather than to the central affirmations of his faith. Fortunately, we can easily discern the essential matters, for the writer took the trouble to set them out in recognisable and memorable form. Certain sentences stand out from the rest by reason of their style and their function of providing summaries and judgments (see on 2:10). Bultmann (pp. 17f.) developed the view that the sentences were part of an existing source (stylistically related to the alleged revelatory discourse source used in the Gospel), commented upon and expanded not only by the writer of the Epistle but also by the supposed ecclesiastical reviser. This suggestion has received both support and criticism (Marshall, pp. 28–30). It is not adopted in this commentary, because (a) it is difficult to suppose that the dismemberment and expansion of an already existing document would be a useful procedure for responding to the threat of unbelief and schism; (b) the limits of an agreed statement by the church leaders can be discerned in 1:1–2:11 (see the commentary) and that provides a sufficient source; (c) the existence of genuinely stylistic and functional parallels in the Gospel is surprisingly rare; and (d) the distinguishing features of these sentences can reasonably be explained as a simple and necessary teaching device. No church congregation or committee (along with other kinds of gathering) feels confident that it has grasped the point until it has heard it three times, and hence the writer sensibly drives home the convictions that must be made to stick.

Here then are the central convictions collected together:

2:10f. He who loves his brother abides in the light,
     and in it there is no cause for stumbling.
    But he who hates his brother is in the darkness
     and walks in darkness,
     and does not know where he is going,
     because the darkness has blinded his eyes.

2:22f. Who is the liar, but he who denies that Jesus is the Christ?
    This is the antichrist, he who denies the Father and the
     Son.
    No one who denies the Son has the Father.
    He who confesses the Son has the Father also.

2:29 Everyone who does right is born of him.
    (cf. 3:9 below)

3:3f. Everyone who thus hopes in him
     purifies himself as he is pure.
    Everyone who commits sin
     is guilty of lawlessness.

3:6–8 No one who abides in him sins;
     no one who sins has either seen him or known him.
    He who does right is righteous, as he is righteous.
    He who commits sin is of the devil.

3:9 No one born of God commits sin.
    (cf. 2:29 above)

3:10 Whoever does not do right is not of God,
    nor he who does not love his brother.

3:14f. He who does not love abides in death.
    Any one who hates his brother is a murderer.

3:24 All who keep his commandments
     abide in him, and he in them.

4:7f. He who loves is born of God and knows God.
    He who does not love does not know God.

4:21 He who loves God should love his brother also.

5:1 Everyone who believes that Jesus is the Christ
     is a child of God,

> and everyone who loves the parent
> loves the child.
>
> 5:4f. Whatever is born of God overcomes the world.
> Who is it that overcomes the world
> but he who believes that Jesus is the Son of God?
>
> 5:10 He who believes in the Son of God
> has the testimony in himself.
> He who does not believe God
> has made him a liar.
>
> 5:12 He who has the Son has life;
> he who has not the Son of God has not life.
>
> 5:18 Anyone born of God does not sin,
> but He who was born of God keeps him,
> and the evil one does not touch him.

This comprises a limited range of themes, driven home by repetition, supported by argument and rhetoric. To reduce it to a summary limits its force but makes clear the outlines.

(i)   Human beings can know God, have fellowship with him and be born of him. That is, they can share the divine nature and so overcome the world. They can abide in him as he abides in them. They can move from darkness to light, from death to life.

(ii) Anyone who abides in God cannot sin – often, no doubt, in the sense 'must not sin' rather than 'is incapable of sinning'. Sin is clearly the antigod. Any one born of God, who knows God, must do what is right and keep the commandments. There are only two commandments: love God and love your brother. To love is to be in the light; not to love is to be in darkness and death.

(iii) If you love the Father, you must love the Son. If you reject the Son, you are rejecting the Father. Therefore you must acknowledge that Jesus is the Son of God and the Anointed One. You cannot be born of God if you do not recognise him who is God's Son. Nor can you behave rightly unless you are pure as he is pure, and right as he is right. To have life, to overcome the world, you must believe that Jesus is the Son of God.

Thus there is considerable agreement between the parties to the dispute. On (i) they vie with one another in proclaiming their knowledge of God and participation in him. The writer of the Epistle rejects the dissidents' claim to have seen God and is reserved about their expectation of a *parousia*. His eschatological language is applied in particular to the schism and the denial of Christ, and in general to the passage from darkness to light, or to the overcoming of the world. The writer overcame the world by rejecting it; the dissidents hoped to overcome the world by saving it.

On (ii) both parties agreed that community members cannot sin. Since all religious communities are subject to error, misjudgment and the results of wilful actions, it is necessary for 'perfectionist' groups (Bogart, pp. 7f.) to find strategies for dealing with negations of their belief in sinless behaviour. The writer of the Epistle thought it could be done by pleading the expiatory work of Christ and defining the limits within which sin is forgivable; the dissidents by defining what they did under the impulse of the spirit as sinless. In one respect, at least, the dissidents were not departing far from the community's general practice. If there are only two command-ments—love of God and love of the brother—a very great deal is left to the individual's imaginative decision or the community's response to new situations. What else could anyone do but rely on tradition or respond to inspiration? The writer chose tradition, the dissidents inspiration. The writer interpreted rejection of tradition as sin and hatred. Though he commended forgiveness and repeat-edly advocated love, he seems not to have extended either to the dissidents – not that he was being hypocritical but was simply falling unknowingly into the habits of a minority-group leader who raises the consciousness of the group by denouncing opponents. The dis-sidents are now often called 'libertines'. Bogart (pp. 124, 129) col-lects passages which accuse the dissidents of immoral behaviour (if that is what 'walking in darkness' means), of ignoring God's com-mandments, of loving the world with its proud and lustful features, of antinomian attitudes, of deceit and hatred of the brethren (1:6; 2:4, 6, 15–17; 3:4ff., 7, 10), and characterises them as 'a group of worldly persons who are morally indifferent'. But that comes from reading moral denunciation uncritically. It is significant and perhaps decisive that the writer of the Epistle brings not a single specific accusation against the dissidents' behaviour. No doubt they were cocksure, complacent and infuriating. They did not provoke the community to love and charity. But to imagine they were gnostic antinomians with an obsessive theory about the irrelevance of behav-iour in the flesh is to create a prurient fantasy.

On (iii) however, the two parties were irreconcilable. The writer brings a specific charge: the dissidents refuse to acknowledge the Son. In fact they may have acknowledged Jesus up to a point (in so far as baptism was concerned), but not to the extent of his death and other elements of the old tradition. They relied on inspiration by the spirit in which the writer of the Epistle had singularly little interest—as is shown by the absence of spirit from the formulaic

sentences. The nearest reference comes in 4:2f. and is very reveal-
ing: 'Every spirit (that is, every prophetic utterance) which confesses
that Jesus Christ has come in the flesh is of God: every spirit which
does not confess Jesus is not of God'. Prophetic utterances are
grudgingly admitted provided that spiritual inspiration is subser-
vient to the community tradition of the flesh of Jesus Christ.

If the dissidents were not libertines (except in an uncontentious
sense), can we still call them gnostics? Yes, if we will also call the
writer of the Epistle a gnostic. He shows no discomfort when pre-
senting our relation to the divine being in terms of knowing God
and of being born of God. He uses the simple dualism of light and
darkness, life and death; and a more specialised contrast of the
community and the world. In the commentary these themes are
illustrated from their occurrence in gnostic writings, as well as such
terms as *chrisma* and *sperma*. It is instructive, for instance, to learn
that an eschatological knowledge of God was rare in the Old Testament but common in the Qumran community and became a standard feature of gnostic hellenistic religion, both in its Christian and
non-Christian forms by the second century AD, when it was equivalent to being born of God. A change of sensibility was taking place
whereby the concept of 'knowing' was becoming dominant in religious awareness.

Knowledge could be expressed as enlightenment and hence compared to the passage from darkness to light. The writer of the
Epistle keeps firm hold of an earlier tradition where darkness had
moral connotations, and so relates illumination and knowledge to
keeping the divine commandments. By so doing, knowledge remains
practical rather than speculative knowledge. There is no evidence,
either in his own teaching or in that of his opponents, of a speculative scheme, a cosmogony, a worked out relation between that
which is above and that which is below. In other words the 'knowledge' of both parties is at the most 'soft gnosis' not the 'hard
gnosticism' of the second century. Some components of this knowledge were indeed taken up into the development of gnostic
schemes, and it may well be that (for example) the descent-and-
ascent imagery of the Gospel shows that development was quite
rapid; but when the Epistle was written there was nothing more
than a grateful borrowing from hellenistic religion and in particular
hellenistic Judaism.

The Epistle, it is true, entirely lacks quotations from the Old
Testament and has only a single reference to it (Cain, in 3:12). Yet
what it contains can be but partly appreciated without some knowledge of the LXX and of Philo, and of the Dead Sea Scrolls (cf.
Boismard, Price). Even simple, unemphatic tricks of speech, such

as using the verb 'walking' for moral behaviour, indicate a writer (and his community) who had half emerged from Judaism. For him knowledge of God can have been no strange thing but the proper fulfilment of an ancient expectation.

The affinity with Judaism is more evident in the Gospel, in particular with the Judaism of Judaea and Galilee. Even so there are few explicit Old Testament quotations when compared with Matthew and Luke. The vocabulary of the Gospel is very common in the LXX and Josephus, reasonably common in Philo, and rather scarce in the Hermetic writings. The Gospel refers to famous Old Testament persons and uses familiar images as developed by the haggadic tradition of synagogue teaching. 'Men with capital, landed property, business and position hardly occur in John, and none of his illustrative remarks is drawn from the world of power and wealth' (Kilpatrick). The Gospel allows the decisive encounters of Jesus to take place in Jerusalem, but reports nothing of his activity in Judaea. It knows one visit to Samaria, but pointedly dissociates Christian worship from either Mount Gerizim or Mount Zion. It knows two visits to Galilee and yet regards Judaea as Jesus' native place. It pictures Jesus as beginning his work with John Baptist in Transjordan, and as retiring there when under pressure. From such indications it may be conjectured that the Johannine community was not led by Galileans, or Judaeans, or Samaritans but by hellenistic Jews from the remoter territories in Syria (cf. Smith, p. 237). They were still in contact with Jewish life but risked excommunication from the synagogue when Judaism was reforming its social life and recovering its strength some time after AD 70.

Among the early Fathers the nearest in thought to the Johannine writings is Ignatius of Antioch in Syria. The first Christian writer to put John's Gospel into a collection of writings is Tatian (c. 160) in northern Syria, and the first to ascribe the Gospel to John is Theophilus of Antioch at the end of the second century. The indications are slender and need to be considered alongside other evidence from tradition (Barrett (1978), pp. 123–34); but at least they suggest the kind of environment in which the Johannine writings were first formulated.

10. THE LOCATION OF THE FIRST EPISTLE

Where the Johannine writings were first welcomed and put to Christian use is another matter. It still seems likely that Christian gnostic communities were bold and that other Christian communities were tentative in their reception of John's Gospel (Moody Smith, pp. 224f.). Although Ignatius expressed his thoughts somewhat in the Johannine manner, he quotes neither the Gospel nor the Epistle (except for a suspect reading in Ign. *Eph.* 7.2). But Polycarp's *Letter to the Philippians* 7.1 reproduces 1 Jn 4:2 in his usual inconsequential manner, without attributing it to anyone. He urges his readers to refrain from false brothers and from those who bear the name of the Lord in hypocrisy, and mislead foolish men. Then he says that anyone who does not acknowledge that Jesus Christ has come in the flesh is antichrist, including any who do not accept the testimony of the cross and who pervert the Lord's sayings to their own desires. His readers are to return to the word that was handed down from the beginning. He has obviously got the gist of 1 Jn, but he had rather heard it than read it.

More than two centuries later, Eusebius (*H.E.* 3.39.17) tells us that Papias, bishop of Hierapolis, who (according to the earlier statement of Irenaeus was a hearer of John and companion of Polycarp), made use of testimonies from the first epistle of John. Eusebius seems to have read at least some of Papias' five books; he does not say that Papias ascribed his quotations to John, and he points out that the information of Irenaeus is misleading. Papias did not claim to be a hearer and eyewitness of the holy apostles, but to have received the doctrines of the faith from their close friends. Eusebius himself placed 1 Jn among the Christian writings recognised as genuine, though 2 and 3 Jn belonged to those which were disputed but well known and approved by many. Despite uncertainties about the two smaller epistles, 1 Jn was firmly established by the end of the second century. It is quoted and explicitly attributed to John the disciple of the Lord (though not clearly distinguished from 2 Jn) by Irenaeus in *A.H.* 3.16.5–8.

Between Polycarp's unattributed quotation and Irenaeus' explicit attribution there is a gap (unless Justin, *Dialogue* 123.9, contains an almost imperceptible reminiscence). Irenaeus as a boy had seen Polycarp (*A.H.* 3.3.4), and was probably a native of Smyrna where Polycarp was bishop. There is no doubt that Revelation, which is related in some way to the Johannine circle, was composed in Asia: Smyrna was one of the seven churches to which John wrote. In a manner unknown to us – though it may be connected with Ignatius' progress as a martyr-designate – the Epistle and the Gospel reached Smyrna. The Gospel perhaps was heard with some surprise and caution; the Epistle was less contentious and could supply phrases that stuck in the mind. When Irenaeus discovered the usefulness of the Gospel Prologue for controverting the growth of gnostic fantasies, he appropriated the Gospel and Epistle for John the disciple of the Lord. From that effective polemic the Fourth Gospel moved towards a dominating position as a source for Christian theology, and overshadowed the Epistle. But perhaps in the cities of Asia Minor the Epistle had served as an introduction to the Gospel, as earlier in Syria it had provided material for the composition of the Gospel.

THE FIRST EPISTLE OF JOHN

A STATEMENT BY THE LEADERS 1:1–2:11

THE TRADITION AND THE DISCLOSURE OF LIFE 1:1–4

The introductory section is differentiated from the rest of 1 John by an emphatic distinction between **we** and **you** and by an incoherent sentence structure. The two features may be connected. A Christian group addresses a group of readers in formal language: they claim to possess an original disclosure and experience and intend to communicate what they possess. The purpose of this communication, surprisingly stated in non-Johannine language, is to promote **fellowship** between the two groups. Since the writing group asserts that **our fellowship is with the Father and with his Son Jesus Christ**, it might be implied that the readers would be deprived of fellowship with the Father and the Son if they rejected the offer of fellowship from the writers. The firm closing words of v. 4 maintain the pressure of this delicate threat, if such it is: it is **we** who **are writing this that our joy** (*hēmōn*, against 'your', *hymōn*, of textus receptus) **may be complete**. (If we, *hēmeis*, read by the Alexandrian text against the widely supported but conventional reading 'to you', *hymin*, is the original text it must be emphatic: 'it is **we**'.) This is a group adaptation of the Elder's stock admonition 2 Jn 12, 3 Jn 13 and, in the context, means 'We wish to be fully satisfied with your response'.

This distinction between **we** and **you** is maintained in v. 5, but in vv. 6–10 **we** includes both the writers and the readers. At 2:1, however, there is a striking intrusion of the first person singular (**I am writing this to you**), which comes again in 2:7 and is then maintained throughout the chapter. It is closely associated with the verb 'to write' (as it is in 5:13, where the first person singular is again explicit). The author quite naturally speaks of himself as **I** and his readers as **you**; though sometimes **we** means 'I and you' (2:1b, 2, 3, 5b, 18d). It does so especially strongly in 2:19 where **we** is put in opposition to **they**. For the rest of 1 Jn it is natural to suppose that one person is addressing a Christian group, regarding himself as their guide and instructor and using various devices to teach and persuade them. It is the more remarkable that 1:1–4 has the formal quality of a corporate not an individual address (cf. Moody Smith, p. 236).

It is presumably important that this is a *written* document. The significance of **we are writing this** in order **that** (cf. 2:1; 5:13, Jn

20:30–31) is reinforced by the extraordinary emphasis on writing in 2:1, 7, 12, 13, 14, 21, 26 (cf. 2 Jn 5, 12; 3 Jn 9, 13). This is somewhat a feature of the Johannine corpus (*TWNT* I, p. 745), as may be seen in Revelation where written communications assure a blessing or convey a curse (Rev. 19:9; 22:18–19); they decide the fate of mankind according as they are inscribed in the book of life (Rev. 20:12–15) or in the scroll containing the terrible judgments (Rev. 5:1, and the unsealing thereof). The John of Revelation is instructed to write what he sees (Rev. 1:11, 19) and to send letters of praise, warning, rebuke and command to the Seven Churches (Rev. 2–3).

In assessing the significance of 1 Jn as a *written* document it is necessary to recall that antiquity was much more habituated to oral than to written communications, and preferred them. The Elder's attitude was typical: 'I had much to write to you, but I would rather not write with pen and ink; I hope to see you soon, and we will talk together face to face' (3 Jn 13–14). Writing was a poor substitute for speech, discussion and debate. A written document was inflexible and not open to questioning; unlike the oral memory of a community, it could easily be tampered with. Ancient pre-literate people and modern semi-literates are suspicious of documents and over-impressed by them. Even literate people were ambivalent towards writing. According to Plato, the written discourse is only a kind of image of the living speech (*Phaedrus* 275D–276A; cf. Hackforth, pp. 162–4). Five hundred years later Papias said 'I did not think that the contents of books would profit me as much as what came from the living and surviving voice' (Eusebius, *H.E.* 3.39). In the third century AD the learned Clement of Alexandria gave due weight to the written word, but 'the secret things, like God himself, are confided to the spoken not the written word' (*Strom.* 1.13.1); and even R. Johanan (d. 279) said, 'The writing down of halakot is equal [in wrongdoing] to the burning of Torah' (b *Tem.* 14b, *Rabbinic Anthology*, p. 131; cf. Gerhardsson, pp. 23–5, 159–60).

Thus it is possible to regard 1 Jn as no mere substitute for a pastoral visit but as an exceptional written communication, prompted by the special circumstances of the recipients, perhaps intended to counter a wayward oral tradition, and purposely introduced by solemn assertions from the sending group. (The eccentric second-century *Epistula Apostolorum* sets out to controvert the gnostic teaching of Simon and Cerinthus by declaring how the apostles 'have written and heard and felt him after he had risen from the dead'; Hennecke I, pp. 191f. The motives for writing are similar though the execution is different.)

The question then arises why the solemn introductory section was so clumsily done, for it reads like a piece of committee drafting. The simplest answer is that an initial short and lucid statement was expanded in successive stages to cover additional points, and was then insufficiently rewritten.

The following stages may be conjectured:–

A.   1*a* **That which was from the beginning,**
     3*ab* **that which we have seen and heard**
     3*c* **we proclaim also to you.**

B.   The first expansion defines the original tradition as the word of life. *Zōē* (*aiōnios*), eternal life, is a dominant theme towards the end of I Jn: it concludes the main discursive argument (5:11, 12), and appears among the miscellaneous final injunctions, when for the last time the writer explains why he has written (5:13, 16, and especially 20, 'This is the true God and eternal life'). Twice earlier it appears in strongly polemical passages introduced by 'what (or, the message) you heard from the beginning' (2:24, 25 and 3:11–15). It may therefore be supposed that, among the recipients of I Jn, there was debate about the means of obtaining or preserving (eternal) life. Hence the second form would run:

     1*a* **That which was from the beginning,**
     3*ab* **that which we have seen and heard**
     1*f* **concerning the word of life**
     3*c* **we proclaim also to you.**

C.   It was then thought necessary to be more explicit about the seeing, to distinguish physical from non-physical perception. (Hearing naturally includes audition, comprehension, and obedience, but this did not call for explicit definition.) The writer uses the two verbs 'see' (*horaō*) and 'look upon' (*theaomai*) (without distinction of meaning, 1:1; 4:12, 20) to introduce one of his prominent polemical themes: that 'no man has ever seen God' (4:12), despite the conviction that 'we shall see him as he is' (3:2); and that 'he who does not love his brother whom he has seen, cannot love God whom he has not seen' (4:20). This seems to be directed against some who claim to have seen God by non-physical perception and to be thereby released from their responsibility to fellow-Christians physically seen. Hence the vigorous modifying clauses are added. For convenience **seen** and **heard** change order, but the connexion with the word of life then becomes awakward since one can hear a word but cannot see or touch it. A very strong motive must have been at work to produce this distortion and yield the following form:

1a **That which was from the beginning,**
 b **which we have heard,**
 c **which we have seen with our eyes,**
 d **which we have looked upon**
 e **and touched with our hands,**
 f **concerning the word of life**
3c **we proclaim also to you.**

D. Once so much has been crammed in, why not more? The final addition begins and ends with **was made manifest** (v. 2). If other statements in the introductory section appear to stress what the writers have experienced and are communicating, this insertion is a balancing statement about the divine initiative. **Life** was disclosed: the particular life which existed in the divine presence was disclosed – and therefore it was disclosed by God, and he disclosed it to us. Thus v. 2 is inserted as a gloss on **life** in 1f to insist on the divine authority of what they testify to and proclaim; it anticipates 3c and requires the resumptive insertion of 3ab. Hence the present form is reached:

1a **That which was from the beginning,**
 b **which we have heard,**
 c **which we have seen with our eyes,**
 d **which we have looked upon**
 e **and touched with our hands,**
 f **concerning the word of life –**
2a **the life was made manifest,**
 b **and we saw it,**
 c **and testify to it,**
 d **and proclaim to you the eternal life**
 e **which was with the Father**
 f **and was made manifest to us –**
3ab **that which we have seen and heard**
 c **we proclaim also to you.**

1–4. That which was from the beginning recalls Jn 1:1, 'In the beginning was the Word', and suggests a number of correspondences between the introduction to the Epistle and the Prologue to the Gospel: **we have seen**: cf. Jn 1:18, 'no one has ever seen' (*heōraken* in both); **we have looked upon**: cf. Jn 1:14, 'we have beheld' (*etheasametha* in both); **the word of life**: cf. Jn 1:1, 14, 'the Word'; **the life**: cf. Jn 1:4, 'the life was the light of men'; **we . . . testify to it**: cf. Jn 1:7–8, 'he came for testimony . . . to bear witness'; **eternal life which was with the Father**: cf. Jn 1:1, 2, 'the Word was with God' (*pros* and acc. in both); **our fellowship is with the Father and with his Son Jesus Christ**: cf. Jn 1:18, 'the only Son, who is in the bosom of the Father, he has made him known'; and, continuing to v. 5, **God is light and in him is no darkness at all**: cf. Jn 1:5, 'the light shines in the darkness, and the darkness has not overcome it'.

There is obviously some connexion between the introduction to the Epistle and the Prologue to the Gospel, for they use a common stock of words, though never exactly in the same sense. In v. 1 the Greek neuter pronoun rendered in English as **that** is scarcely suited to the personal treatment of the masculine 'Word' in the Prologue; contrast 'him who is from the beginning', 2:13, 14. In the Prologue 'in the beginning' recalls the opening words of Genesis in LXX and directs attention to the creative initiative of God with whom the Word was clearly existent, not the object but the agent of creation. 'In the beginning' has this special meaning only in Jn 1:1, 2 (elsewhere it refers to the beginning of the Christian movement, Ac. 11:15, Phil. 4:15); **from the beginning** may also refer to the creation if an appropriate genitive is added (of creation, of the world, Mk 10:6; 13:19, 2 Pet. 3:4; and possibly the unqualified variant reading in 2 Th. 2:13), but otherwise it simply means 'from the start', in whatever sense is appropriate (Ac. 26:4; Lk. 1:2). The other references in 1 Jn lean in that direction. 'The old commandment you had (or the message which you have heard) from the beginning' (2:7, 24; 3:11; 2 Jn 5, 6) refers to the earliest stages of the Christian community, and is parallel *mutatis mutandis* with 'you have been with me from the beginning' in Jn 15:27. The statement in 3:8 means that the devil is a sinner from the start (*RSV* translates the present tense of *hamartanei*, 'is sinning', by 'has sinned', because it thinks of *archē* (**beginning**) in too precise terms: cf. Jn 8:44). On the other hand, 'him who is from the beginning' (2:13, 14) is ambiguous: it may be intended to refer to the pre-temporal existence of God or Christ, or to the significance of Christ for the Christian community from the beginning of its existence.

Therefore in considering the meaning in 1:1 of **that which was from the beginning** a choice must be made between the pre-temporal existence of Christ (in which case it is hard to understand why the neuter form was used) and the set of convictions present in the Christian community from its beginning (which sense is confirmed by **the word of life** and the general drift of 1 Jn). If the latter

interpretation is accepted, the writers intend to set out the original
Christian convictions in opposition to novelties that are proving
attractive to the recipients. Some of those convictions are indicated
in subsequent references to what the community had heard: the
commandment of love in 2:7; 3:11; 2 Jn 6; the knowledge that
antichrist was coming 2:18; 4:3; and the confession of Father and
Son, 2:24. In what sense, however, could such convictions be **seen
with our eyes, looked upon and touched with our hands?** And
what strong motive could have thrust such additional phrases into
the originally perhaps simpler formulation of the introductory
section?

It has commonly been supposed that these words were an allusive
reference to Jesus whom the writers had seen and heard during his
ministry and touched with their hands after his resurrection.
According to the resurrection episode in Lk. 24:39, where the same
verb *psēlaphaō* for 'touch' or 'handle' is used as here, Jesus deliberately asked the disciples to handle him in proof that he was flesh
and bones and not merely a spirit. It may be that the writers of the
introductory section were dropping a hint that the risen Jesus was
not disembodied, though the Johannine resurrection stories lack the
direct Lukan stress on embodiment.

The two Johannine incidents are more elusive. In Jn 20:17 Jesus
says to Mary, 'Do not hold me, for I have not yet ascended to the
Father' (the verb for 'hold' is *haptomai*), with perhaps the odd
implication that she might be able to hold him if he had ascended.
In 20:27 Jesus says to Thomas, 'Put your fingers here, and see my
hands; and put out your hand, and place it in my side'; though in
fact it is not said that Thomas did so, and it may be the evangelist's
intention to indicate that the person who appeared to the assembled
disciples on both occasions was the ascended Christ. Within the
early Church there were those who read this narrative in a materi-
alistic sense, muddled as they may have been. In the *Adumbrations*
(GCS 17, p. 210, Stählin) Clement of Alexandria on 1 Jn 1:1
expressly mentions traditions associated with the name of John: 'In
the traditions it is reported that John touched the outward body (of
Jesus) and put his hand deep within and that the solidity of the
flesh in no wise offered resistance but yielded to the disciple's hand'
(cf. the third century *Acts of John* 93).

Yet the confident opening words of the Epistle are a very oblique
way of introducing such an imaginative idea about the resurrection,
and indeed the introductory section as a whole would be a curiously
diffident set of references to the Jesus who was known to his first
followers. If the introductory section were intended to call the
historical Jesus to mind – and 4:2 stresses the importance of con-

fessing that Jesus Christ has come in the flesh – why does 1 Jn provide no unambiguous reference to any historical action (including the resurrection) or to any saying? There are references to his commandments and to the injunction 'to walk in the same way in which he walked' (2:6). But the writer's commendation of love is not directly rooted in Jesus' love command as recorded in the Synoptic Gospels, and the command 'that he who loves God should love his brother also' (4:21) is more restrictive than Jesus' commandment of love to one's opponent in the Great Sermon. It seems unlikely that the introduction was intended to bring before its readers' eyes a picture of the historical Jesus.

Therefore the words about seeing and touching must refer to such perception and experience of the original Christian convictions that placed them firmly in the physical life of Christians and not in a realm of non-physical religious awareness. Such an intention may have been formed in order to set aside a non-physical version of Christian truth. Two kinds may be illustrated, one from Col. 2:21, which records the slogan 'Do not handle (*haptomai*), Do not touch (*thinganō*)' of a group who wish to force their views and practices on the Church as the price of entry into ecstatic visions (Martin, pp. 91–8). In that case, against the temptation to renounce some features of physical existence for the sake of promised visions, the writers of the introductory section would be asserting the superior claims of what they had indeed handled and seen as well.

The other non-physical version of Christian truth may be discerned in developments from the *NT* in two second-century texts. Logion 17 of the *Gospel of Thomas*, which looks like a modified version of 1 C. 2:9, reads: 'Jesus said: I will give you what eye has not seen and ear has not heard and hand has not touched and which has not come into the heart of man'. The saying was widely reproduced (see Ménard, p. 105) and expresses the conviction that the heavenly Jesus could be apprehended only by non-physical perceptions. In similar fashion the *Gospel of Truth* 30.25f. says: 'The knowledge of the Father and the revelation of his son gave them the opportunity to perceive. For when they saw him and heard him, he granted them to taste of him and to smell him and to take hold of the beloved son' (Foerster II, p. 62). Against such claims that only gnostic spiritualising could give access to the true Jesus, the writers of the introduction would be asserting that they had heard, seen and handled the truth about him. For the writers, as much as for those they were opposing, this was not a speculative debate but **the word of life**.

Once the temptation has been resisted to assume that *logos* here in v. 1 has the same speculative meaning as in the Prologue to the

Gospel, it is possible to give full weight to the use of *logos* in the rest of 1 Jn. In 2:5 'keeping his word' is the opposite of 'disobeying his commandments' in the previous verse; and in 2:7, 'the old commandment is the word which you have heard'. The **word** dwelling in the community is the means of recognising sin and of overcoming the evil one (1:10; 2:14). It is in fact the commandment of mutual love and must not remain an idea in the mind or a spoken statement, but must become the activity and inmost conviction of the community (3:18). Hence *logos* means here what it also means in the Gospel outside the Prologue: that instruction provided by Jesus which marks the passage from death to life for the person who accepts and practises it (Jn 5:24; 8:51). Those who live by his word are truly his disciples. They come to know the truth and the truth sets them free (Jn 8:31). 'If a man loves me, he will keep my word, and my Father will love him, and we will come to him and make our home with him' (Jn 14:23) – which is precisely the claim made in 1 Jn 1:3. Hence **the word of life** means the life-giving instruction (taking the gen. as descriptive, though it might be subjective 'the message about (the) life'; cf. Jn 6:68, 'You have the words of eternal life'; i.e., you have the instructions that make eternal life possible. *JB* wrongly takes the genitive in 1 Jn 1:1 as appositive, 'the Word, who is life'. We heard it, say the writers, we saw its effects, we observed it, and our hands handled it, i.e., we actually practised it (cf. Leaney, pp. 199–200, on 1QS 6.24).

Finally, is it possible to discern the relation between the introduction to 1 Jn and the Prologue to the Gospel? Does 1 Jn echo the Prologue, faintly and with some confusion; or is the Prologue an elaborated form of the introduction to 1 Jn? Of those possibilities, the latter is to be preferred. The Prologue is three times as long as the Epistle's introduction and contains many more key words. Some of them, though absent from the Epistle's introduction, appear elsewhere in 1 Jn and the Gospel (e.g., believe, children, flesh, truth, world); some are absent from 1 Jn though found in the Gospel (glory, his own); and some are absent from both 1 Jn and the Gospel ('dwell' translating *skēnoō*, grace, and 'make known' translating *exēgeomai*, rather than 'make manifest', *phaneroō*, in the Epistle's introduction). 'Only son' appears at Jn 3:16, 18, at 1 Jn 4:9, and twice in the Prologue Jn 1:14, 18 (though in the latter *monogenēs theos* is a strongly-supported variant). The writer of the Prologue was fusing Johannine and non-Johannine terminology into a coherent structure (or so it may be argued), dominated by the theme of creation: he converted the common Johannine **word** into the speculative Logos and thus could say that 'the world was made by him' (Jn 1:10, *ho kosmos di autou egeneto*—apart from 1:3, the only

Johannine use of *ginomai* to mean 'create'). *Kosmos* is frequent in 1 Jn (though not 'all things' of Jn 1:3); its passing away is mentioned at 2:17, but the creation of the *kosmos* plays no part whatsoever. Speculation about the creation has not touched 1 Jn (hence the irrelevance of the treatment in Ehrhardt, pp. 193f.); the community has not yet made the shift from eschatology to protology. It is not likely that the writers of the Epistle's introduction would have borrowed from an already existing Prologue, suppressing the creation theme and producing a very oblique christological allusion; it is more likely that the Prologue came later and universalised the particular assertions of the Epistle's introduction.

2. The parenthesis is introduced by *kai*, usually left untranslated; but it might be represented by 'indeed', or even by 'though', if the clause is intended to stress disclosure rather than perception of **the life**. It is taken for granted that the readers will know what is meant, at least formally, by **life** and **eternal life**; the whole of the Epistle is an attempt to argue that a particular life-style alone corresponds to **eternal life** which the community has possessed from the first. It has two interrelated components which are discernible in 1 Jn, though references in the Gospel give substance to these brief indications.

(i) 'The darkness is passing away and the true light is already shining' (2:8 cf. 2:17, 18, 28; 3:3; 4:17). The *kosmos* has reached its last hour. Whatever it contains belonging to the devil will be destroyed; whatever it contains belonging to the true God will be transformed. This transformation is the passage from light to darkness, from death to life. **Eternal life** is the new existence which not only replaces the present *kosmos* but which is anticipated in the Christian community and is evidenced by love of the brethren (3:14). This is written out more explicitly in Jn 5:24–25: 'He who hears my word and believes him who sent me has eternal life; he does not come into judgment, but has passed from death to life. . . The hour is coming (that is the traditional eschatological statement), and now is (that is its anticipation in the Christian community) when the dead will hear the voice of the Son of God, and those who hear will live'. Hence eternal life, so far as preaching and moral instruction are concerned, has its origin in the Jewish eschatological expectation.

(ii) But it has its spiritual and liturgical origin in reflexion on the divine being: **the eternal life which was with the Father** (*ēn pros ton patera*, had its existence only in relation to the Father). This is explained in Jn 5:26: 'As the Father has life in himself, so he has granted the Son to have life in himself' – and therefore the Son has authority to execute judgment, to call forth the dead to the resurrection of life or of judgment. God alone is independent self-existent being; by divine gift, the Son is dependent self-existent being. Those who believe on the Son and on the Father who sent him share the Son's dependent self-existence, which is **eternal life**. So in Jn 6:53–54: 'Unless you eat the flesh of the Son of man and drink his blood, you have no life in yourselves; he who eats my flesh and drinks my blood has eternal life, and I will raise him up at the last day'.

Consequently, to return to 1 Jn, 'If what you heard from the beginning abides in you, then you will abide in the Son and in the Father. And this is what he has promised us, eternal life' (2:24–25; cf. 5:11–13). Thus the two components of eternal life are the existence of the new world and the existence of the divine being. They belong together because God had sent his Son to manifest and make available the divine life in the present *kosmos*; this the Son had done by passing from death to life in his resurrection and so setting in train the great transition. 'He sent his only Son into the world, so that we might live through him' (4:9). The author of 1 Jn writes 'in order that you may know that you have eternal life' (5:13), and the author of the Gospel follows the same programme, though with a different manner and in other circumstances: 'these are written that you may believe that Jesus is the Christ, the Son of God, and that believing you may have life in his name' (Jn 20:31).

The writers of the introduction are insistent that this life was disclosed to them (here and at 4:9 *RSV* preserves the archaic **made manifest** to translate *phaneroō*). Elsewhere the verb refers to the past appearance of the Son of God to take away sin, destroy the devil's activities, and give life to the community (3:5, 8; 4:9); and also to the future divine appearance at the parousia and (perhaps) to the consequent disclosure of the true nature of Christians (2:28; 3:2). (The unmasking of the dissident group in 2:19 may imply a more neutral sense of the verb, but it may equally be the converse of [one interpretation of] 3:2*a*: there is a disclosure of their radically false nature.) These are important stages of disclosure in the apocalyptic drama; they are not merely episodes that provide religious information that has become the property of a sect. Hence the disclosure of **the word of life** to this Christian group is not essentially different; it also is a necessary stage in the eschatological drama. (The use of *phaneroō* in the Gospel scarcely bears this weight, except perhaps in 21:1, 14 of the Resurrection disclosure.) That is why they must **testify** (*martyreō*) and **proclaim** (*apangellō*, though *anangellō* in 1:5). The latter verbs are used again in that section (or version) of the Farewell Discourse which appears in Jn 16:12–33 and deals with matters yet to be disclosed. The Spirit of truth will not speak on his own authority, but whatever he hears he will speak (cf. therefore the emphasis on hearing in 1 Jn 1:1–3) and he will declare things that are to come. He will take what belongs to Jesus and declare it to the community (Jn 16:13–15; cf. 1 Jn 4:1–3, where the same subjects are mentioned because the writer wishes to exclude false declarations).

As the Discourse proceeds with veiled statements about the 'little while' when they will no longer see Jesus, and the period of sorrow that will be turned into joy, even more is promised: that the hour is coming when Jesus will speak to them no longer figuratively but plainly about the Father, when they themselves in his name will speak directly to the Father (16:25–26). The verb **testify** is of larger importance in the Johannine writings and naturally appears when the eschatological drama includes imagery of trial and judgment. 'In chapters one to twelve John uses language to describe a cosmic lawsuit between God and the world' (Trites, p. 112), and indeed the whole of chapter 8. In 1 Jn 4:14; 5:6–12 the testimony, of the we-group ('we have seen and testify . . .') or the more complex threefold testimony of Spirit, water and blood, is exclusively given to the Son, though in 5:11 the testimony embraces both God's gift of eternal life and its character as life in the Son. The responsibility laid on the community or on one of its members to bear witness appears in a few intrusions in the Gospel: Jn 19:35, the witness to the emission of both blood and water; 21:24, the witness to the authorisation of Peter and its confirmation by a we-group; 3:11, the rueful admission by a we-group, in the setting of Jesus' poor success in enlightening Nicodemus, that their testimony to what they have seen and known is not accepted by the Jews. This experience is generalised and given a reflective explanation in 3:31–36: Jesus who comes from above bears testimony to what he has seen and heard (like the we-group of 1 Jn 1:2), but those who belong to the earth do not accept his testimony. *Anyone* who does accept his testimony certifies that God is true; *anyone* sent by God speaks God's word, for God does not restrict the gift of his Spirit to a few but gives to all believers (so, with the problems of 1 Jn in mind, may 3:34*b* be interpreted). The passage ends with the credal assertion in 3:35–36 which is very close to the testimony of 1 Jn 5:11–13. As elsewhere, a reading of 1 Jn shows what problems the evangelist was trying to solve in the Gospel.

3. Apart from 1:3, 6, 7 the word fellowship does not appear in Johannine writings; indeed *koinōnia* and related words are almost confined to the Pauline corpus, where they are mainly used in a practical and commonplace manner. A *koinōnos* is a partner in some enterprise; *koinōnia* is a close relation between partners who share something—either by retaining it in common or by taking separate portions. In various Pauline passages, Christian partners share the faith, the preaching task, financial arrangements, charity to the destitute, the sufferings of Christ, and the Holy Spirit. This usage is entirely natural and its application to a religious group does not thereby make it theologically significant. Yet the character of a group is moulded by what it shares in common, and in I C. 10:14–22, moved by pressures on the Corinthian community, Paul takes some steps towards a more theologically significant sense of *koinōnia*. The passage begins, as I Jn ends, with a warning against idolatry and leads to a sharp distinction between the Lord and the lords (here called demons) because they have no *metochē*, nothing they share in common—just as light and darkness have no *koinōnia* in I Jn 1:5–6. Worshippers who share cultic meals share more than the group enhancement of ritual actions and more than the benefits promised by the deity: they also share an understanding of the world and human existence. This is true of Israel's sacrificial system, of hellenistic cults, and of the Lord's Supper. The Christian *koinōnia* is therefore formed around Christ, shares his benefits, and understands its existence in the world exclusively in terms of his death and resurrection, his blood and his (resurrection) body. 'The cup of blessing which we bless, is it not a participation in the blood of Christ? The bread which we break, is it not a participation in the body of Christ?' Paul's argument is used not only to warn against idolatry but also to commend unity within the community; perhaps for a similar reason he writes in the letter that his readers 'were called into the fellowship of his Son' (I C. 1:9). The translation implies 'into the community belonging to, constituted by his Son', but *eis koinōnian* might be translated 'into close relation', i.e., 'communion with', or 'to participate in' his Son.

Whatever Paul may have intended, it is clear that his ventures with *koinōnia* never led him to talk, as I Jn does, of **fellowship with the Father**. The first use of *koinōnia* in v. 3 is straightforward: **that you may have fellowship with us** means that the writers and the readers may share **the word of life** in common. Their **fellowship with the Father and with his Son Jesus Christ** undoubtedly implies a close relation between the writers, God and Christ, but it is likely to be a relation between partners who share something in common. What is it that they have in common? Surely it is the eschatological drama, from the sending of the Son to his passion, which includes the disclosure to the community and the responsibility which is thereby laid upon them. The insistence that the *koinōnia* is with both the Father and his Son implies a different or more restricted *koinōnia* claimed by others (cf. therefore 2:22).

The grammatical form of **our fellowship** may be significant. In *kai hē koinōnia de hē hēmetera* the word *kai* is intensive 'and indeed', and the phrase may imply: 'and indeed our fellowship in contrast to someone else's'. *hēmetera*, 'our', like other possessive adjectives, is uncommon in *NT* and is usually said to be unemphatic in post-position. Some forms, especially *emos*, 'mine', are fairly frequent in Jn: though not necessarily emphatic, they often express a contrast; cf. 1 Jn 2:2, 'not for ours (*hēmeterōn*) only, but also. . . . ' Finally, the use of this non-Johannine word *koinōnia* may imply that the writers were using the words of others to state their own claim before expressing it in their own preferred language. It is often said that, despite the rarity of the *koinōnia* words in Jn, communion is central in Johannine teaching. So it is, but it is a rather different thing from *koinōnia* (cf. Moule, pp. 64–6. The discussion of *koinōnia* has not advanced much beyond Hauck, *TWNT* III, 1938, and A. R. George, *Communion with God in the New Testament*, London, 1953).

4. The sentence is a polite convention; see the introductory paragraph to the commentary on 1:1–4.

THE MORAL CONSEQUENCES 1:5–2:11

Verse 5 stands somewhat by itself. The remaining verses 6–10 are an interconnected tissue of words, such that almost every clause is echoed in another clause, e.g., **fellowship** in 6*a* reappears in 7*c*; **we walk** (6*b*) in 7*a*; **we lie** (6*c*) in 10*b*; **the truth** (6*d*) in 8*d*, and so on. Only two phrases lack this integration with the characteristically Johannine progressive argument, viz. 7*d*, **the blood of Jesus his Son**, and 9*b*, **he is faithful and just**. Moreover, the passage is composed of five if-clauses which are common in the Epistle (but not elsewhere concentrated as they are here) and often introduce a condition for knowing or experiencing a religious truth, e.g., 2:3, 24, 29 and 4:12. To this group the if-clauses of 1:7, 9 also belong: **if we walk in the light** or **if we confess our sins** then certain benefits will follow. But the remaining if-clauses of this passage (1:6, 8, 10) have the opposite effect: they introduce conditions which prevent the desired benefits; cf. 2:15; 4:20. Specifically they introduce destructive statements by the formula **if we say**; and so may be put alongside 4:20, 'if any one says', and 2:4, 6, 9, 'he who says'. In each case the writing appears to be polemical, not simply warning the community against thoughts that may occur to them, but repudiating views actually expressed by a dissident section of the community.

5. Although the original tradition has been defined in 1:1 as 'the word of life', which might naturally lead to a dualism of life and death as in 3:14–15, the writers turn away from that designation to a dualism of light and darkness. They introduce it with a favourite assertive formula: **this is the message** (or testimony, or confidence) **that God** . . . (1:5; 5:9, 11, 14 using *hoti*, 'namely, that'; there is a variant of the formula using *hina* ('in order that') to state what Christians should do in 3:11, 23; 5:3, and another variant rather awkwardly using apposition in 2:25; 5:4). The essential assertion is a sharp distinction between light and darkness which associates God exclusively with light. This, the writers claim, **we have heard from him** (i.e., from the Son). They are presumably stating common Christian belief since the remaining references to light and darkness in 2:8–11 are not in themselves polemical. Both they and the dissident group proceed from this common affirmation though drawing different consequences from it, and this becomes plainer in vv 6–9; but for other readers of the epistle the meaning of the essential assertion is not immediately clear.

Is it significant that the positive affirmation says that God is light, whereas the negative affirms that **in him is no darkness at all** (as if the divine person might perhaps include both darkness and light, somewhat in the manner of the Qumran belief: God 'created the spirits of light and darkness and founded every action upon them and established every deed upon their ways', 1QS 3.25–26; Leaney, pp. 37–46)? The answer must probably be no, since in him (*en autō*) readily means 'in his case' (2:10; 3:5, 'in him there is no sin'; Jn 1:47; 4:14; 7:18; 8:44; 9:3; 18:38, 'I find no crime in him'; 19:4, 6): the writers are using emphatic variation to assert that so far as God is concerned there is no darkness at all. They oppose a widely held belief in the permanent existence and equal powers of light and darkness – intruded awkwardly into the *Community Rule* of Qumran and turning up in gnostic sources; e.g., Basilides is reported to have written that certain barbarians say that the origins of all things 'are without origin and unoriginate, that is, that in the beginning there were light and darkness, which existed of themselves' (Hegemonius, *Acta Archelai* 67.7; in Foerster I, p. 75). Their opposition would include Mandean religious conceptions (supposing that the oldest sources could be securely identified and regarded as witnesses from the oriental milieu of early Christianity) despite the initial similarity between 'the world of radiance and light in which there is no darkness' of the Right Ginza and the conceptions of the Epistle. It is in any case difficult to believe that the luxuriant verbiage of the Mandean texts (an English translation of which is now available in Foerster, *Gnosis*, II) can have influenced the controlled rhythmical austerity of the epistle.

The imagery of light and darkness is widespread in the religion and philosophy of antiquity, either in speculation about divine beings or attempts at cosmogony or descriptions of human activity. The Hermetic tractate *Poimandres* begins with a vision of light followed by a vision of darkness, and the divinity Poimandres explains 'That Light is I, Mind, Your God'. Later he teaches that 'God the Father is light and life' and warns that 'he who loves the body which comes from the seduction of passion remains in the darkness'. In the final offering of praise the initiate says, 'I believe and testify: I go to life and light' (*Corpus Hermeticum* I.6, 12, 18, 20, 32).

The seventh Tractate includes an appeal: 'Seek a guide who will lead you to the gates of knowledge, where the bright light is, uncontaminated by darkness, where not one is drunk, but all are sober, because they look with their heart at him who wishes to be seen' (*Corpus Hermeticum* VII.2). This mystical awareness of God as light is not remote from Philo's conception (which he reaches by a different route) that God is 'the sun of the sun, the mental concept corresponding to the object of perception (*noētos aisthētou*), providing from invisible sources the visible rays of the sun that we see' (*Special Laws* I.279). In the treatise *On Dreams*, Philo cautiously explores the senses in which God can be likened to the sun, although in reality nothing is like God. 'God is light, for there is a verse in one of the psalms, "the lord is my illumination and my saviour". And he is not only light but the archetype of every other light. . . As the sun makes day and night distinct, so Moses says that God kept apart light and darkness. . . Above all, as the sun when it rises makes visible objects which had been hidden, so God when he gave birth to all things, not only brought them into sight, but also made things which before were not, not just handling material as an artificer, but being himself its creator' (*On Dreams* I.75f.). The figure of light can be regarded as the primary guide to Philo's philosophy and mysticism, and it typifies the highest reality as much to Plato and Aristotle as to the religious devotees of Egypt (Goodenough (1962), p 101; cf. *By Light, Light*, p. 8).

Despite these affinities, light mysticism plays no part in the Epistle. The words **God is light** are not intended as a statement about God's nature since they are immediately followed by the assertion that God is **in the light** (1:7). Light and darkness signify two contrasted structures of human existence, such that God in his proper being is associated exclusively with light. (In the Gospel, light is associated with the Logos and with Jesus but not directly with God; and Barrett (1982), p. 106, draws attention to the contrast between the dynamic references in the Gospel and the static proposition of 1 Jn 1:5).

The first idea suggested by light is illumination: Christians know the truth and know that they have eternal life. This conviction plays some part though not a dominating part in the Epistle (e.g., 2:20–21; 3:19; 5:13) and reassuringly provides its closing paragraph: 'We know that the Son of God has come and given us understanding, to know him who is true; and we are in him who is true . . . This is the true God and eternal life' (5:20). There are good grounds in Scripture for interpreting the divine light as truth and life (and Scripture is doubtless the source of what they **have heard from him**, since there is no reason to suppose that Jesus is referred to or indeed gave such teaching): 'Send out thy light and truth . . . let them lead me to thy holy hill and to thy dwelling' (Ps. 43:3); 'For with thee is the fountain of life; in thy light do we see light' (Ps. 36:9). But the writer of the Epistle far prefers to interpret Christian life as righteousness and love; 'Whoever does not do right is not of God, nor is he who does not love his brother' (3:10). It is therefore significant that the passage just quoted from Ps. 36 is set in a context of God's steadfast love (*eleos*), faithfulness (*alētheia*), and righteousness for those who know him (Ps. 36:5–10). Compare also Ps. 89:14–15:

> Thy throne is built upon righteousness and justice,
> true love and faithfulness herald thy coming.
> Happy the people who have learnt to acclaim thee,
> who walk, O Lord, in the light of thy countenance. (*NEB*)

In agreement with traditional Jewish piety, the writer of the Epistle puts a limit to the interpretation of light-imagery in individual speculative mysticism though without repudiating it, and instead powerfully develops an interpretation in terms of social morality, simply replacing the Septuagint's *eleos* (which translates Hebrew *ḥesed*, covenant love) with the Christian *agapē*.

6–7. The first general conclusions for human behaviour are here drawn from the previous assertion about God. The word **we** now extends from writers to readers. On **fellowship**, see 1:3. **Walk** has the characteristically Jewish figurative meaning 'to conduct one's life' (not normal Greek usage; occasionally *peripateō*; frequently *poreuomai* in LXX for the figurative sense of the Hebrew *hālak*) and is common in Paul, fairly common in the Johannine writings: walking in the darkness/light, 2:11; Jn 8:12 and 12:35 (where however Jesus is the light); 11:9–10 (day or night); cf. walking in the truth 2 Jn 4; 3 Jn 3, 4, and walking according to his commandment, 2 Jn 6. The phrases are examples of one type of Johannine construction using the preposition 'in' mostly for describing persons being,

walking, or remaining in various situations: being or remaining in
the darkness or the light (2:9–10); being in the world (4:3–4, 17)
and remaining in death (3:14); remaining in love (4:16). In Jn the
construction is used in more varied manner; in the Epistle it is fairly
closely confined to the contrasting structures of human existence
which can be indicated by light and darkness, life and death, sight
and blindness, love and hatred, God and the Evil One.

According as we belong to one side or the other, either **we lie** or
we live according to the truth. 'Speak falsely' would better convey
the meaning of the former words and 'perform the truth' of the
latter, for they are more practical than theoretical. 'Performing the
truth' occurs again in Jn 3:21 and seems to be based on the occa-
sional appearance of *poiein tēn alētheian* in LXX to translate Hebrew *'aśâh 'emet*, 'to act loyally'. In Tobit, however, a popular
romance commending strict observance of Torah, generosity of
spirit, and the superiority of Jewish magic, 'doing the truth' is a
matter of specific practices:

> Perform good deeds all the days of thy life
> and do not walk in the ways of wickedness;
> For those who perform the truth
> will prosper in their activities.

(Tob. 4:6 א ; the text of BA makes the point even more strongly.)
Similar references occur in *Test. Reub* 6.9 and *Test. Benj.* 10.3, and
this may therefore be a popular usage extending from 200 BCE to
200 CE. It is dominant in the writings of Qumran: the *Community
Rule* begins with the Master's duty of instructing the members 'to
practise truth, righteousness and justice', so that they become 'a
community of truth and virtuous humanity, of loving-kindness and
good intent one towards the other' (1QS 1.5; 3.24f.). The *Rule*
includes instructions for admission to and behaviour within the
community, teaching about the spirits of truth and falsehood, and
instructions about calendrical worship. The Master is required to
conceal the teaching of the law from men of falsehood, but to impart
knowledge of the truth and right judgment to those who have chosen
the Way (1QS 9.17). That is, truth is the Law as revealed to Moses
and interpreted by the sect. This interpretation which told them
what to believe and how to act was not a matter of opinion or
preference: it was the truth recently disclosed for use in the last
days. Their rules and convictions corresponded to the structure of
the world; hence their actions and thought if true maintained the
world, if false destroyed it. Something similar is present in 1 Jn's
concern with truth and falsehood. 'The desire to live according to

the structure of the universe is found everywhere in the ancient world, differing only in the forms which it takes' (Leaney, p. 26). In the Epistle, one of the central matters in debate is whether living according to the structure of the world is possible or desirable, whether rules and convictions are disclosed, and whether they are necessary and compulsory.

An example is immediately available in v. 7*d*. Verses 6–7*c* form a complex but satisfactory antithesis:

6*a* **If we say we have fellowship with him**
  b   **while we walk in the darkness,**
  c **we lie and do not live according to the truth;**
7*a* **but if we walk in the light,**
  b   **as he is in the light,**
  c **we have fellowship with one another.**
  (*d* **and the blood of Jesus his Son cleanses us from all sin.**)

Verse 7*d* is not necessary to the argument and is unexpected, since sin has not yet been mentioned. It is also contradicted by v. 9, which presents standard Jewish teaching that God forgives those who confess their sins (e.g., Isa. 55:7; 1QH 14.24; Vermes, p. 194) 'Thou art a merciful God and rich in favours, pardoning those who repent of their sin'; in Tannaitic Judaism: 'No matter how numerous a man's transgressions, God has provided for their forgiveness, as long as he indicates his intention to remain in the covenant by repenting and doing other appropriate acts of atonement' (Sanders, p. 157).

Thus there is a strong case for regarding v. 7*d* as an addition to the original formulation or at least as an afterthought; and it clearly belongs to a different way of thinking from that contained in vv. 6–7*c*. In fact the cleansing effect of the blood of Jesus is meaningful only if particular convictions are held about the structure of the world, and those convictions were by no means generally held in the Johannine community, which was uncertain what to make of the death of Jesus, if anything. Hence the writer later has to plead that Jesus Christ came 'not with the water only but with the water and the blood', though without indicating why the blood had such importance. In 3:16 the death of Jesus is purely exemplary: 'By this we know love, that he laid down his life for us; and we ought to lay down our lives for the brethren'; and there is no other explicit mention of his death in the Epistle. If 4:10 is interpreted by 3:16, the death of Jesus is an expiation for our sins which is also asserted in 2:2 where, however, the expiation is attached to Jesus as paraclete. For further discussion, see on 2:2. The impression cannot be avoided that reference to the blood of Jesus sits rather uneasily alongside the simple metaphor of light and darkness; perhaps this apparent intrusion therefore raises the question whether the metaphor can be allowed to remain as simple as it seems.

In this connexion it is worth noticing how the other Johannine writings treat the death of Christ. There are no references to it in 2 and 3 Jn. The Apocalypse is single-minded: the blood of Jesus means his martyrdom and relies on the martyrdom theology deriving from the Maccabean deaths. 'They who have come out of the great tribulation and have washed their robes and made them white in the blood of the Lamb' are Christians who have regained their innocence by sharing his martyrdom (Rev. 7:14). Of this there is no trace in the Epistle. The Gospel contains premonitions in Jn 15:18–20 and 16:2, possibly also in the surprising intrusion of drinking the blood of the Son of man (Jn 6:53–56), but otherwise martyrdom theology is not significant. Any reader of the Gospel can readily hear the death of Christ as an undertone; but references are surprisingly oblique.

The Passion and Resurrection narratives devote proportionately more space to the Resurrection than any other Gospel, the section Jn 18:1–19:16 is mainly a Johannine-type dialogue about the non-political authority of Jesus, and Jesus finally dies as the model wise man. Thomas's request shows that continuing evidence of crucifixion is available but unnecessary. The action and discourses in Jn 13–17 contain no explicit reference to the death of Christ, and the indirect reference in 15:13 is in the form of a general truth. In Jn 1–12 there are long sections relating the animosity of 'the Jews' to Jesus and so accounting for his death (cf. Harvey, 1976, *passim*), references to the predetermined 'hour' at which it took place, and interpretations of the death as exaltation. In the centrally significant narrative of Jn 9, when Jesus confers sight on the man born blind, which may be regarded as symbolic of what Jesus does for mankind, mention of his death would doubtless be dramatically inappropriate; but the writer has felt it necessary to append the *paroimia* of the good shepherd, and extend it by Jesus' statement that he lays down his life for the sheep (Jn 10:15, linked to the miracle by 10:21). That Jesus' death is in some way related to the benefits he confers is presumed but not readily demonstrated. Likewise in the narrative of Lazarus, Thomas says beforehand, 'Let us also go, that we may die with him', and afterwards Caiaphas judges 'that it is expedient for you that one man should die for the people, and that the whole nation should not perish'; yet Jesus performs the miracle because he is the resurrection and the life (Jn 11:16, 50, 25). The Baptist's disclosure of Jesus as 'the Lamb of God who takes away the sin of the world' (Jn 1:29) may throw some light on I Jn 1:7*d*, if combined with I Jn 2:2 where Jesus is the 'expiation. . . . .for the sins of the

whole world'. Presumably the designation refers to a sacrificial offering but no exegete has yet satisfactorily identified what it is, and
as it stands there is no explicit reference to the death of Christ. The
evidence suggests that traditional language about the atoning value
of the blood or death of Christ was known but not entirely at home
in the Johannine community. Those responsible for the Epistle were
more than willing to incorporate such language; those responsible
for the Gospel were more reluctant.

8–10. Like vv. 6–7c, these verses are rhythmically phrased in
such a way that 10 repeats 8 with appropriate variations and both
enclose 9 which may originally have omitted **he is faithful and just,
and** (since these words destroy the rhythm and play no part in the
interconnected linkage of words in the whole passage). To **have (no)
sin** is Johannine only and is more appropriately translated 'to be
(not) guilty'. **The truth** (or **his word**) **is not in us** belongs to the
type of Johannine construction using the preposition 'in' to indicate
that something divine is or remains evident *within* the Christian's
individual or communal life: namely, God's **word** (1:10; 2:14); 'what
you heard from the beginning' (2:24); 'the testimony' (5:10); 'the
truth' (1:8; 2:4); 'the anointing' (2:24); 'his seed' (3:9, *RV*); 'the
love of God' (2:5, 15; 3:17; 4:12, 16); 'eternal life' (3:15). This use
is also common in the Gospel and it presumes that the Christian life
is constituted by features of the divine activity. Thus God's **word**
and **truth** (the two are equivalent and mean instruction for living in
the light) are not simply addressed *to* the Christian but are also
displayed *in* the Christian.

This surely was common ground in the Johannine community.
From it could easily be drawn the conclusion that Christians, indwelt by the divine activity, could do no wrong. That indeed is
clearly affirmed at 3:6, 9: 'No one born of God commits sin; for
God's nature abides in him, and he cannot sin because he is born
of God'. A later gnostic wrote: 'As for those who have put on the
perfect light, the powers do not see them and cannot seize them.
But one will put on the light in the mystery, in the union' (*Gospel
of Philip* 77). Some Christians at least insisted that we have no sin
and we have not sinned; the writers of the letter denied their claim.

Anyone familiar with the ways of the churches and their members
scarcely needs persuading that Christians can sin and require forgiveness. It is not easy to be patient with an 'enthusiastic' Christianity which regards sinlessness not merely as a possibility but as an
accomplishment, especially when the 'enthusiasts' admit no criticism of their own actions. Apart from that hindrance, simple ob-
servation of Christian communities would show their fallibility. In
2 Jn 4 only some are 'following the truth', and in 3 Jn 11, with the

objectionable Diotrephes in mind, they must be urged 'Do not imitate evil but imitate good'. Of the seven churches addressed in the Apocalypse, only the second and sixth are not told to repent; and in the dialogues of Jn 13–17, written for the nurture of the Christian community, the disciples are subject to rebuke and reproach.

The writers of the Epistle, however, go further: not only are those who claim to be sinless self-deceived but they make God out to be **a liar** (cf. I C. 4:4, 'I am not aware of anything against myself, but I am not thereby acquitted. It is the Lord who judges me'). In 5:10 the same verdict is passed on those who reject 'the testimony that God has borne to his Son' by which the writer indicates the congruent testimony of 'the Spirit, the water, and the blood' (see on 5:8). So also in this passage, the dissidents are repudiating God's intention to **forgive our sins** and refusing the provision he has made to **cleanse us from all unrighteousness** by **the blood of Jesus**. Forgiveness and cleansing are not equivalent but complementary. Forgiveness belongs to that view of offences which supposes they can be covered, removed or put from the mind by repentance on our part and by generosity on the part of God who is **faithful and just**. Cleansing belongs to that view which regards offences as having polluted an environment so that all actions and relationships within its range are affected. The remedy for this is some form of cleansing or atonement. There is an old rabbinic tradition that sins against God are more easily forgiven than sins against one's fellow men (Sanders, p. 179). If forgiveness were thought appropriate for sins against God and cleansing for sins against fellow Christians, the distinction would lead naturally to the passionate pleading that we should love one another. However that may be, the opening statement ends by withdrawing recognition from dissidents who claim to be sinless, for they are judged not to possess God's **truth** and **word**.

To say that God is **faithful** (*pistos* is occasionally used elsewhere in Johannine writings, but never of God) **and just** means that he stands by his own promises of mercy (e.g., Exod. 34:6–7; Dan. 9:9–19). According to common *OT* teaching, if we confess our sins God forgives us because he is *pistos* and *dikaios*, i.e., we can trust him to do what is right. The rendering of *dikaios* is not easy since 'righteous' is now merely opaque, and 'just' is misleading. The problem arises from the structure of Hebrew thought about ṣᵉdāqâ, commonly rendered 'righteousness' (cf. Hill (1967) IV). The word *dikaios* is applied to God because he can be thought of as judge in a case between a person and his enemies or accusers. In Ps. 7 the psalmist pleads for God's support against his enemies, protests his own blameless conduct, and begs God to arise in anger at this example of oppression (1–8). 'God is a righteous judge' (11), and the psalmist ends by giving thanks for his righteousness (17). He means that God has the power to give him the verdict and to put a stop to his enemies; indeed, it is God's responsibility to support the oppressed and thwart the oppressor (Ps. 10:18). '*Righteous* art thou, O Lord, and *right* are thy judgments. Thou hast appointed thy testimonies in *righteousness* and in all *faithfulness*' (Ps. 119:137f.; cf. Dt. 32:4). The psalmist's forensic pleading, however, tells us nothing about the actual merits of his case: it is rhetoric intended to get God on his side. What can be said if his case is weak, or if he cannot pretend to be blameless? 'Thou hast been *just* in all that has come upon us, for thou hast dealt *faithfully*, and we have acted wickedly' (Neh. 9:33; cf. Ezr. 9:15). In that case he must still put himself in the hands of God who is *ṣaddîq* or righteous, because his *ṣᵉdāqâh*, or righteousness, is his property of maintaining the covenant by which people live. 'In thy *faithfulness* answer me, in thy *righteousness*! Enter not into judgment with thy servant; for no man living is *righteous* before thee' (Ps. 143:1, where LXX translates 'faithfulness' by *alētheia*, truth; cf. 1 Jn 1:6, 8). This initial pleading is an important stage beyond the similar beginnings of Ps. 31 and 71; it recognises that nothing we are able to say can bring God onto our side – only God's steadfast love (Ps. 36:5f.), his grace and mercy (Ps. 116:5). His righteous acts are his deeds of salvation (Ps. 71:15f.). He is 'a righteous God and a saviour', even to those who 'were recently incensed against him' (Isa. 45:21–24).

This type of piety is strongly developed in some parts of the Qumran material (discussed by Black, pp. 125–8, and repeated by Hill (1967), pp. 112–14). The concluding psalm of the *Community Rule* contains characteristic admissions of sinfulness with a turning towards the righteous God who alone can answer the need: 'I will declare his judgment concerning my sins, and my transgressions shall be before my eyes as an engraved precept. I will say to God 'My Righteousness', and 'Author of my Goodness' to the Most High' (1QS 10.11; Vermes, p. 90). 'I belong to wicked mankind, to the company of ungodly flesh, my iniquities, rebellion and sins, together with the perversity of my heart belong to the company of worms and to those who walk in darkness. . . If I stagger because of the sin of flesh, my justification shall be by the righteousness of God which endures for ever. . . He will judge me in the righteousness of his truth and in the greatness of his goodness he will pardon all my sins. Through his righteousness he will cleanse me of the uncleanness of man' (1QS 11.9–14, Vermes, pp. 93f.; the *Hymns of Thanksgiving* have equally powerful passages; Vermes, pp. 164, 175, 198).

Those are very much the sentiments of 1 Jn, though recorded here in a more reticent idiom. God is **faithful and just** (the phrase is almost a hendiadys) because he alone restores the penitent sinner to the community of godly persons. *Dikaios* (RSV, **just**) cannot easily be translated, but it is somewhere near to 'well disposed', which indeed is an Old English meaning, now rare, of the adjective 'right' (*SOED*). See further, on 2:1.

The statement by the leaders group has probably not yet ended. Despite the sudden change in person at 2:1, the we-style (which is used to express common Christian convictions) is maintained in 2:3-6. It then disappears until 3:1-2 and thereafter appears throughout the rest of the Epistle. It is suggested that the initial 'agreed statement' in fact extended from 1:1 to 2:11, that it is interpolated in 2:1-2 and 2:7-8 by two statements from the writer, and that its end is marked by the change from 'I am writing' to 'I write' in 2:12-14 (for the difference, see the commentary on these verses).

2:1-11. The deliberate formality of the opening address and statement is for the moment replaced with something more intimate. The first person plural yields to the first person singular. The readers are **my little children** and later, in pleading with them, the writer calls them **beloved**. His qualifying comments in vv. 1 and 2 refer to the theme of repentance and forgiveness in 1:8-9; they also transfer the adjective *dikaios* from God in 1:9 (*RSV*, **just**) to Jesus Christ in 2:1 (*RSV*, **righteous**) and so give content to the relation between Father and Son, briefly stated in 1:3. Further, the reference to **expiation** in 2:2 is presumably linked with **the blood of Jesus** in 1:7; but, by contrast, **world** introduces one of the main themes of the Epistle and is a mark of the writer's special interest.

In 2:3-5 the first person plural is resumed, and presumably with it the agreed statement. The thought flows on from 1:10 (**word** in 1:10 and 2:5, **truth** in 1:8 and 2:4, **walk** in 1:7 and 2:6) and introduces further leading thoughts: **know**, **commandments**, **love**, being **in him** and the verb **abides**. In 2:7-8 the first person singular reappears in order to comment on the commandment introduced in 2:3-4. Verses 9-11 are written in a formal style using the third person singular, a style which frequently recurs later in the Epistle. Its first occurrence may of course be due to the writer, already operating a favourite device; but it may equally be the model on which he created numerous succeeding examples. Since the main theme of these verses is the contrast between light and darkness which dominates 1:5-7, they may plausibly be attributed to the agreed statement which therefore ends at 2:11 and suggests some reason for the otherwise inexplicable passage 2:12-14.

1-2. A perverse conclusion that might possibly have been drawn (by the dissidents?) from the remarks about sinning in 1:7–10 is promptly dismissed. Christians are not to sin; but, if anyone does, there is a remedy. That position is defensible (e.g., by analogy: those who work with toxic substances must strictly avoid contamination; but, if they do become contaminated, the matter can be dealt with). Yet the impression remains that the writer is not comfortable with it. On the one hand, he mentions remedies for sin here and at 2:12 (forgiveness), 4:10 (expiation), and 5:16 (intercession for sin which is not mortal); on the other hand, he insists that 'no one who abides in him sins' (3:6). In that context, 'he appeared to take away sins' must mean 'to take away the possibility of sinning'; cf. 5:18.

This second aspect of the writer's thought seems to depend on his simplistic statement that sin is lawlessness (3:4), i.e., sin means a prohibited action. If the writer merely intends to say that no Christian deliberately defies God by doing prohibited actions (rather like sinning 'with a high hand' in *OT*), nor can he remain a Christian if he does, the sentiment is acceptable but not very useful. A great many morally wrong actions are not prohibited and cannot be. By lawlessness (*anomia*), however, the writer may mean the careless or unfortunate infringement of those rules which maintain the structure of the world (see 1:6–7, on 'performing the truth'). Such infringements would not merely be shameful to the Christian community but would be destructive of the world, that is of society as a whole: hence **for our sins, and not for ours only but also for the sins of the whole world.** That suggestion turns upon the meaning of **world** (*kosmos*) which in this Epistle totally lacks any hint of cosmic speculation. Least of all is the writer contemplating the world-wide scene. His horizon extends little further than the village and even today can be illustrated by attitudes and word-usage common in remote, traditional Greek communities. In *Portrait of a Greek Mountain Village*, J. du Boulay quotes modern examples of *kosmos* as meaning 'people'. For instance, 'You cannot stop the mouth of the *kosmos*', means 'You can't stop people gossiping', and of course 'maliciously' is implied. '*Kosmos*', says the author, 'the word used in Greek both for "people" and "world", is therefore on the whole used for the people with whom the villager is able to identify, and may be extended to cover a wider concept of humanity when this identification is made less in the narrow religious sense as in the awareness of common proneness to sin and liability to suffering' (loc. cit., p. 42).

This modern usage is familiar in the hellenistic world and in *NT* (see *TWNT* III, pp. 889–96): thus, 'the world has gone after him' (Jn 12:19); and 'I have spoken openly to the world' (Jn 18:20).

Since *kosmos* means 'other people', people outside your own family
or group, the words of Judas (not Iscariot) in Jn 14:22 can be
translated: 'How is it that you will manifest yourself to us and not
to other people?' 'Us' and 'other (potentially hostile) people' exactly
captures the attitude to *kosmos* in many parts of the Epistle, though
here our sins and those of society as a whole are the object of
Christ's expiation.

The life of a social group is a complex system, depending on
conventions and seldom-explicit social rules. If conventions are de-
fied, if the psychological mechanisms of the social rules are hin-
dered, or if changes of attitude and feeling bring abnormal pressures
to bear, the *kosmos* begins to undergo dissolution. In that situation,
the infringement of rules – even when it is necessary and inevitable
– is fraught with danger. In such circumstances, special intercession
or expiation may be required. No one who has shared the life of a
community undergoing rapid change or forced to respond to alien
initiatives can be unaware of the skills, concessions and sacrifices
that are necessary to preserve the community from disintegration
and to make possible the transition to a new phase of the community's life.

Such a situation, rather than the much simpler problem of individual wrongdoings, may well be the proper context for viewing the
two statements about Christ's relation to sin and sinning. He is
given what appear to be incompatible roles: intercessor and victim
(though of course the roles are ingeniously combined in the Epistle
to the Hebrews). First, **we have an advocate** (*paraklētos*) **with the
Father, Jesus Christ the righteous; and he is the expiation** (*hilasmos*) **for our sins**. In other words, God takes into account not only
that we have sinned but also that we are in the company of Jesus
Christ and he is thereby moved to hinder the destruction we have
brought about by sinning. That interpretation depends on an understanding of *paraklētos* and *hilasmos*. Neither is common: *paraklētos* occurs only here and Jn 14:16, 26; 15:26, and 16:7 where it
is translated 'Counsellor' and applied to the Holy Spirit (and, in the
first quotation, by implication to Jesus); and *hilasmos* appears again
only at 1 Jn 4:10 (though *hilastērion* occurs with theological meaning
at Rom. 3:25, and the verb *hilaskomai* at Lk 18:13 and Heb. 2:17).

The translation of *paraklētos* by 'advocate' is not misleading, if
advocate is understood in its non-technical (or indeed its original
Latin) sense; but the common statement that *paraklētos* was a
technical legal term is wrong. The term first appears in extant Greek
literature in a single use by Demosthenes (4C BC) to describe partisan
supporters who had tried to influence the choice of jurors. There
are some sixteen further occurrences in sources from the fourth

century BC to the third century AD, including nine in Philo (none in LXX), some on legal and some on non-legal occasions. Everywhere the word means supporter, sponsor, or the patron who 'lends his presence to his friend' (according to a comment on Cicero by a Latin writer of the first century AD). In the ancient world it was sensible, when approaching an important person to have the support of an influential patron. Philo tells two apposite stories. One concerns Flaccus, the prefect of Alexandria who fell into disfavour with the emperor Gaius and needed the well placed Lepidus as his *parakletos* to propitiate (*exeumenizein*) the emperor and get him less harsh terms of banishment. The other story retells the biblical narrative of Joseph, the Egyptian governor, receiving his unsuspecting brothers. One brother attempts to propitiate (*exeumenizein*) the apparently harsh governor by offering to be enslaved in place of the youngest brother, whereupon Joseph abandons the pretence and says that he himself will be their *parakletos*. It is his own generosity and family feeling that makes him well disposed to his brothers, despite the ancient wrong, and prompts him to become their supporter. Hence in general a *parakletos* seeks to gain good will for his friend or protégé, perhaps by what he says and does, but chiefly by his presence and reputation (Grayston, *JSNT*).

The reputation of Jesus Christ is that he is **righteous** (*dikaios*; see on 1:9; in the phrase *Iesoun Christon dikaion*, the adjective is not a simple epithet, as *ton dikaion* would be, but a predicate). The translation of *dikaios* is again not easy: 'just', preferred by *NEB*, *JB*, is unsuitable in this passage. It can indeed be rendered 'innocent' (AGB, s.v. 3), perhaps 'sinless'; and this leads Houlden, p. 64, to connect it with references to sacrifice in 1:7; 2:2, and with the ceremonial purity of priests in Israel. He adds: 'Jesus, now exalted to heaven, after carrying out the sacrificial task, can speak the more effectively to the Father on his followers' behalf: his sinlessness matches that of God himself and enables him to approach him (cf. the use of *dikaios* to describe God in i.9)'.

But there are strong objections to this explanation: (i) it mistakes the meaning of *dikaios* when used of God; (ii) it assumes a literal reading of obviously metaphorical sacrificial language; and (iii) it attributes to the writer a view—that innocence speaks only to innocence—which is surprising in one who claims fellowship with God while yet admitting sins. It is indeed true that *dikaios* here and in 1:9 has the same meaning, but in the sense that Jesus has the power and the will to join God in setting the sinner to rights. According to 3:7, 10, 'He who does right (*dikaiosyne*) is righteous'. Righteousness is practical virtue, almost entirely comprehended in loving one's brother. God himself is righteous and 'everyone who does

right is born of him' (2:29). Hence, Jesus Christ is in good standing
with God and fully acceptable to him as the sponsor of penitent
sinners. Gregory of Nazianzus (*Or.* 30.14) comments as follows:
'Thus we have a paraclete Jesus Christ – not as if he prostrated
himself before the Father or slavishly fell at his feet. Away with a
thought so servile and unworthy of the Spirit! It is not for the
Father to seek such servility nor for the Son to suffer it, nor is it
proper to suspect it of the Father. But by the things he suffered as
a man, now as Word and Adviser he persuades him to be patient.
This, it seems to me, is the meaning of his intercession'.

That way of dealing with sin regards wrongdoing as a voluntary
activity. The writer can appeal to his readers not to sin: since 'the
darkness is passing away and the true light is already shining' (2:8),
his readers are illuminated and therefore they *can* do what is right
even if they do not always so decide. But if wrongdoing is thought
to be the devil's work in those who are his (3:8), then something
more than sponsorship is needed to make sinners and God at one.
If sinners are in the grip of destructive forces, they need God's
powerful intervention to protect them from the danger, and the
hilasmos (**expiation**) is that which brings God in on their side. If the
hopeful conviction that darkness is giving way to light should be
overwhelmed by the dreadful awareness that 'it is the last hour'
when antichrists abound (2:18), then the *hilasmos* is needed to preserve the Christian community within a disintegrating *kosmos*. This
meaning of *hilasmos* is justified by its use in secular Greek (to
conciliate, and hence to gain the favour of someone), by the above
examples from Philo (where an equivalent word is used), and by
the context in the Epistle. It may be possible, however, to explore
further. Both here and in 4:10, Jesus is a *hilasmos* for our sins, and
in 1:7 'the blood of Jesus cleanses us from all sin'.

Even though the Johannine community does not show much
influence of the Jewish cult, these statements suggest that we should
examine the association of sin, blood and *hilasmos* in the Pentateuch
where the great majority of references to expiation occur. The association has deep roots in the ancient Israelite conviction that no
living creature may be killed except by direct command of God, or,
if an animal is killed for food, provided that ritual protection is
sought. The ritual protection is obtained by strict abstention from
consuming blood, which instead is smeared on the altar, so that the
hands of the killer and the altar of God are both stained with blood.
In that way God accepts responsibility for the slaying, exonerates
the slayer and protects him from the consequences of having shed
blood. See Lev. 17:3–14, which includes the following:

CAMROSE LUTHERAN COLLEGE
LIBRARY

The life of the flesh is in the blood;
and I have given it for you upon the altar
to make atonement for your souls;
for it is the blood that *makes atonement*
because of the life (Lev. 17:11).

('to make atonement' is *hilaskesthai*, the verb associated with *hilasmos*). Here there is no sense of appeasing God (hence 'propitiation' is inappropriate) but of securing God's protection against the mysterious dangers released by a killing.

In the developed Jewish ritual this exculpatory action was widely extended for dealing with unintentional offences against moral and ritual laws (see Lev. 4:1–5:9), and for the religious risks of operating the cultic system (see Lev. 8:1–10:20). In no circumstances were these blood sacrifices available for intentional sins or for human killing (only the blood of the killer can remove that pollution, Num. 35:33). But in reflection on Jewish martyrdoms during revolt against Antiochus in the second century BC, some Jews began to suppose that God might accept the death of some of the faithful and stay his wrath against all Israel (2 Mac. 7:37f.—why did God allow the most devout to die and not the renegades?). By their death the country was purified. They were a compensation for the national sins: 'by the blood of these righteous men and the atonement (*hilastērion*) of their death, the divine Providence delivered Israel hitherto persecuted'. Thus early Christian theology, by analogy with ancient blood ritual, helped perhaps by description of Jesus as the Lamb (Jn 1:29, 35) and made possible by the martyrdom theology of the Jews, regarded God as accepting the blood of Jesus and thereby binding himself to exonerate those who betrayed and killed him. In this sense, certainly in Paul and perhaps in John, the death of Jesus may sometimes be represented as an atoning sacrifice (Grayston, *NTS*).

3–5. This is a self-contained unit beginning and ending with **by this we may be sure**: the first use of the phrase looks forward, the second backwards. (This use of *en toutō*, though not found in Jn or in 2 or 3 Jn, is common in 1 Jn. In 3:16, 24; 4:2, 9, 10, 13, it is prospective; in 3:10, 19 and 5:2 it is retrospective, and in 4:17 it may be either. It points to conditions by which something is known, identified or distinguished.) After the interruption of vv. 1–2, the group statement continues by setting down the condition for knowing that we know God (the Greek uses first the present tense and then the perfect of the same verb *ginōskō*: 'we know that we have come to know', i.e., we are sure that we know him). What is formally presented, however, as a condition for knowing God is

actually a description of knowing him: to know God is to obey him
and to obey him is to know him.

That perception is obviously congenial to Jewish piety; from the
Torah-devotion of Ps. 119 to the rabbinic passion for studying
Torah: 'R. Hananiah b. Teradion said: If two sit together and the
words of the Law [are spoken] between them, the Divine Presence
rests between them' (*Aboth* 3.2; Danby, p. 450). The oracle of Jer.
31:33-34 expected the new covenant to provide this kind of knowledge: 'I will put my law within them, and I will write it upon their
hearts; and I will be their God, and they shall be my people. And
no longer shall each man teach his neighbour, saying, 'Know the
LORD,' for they shall all know me, from the least of them to the
greatest, says the LORD; for I will forgive their iniquity, and I will
remember their sin no more'.

This eschatological expectation of the knowledge of God, rare in
the Old Testament, seems to have found fulfillment in the experience of the Qumran sectarians. 'Grace and knowledge were the twin
foundations of the sect's spirituality' (Vermes, p. 42). It was the
duty of the community's instructor to conceal the teaching of the
Law from men of falsehood but to impart true knowledge and
righteous judgment to those who had chosen the Way (1QS 9.17;
Vermes p. 88). Therefore the hymn-writer thanks the Lord that
'Thou hast enlightened me through Thy truth. In Thy marvellous
mysteries, and in Thy loving-kindness to a man of vanity, and in
the greatness of Thy mercy to a perverse heart Thou hast granted
me knowledge' (1QH 7.26; Vermes, p. 175). Moreover, those who
keep God's commandments expect to stand in his presence for ever
and can pray that he will purify them by his Holy Spirit and draw
near to them by grace (1QH 16.12; Vermes, p. 197). Thus it appears
that the Epistle's interest in knowing God through obedience is
somewhat similar to the piety of Qumran (without suggesting a
closer relation between the two), though it has to be acknowledged
that Qumran 'placed a greater emphasis upon the concept of knowledge, whatever its exact connotation, than the more strictly Jewish
circles, whose literature across the centuries is preserved in the Old
Testament. This may well be due to the influence of Hellenistic
factors', according to W. D. Davies, pp. 140f.

It is therefore appropriate to recall that 'knowledge' had become
a familiar feature of hellenistic religions at least by the second
century AD, and possibly earlier. In many writings the reference is
to a form of self-knowledge. The Valentinian teaching about baptism
(according to Clement of Alexandria, *Exc. Theod.* 78.2) says that
'It is not the washing alone that makes us free, but also the knowledge: who were we? what have we become? where were we? into

what place have we been cast? whither are we hastening? from what are we delivered? what is birth? what is rebirth?' According to the *Book of Thomas*, probably composed in Syria during the first half of the second century (Nag Hammadi Codex II, 138.5), the Saviour says to his twin Thomas: 'You have already come to knowledge, and you will be called "the one who knows himself", for he who has not known himself has known nothing. But he who has known himself has already come to knowledge concerning the depth of the All'. Thus self-knowledge is also knowledge of the All. In the *Gospel of Truth* (Nag Hammadi I, 22.1–35) self-knowledge is also knowledge of the self-revealing Father.

So much for Christian tradition in the second century; it is also present in non-Christian tradition. Something similar appears in the non-Christian *Apocalypse of Adam* (Nag Hammadi V) which probably originated in the first or second century, according to Krause (*Gnosis* II, p. 15). It contains a characteristically gnostic distinction between God the eternal and God the creator. Adam explains to his son Seth how knowledge of the former had been sacrificed for knowledge of the latter and his powers. In the Sethian tradition this disaster is repaired by 'the illuminator of knowledge', 'the man upon whom the holy spirit has come', who is ill-treated by the God of the powers (76.10–77.15), but is able 'to enlighten those whom he chose'. 'Blessed is the soul of those men, because they have known God with a knowledge of the truth. They shall live for ever, because they have not been corrupted by their desire, along with the angels, nor have they accomplished the works of the powers, but they have stood in his presence in a knowledge of God like light that has come forth from fire and blood' (83.1–20). This knowledge is thus saving knowledge: not only information about God the eternal but knowledge that transforms the possessor and removes him from the destructive powers of creation and creation's God.

In the simpler scheme of the pagan Hermetic writings, the initiates say, 'We rejoice because while we were in the body, thou hast made us divine through thy knowledge' (Nag Hammadi VI, 64.15). *Corpus Hermeticum* XIII is explicitly concerned with the need to transform existence as man into existence as God before God can be known ('none can be saved before regeneration', 1.6; Grese, pp. 70f., 121–3, 144). Since the Epistle explicitly associates being born of God with knowing God (4:6–7), its intention can at least be illustrated by *Hermetic Tractate* XIII; and the conviction that 'whatever is born of God overcomes the world' (5:4) is not alien to the *Apocalypse of Adam*. Yet the Epistle sharply distinguishes itself from these apparently equivalent concerns by stating that to know God is to keep his commandments.

Throughout the Epistle the process and results of knowing or not knowing are in the forefront. Two verbs are used, *ginōskō* and *oida*, somewhat distinguished in their areas of application but not in their basic meaning. Apart from the conventional truism that God knows all things (3:20), the occurrences always refer to human knowing.

(i) The verb used with a direct object: Christians know God or claim to know him (2:3-4; 4:6-7); they know the Father, him who is from the beginning (2:13-14), him who is true (5:20), as indeed they knew the truth (*oida*, 2:21). Others know neither him nor the truth (3:1, 6; 4:8). Knowledge of God is associated with keeping his commandments (2:3-4), with not sinning (3:6), and with practising love within the Christian community (4:7-8), which has come to know and put its faith in the love which God has for them (4:16). The kind of love required is known from the fact that 'he laid down his life for us' (3:16); correspondingly the spirit of truth is known and distinguished from the spirit of error by observing whether it produces an obedient hearing for the leader of the community and the group in whose name he writes (4:6).

(ii) The verb used with the conjunction 'that' to express two classes of statement: (a) *Theological convictions*: that God is righteous (2:29), that he hears and grants our requests (5:15), that 'he appeared to take away sins and in him there is no sin' (3:5), 'that the Son of God has come and has given us understanding to know him who is true' (5:20), and 'that it is the last hour', because many antichrists have come (2:18—the last is *ginōskō*, the rest *oida*). (b) *Expressions of self-awareness*: (first *oida*) 'that we shall be like him, for we shall see him as he is' (3:2), 'that we have passed out of death into life because we love the brethren' (3:14), 'that no murderer has eternal life abiding in him' (3:15), though the true believer does (5:13); (then *ginōskō*): that we know God and are in him if we keep his commandments (2:3, 5), that we are born of God if we do what is right (2:29), that we belong to the truth if we show genuine love (3:18-19), that we abide in him and he in us by keeping his commandments, receiving his Spirit, and loving one another (3:24; 4:13), that we really love the brethren if we love God and keep his commandments (5:2). Hence various expressions are equivalent in meaning: knowing God, being in God, abiding in God and he in us, possessing the Spirit, being born of God, belonging to the truth and loving God. The tests of these forms of religious awareness are similarly described by a group of equivalent phrases: keeping his commandments, doing what is right, practising love within the community. In short, knowledge of God which at first is described

as obeying him comes to carry the implication that this obedience
is a sharing of the divine activity within the community.

Verse 4 begins with **He who says** (in Greek the article with the
present participle, *ho legōn*); the same words appear also in 2:6, 9,
but not elsewhere. Most probably they refer to what was actually
said by members of the dissident group, namely: I know him, I
abide in him, and I am in the light (cf. 1:6, 'If we say we have
fellowship with him'). At this point, the writers are reiterating 1:6–
7 and making it plain that truth is a matter both of perception and
practice. Anyone who fails to practise, while claiming Christian
perception, **is a liar** (cf. 4:20): not necessarily someone who makes
false statements with intent to deceive (for how could it be said that
anyone makes God a liar in that sense, 1:10; 5:10?), but perhaps
someone who deceives by stating what he falsely believes to be the
truth. I Jn is much concerned (more explicitly than the Gospel—
only 8:44f.) with how to distinguish truth from plausible and sin-
cerely held falsehood. This arises from the statements of the dissident group (2:18–22, 27) and the answer is not given when they
claim spiritual authority for their convictions (4:1–2).

The decisive test at this point is whether they **keep his commandments** or **his word**. Neither at this stage nor later are the
commandments identified: it is taken for granted that they are
known, and (more important) when stated they will be recognised.
(The Farewell Discourses of the Gospel, too, powerfully insist that
keeping the commandments of Jesus is a test of loving him (14:15,
21; 15:10), but the commandments are not specified except when
the plural 'commandments' is replaced by the single commandment
of mutual love; cf. 13:34; 15:12). The similarity of keeping his
commandments and keeping his word suggests that 'commandment'
and 'word' are at least closely related (in Jn 14:21, 23–24, love for
Jesus is evidenced by keeping his commandments or his word(s);
but whereas the commandments give the impression of coming to
us from another source, the word of God can be regarded as within
us (1:10; 2:14; cf. Jn 5:38). It may be conjectured that the dissident
group preferred the indwelling word of God to apparently external
commandments, and that the writers deliberately identified word
and commandments (cf. 2:7). The danger of such identification is
that 'word' loses its inherent freedom and is reduced to the narrow
limits of 'commandment'; but for the writers of I Jn the word of
God really (or **truly**) is one word, namely, 'love'.

The introduction of **truly** into the sentence is not merely for
emphasis: the writers are marking this statement about love as an
authoritative declaration. Compare the assurances about the true
God and the one who is true in I Jn 5:20, and the true knowledge

conveyed by Jesus to the men who were his in Jn 17:8. Note also
that the comment which immediately follows the present passage
echoes the authoritative note by applying 'true' to the effect of the
commandment and to the light that is shining (2:8). Somewhat in
the Qumran fashion, the writers are giving their interpretation of
the tradition and ruling that it is obligatory. Nothing less does
justice to the confidence and solemnity of these pronouncements.

The significance of **love** within the Christian community is ex-
plored in 1 Jn 3 and (especially) 4, where, as here, **love** is spoken
of as being **perfected** (cf. 4:12, 17, 18). The verb *teleioō* means to
cause somebody or something to be *teleios*, i.e., the state of being
no longer incomplete and imperfect. English versions commonly
translate by 'perfect', with the effect of introducing preformed ideas
of (moral) perfection into the exegesis of this passage. To translate
'love has reached its consummation' would allow the inner dynamic
of the love in question to decide its appropriate completeness and
perfection; and this has a bearing on the phrase **love for God**. That
indeed may be the meaning of a more literal translation of the Greek
('the love of God'); but equally possible is God's love for his people,
and even (in view of the teaching in 1 Jn 4) love for one another
prompted by God. At this stage in the Epistle, 'God's love' would
be the best translation (allowing room, as so often in Johannine
writings, for the reciprocal nature of concepts); and the pregnant
statement that 'God's love has reached its consummation' in anyone
who keeps his word may have been spoken against members of the
dissident group who perhaps sought consummation in another
fashion (see also on 3:11).

However that may be, it is by this test (say the writers) that **we
may be sure that we are in him**, thus for the first time using the
'in him' formula which (with its variations) is a mark of Johannine
writing. (For a full, though over-elaborate study of this formula, see
Malatesta.) Already 1:6-7 has marked out the two contrasting structures of human existence, which can be indicated by light and
darkness and hence by God and the Evil One. At this point, the
language of 'knowing God' (2:3-4) is changed to the language of
'being in God', in order to bring in the associated thoughts of light,
life and love.

6. At once the phrase undergoes significant development when it
is changed to **abides in him**. The verb **abides** (which in a modern
translation is an example of translator's paralysis) represents the
Greek *menō* with the meaning 'to stay where you are, to remain in
your present situation, to continue in an allegiance or relationship'.
It is used with exceptional frequency in Johannine writing. At one
end of the range of application there is Jn 11:6, 'he stayed two days

longer in the place where he was'; and, with a special meaning, Jn 1:38, 'Rabbi where are you staying?' (hence *NEB* in the present passage: 'whoever claims to be dwelling in him'). Further along the range, there is 'remaining in the light' (that is, not moving away from your conviction of illumination, 1 Jn 2:10), and remaining in the teaching of Christ, 2 Jn 9. At the far end of the range is a rich development whereby we remain in (allegiance to) God and he remains (actively at work) in us.

For 'we remain in God' or 'in Christ', cf. 2:6, 24, 27, 28; 3:6, 24(R); 4:12, 4:13(R), 15(R), 16(R), where (R) indicates that the relation is reciprocal, namely, 'God also remains in us'. (To 2:5, 'we are in him', add 5:20.) The means by which God remains in us is indicated by passages where something of the divine being is or remains in those who are unshaken in their allegiance to him: God's word, 2:14 (cf. 1:10); what was heard from the beginning, 2:24; the anointing, 2:27; God's nature (in Greek, 'his seed'), 3:9; eternal life, 3:15; God's love, 3:17 (cf. 2:5, 15; 4:12, 16—and note also: the truth 1:8; 2:4; the new command, 2:8; and the testimony, 5:10).

Since the 'remaining in him' formula goes far beyond the implications of the 'being in him' formula, the change from one to the other is likely to have been deliberate. The cause must have been the departure of the dissident group who had not remained members of the community but had left it. Nor had they continued in that allegiance which the writers of 1 Jn considered essential or in that network of relationship that constituted the community. ('If they had been of us, they would have continued with us', 2:19.) Therefore they no longer walked in the light, as he is in the light (1:7), and to remain in God you must **walk in the same way in which he walked**. The word **he** represents the Greek demonstrative pronoun *ekeinos* meaning 'that person', commonly indicating *that* person rather than *this*, or the person recently mentioned. But in the Epistle it is used in six passages which refer to Jesus without actually naming him (3:3, 5, 7, 16 and 4:17—his purity, sinlessness, acceptability to God and demonstration of love, with the consequence that 'as he is so are we in this world'). The person who claims a continuous relationship to God must conduct his life as Jesus conducted his. The same conviction appears more dramatically in the words of Jesus about the footwashing: 'I have given you an example, that you also should do as I have done to you' (Jn 13:15); but that conviction has to be interpreted within the Johannine circle of ideas. It is the Johannine Jesus, not some other Jesus, who is the example to be followed.

7–8. At this point the writer resumes the first person singular and addresses his readers as **beloved**, appropriately enough in view of

the appeal for brotherly love in 2:10. The connexion is even stronger
in 4:7, 11, though less obvious in 3:2, 21; and the widespread use
of this address (in the singular in 3 Jn 1, 2, 5, 11; in the plural in
Paul, Hebrews, 1 and 2 Peter, Jude) in *NT* letters indicates that it
was common fashion in the primitive church. The commandments
of 2:3–4 (as again in 5:2–3) are now reduced to the singular **commandment** which is both old and new. This change can best be
understood by looking ahead to 4:21: 'This commandment we have
from him, that he who loves God should love his brother also'. In
that formulation love for one's brother is explicit and love for God
is implicit. Hence, for those who know the Christian tradition the
two commandments of Jesus (Mk 12:29–31) spring to mind and
need no identification; and these two commandments contain all the
rest (see on 2:4).

The Johannine tradition nowhere preserves the Synoptic pericope
in explicit form, yet it undoubtedly stands behind Jn 15:10–17; and
whereas the Synoptic logion puts the commandments of love to God
and neighbour side by side, the Johannine interpretation co-ordi-
nates them: Jesus keeps the Father's commandments and abides in
his love, while disciples correspondingly keep Jesus' commandments
and so abide in his love (15:10). When the Gospel specifies a new
commandment it fixes attention on love for neighbour and in effect
redefines 'neighbour' by 'one another' (i.e., members of the Christian community) and qualifies 'love' by 'as I have loved you'. The
Epistle similarly devotes most attention to love for one another, yet,
under theological pressure from the dissidents, does not ignore love
for God. In 3:22 and 24 the writer insists on keeping God's commandments, but in v. 23, 'this is his commandment, that we should
believe in the name of his Son Jesus Christ and love one another,
as he gave us commandment'. Love for God includes, indeed is
expressed by, believing on his Son (cf. 1:3); and consequently love
for God and love for one another is one commandment.

In any case, the community possessed that commandment **from
the beginning** of its existence, it was (part of) the statement of
convictions which they had heard (see on 1:1). The insistence that
it was old rather than new suggests opposition to novelties introduced by the dissidents, for which impression support may be found
in the tense of the verb translated **had**. The Greek has the imperfect
(*eichen*), where the perfect might have been expected, and it should
mean 'you used to have'. If *echō* is given the meaning 'to have
something over one' (AGB, p. 333, I.2.i), the translation could be
'an old commandment which you were previously subject to from
the beginning'. And yet when you consider the matter again (*palin*
rather than meaning 'on the other hand' (AGB, p. 611, 4), suggests

going a little further), it really is a new commandment; and that perception (not the commandment, which is ruled out by the neuter *ho* and *alēthes* which do not match the feminine *entolē*) is true in relation both to him and you. In other words, the first part of the old commandment, love for God, is made new by incorporating faith in Jesus; and the second part, love for neighbour, is made new by practice of love for one another.

No doubt this renewal, as it were, of the old commandment had long been known to the community, but the urgent demands of a new situation—**because the darkness is passing away and the true light is already shining**—made it particularly necessary. The new situation was new in fact though not in expectation: from the beginning, Christians had expected the present age to be replaced by the new age, for darkness to be replaced by light. Even if it was possible to live in the light though surrounded by darkness (see on 1:5–7), sooner or later that must be resolved in favour of the true light (rather than the false light, perhaps, of the dissidents). When the expected transformation was thought to be near (cf. 2:18), the writer directed his readers, on the lines of **in him and in you**, to questions of christology and community life. The latter appears in the immediately following verses.

9–11. He who says he is in the light is no doubt the person who claims to abide in God (2:6). If however he hates his brother instead of loving him, his claim is rejected. Hatred belongs with darkness and love with light (cf. 4:20); it is what the world offers to Christians and is equivalent to murder (3:13–15). 'Hate' therefore is a hostile and violent word but it need not and here does not carry the strongly emotional sense of detestation. Absence of emotional hatred towards one's brother is no defence against the writer's condemnation, for hatred is the opposite of love and he who does not love his brother **hates** him. **Brother**, used in Judaism and the hellenistic world for members of a religious community, is much favoured in *NT* for fellow Christians; so it is in the Epistle where, however, the meaning 'neighbour' (AGB, p. 16, s.v. *adelphos* 4) cannot be dismissed.

The judgment voiced in v. 9 is then supported by the general statements of vv. 10–11 which are expressed in a common Johannine formula, characteristically beginning with definite article and present participle. Here **he who loves** (*ho agapōn*) is paired with its opposite: **but he who hates** (*ho misōn*). A similar pairing of opposites is found in 2:23a,b (strengthened with 'everyone', *pas*, in the first member), 3:7–8; 4:7–8 (with *pas* in the first member), 5:10a,b and 5:12a,b. The formula can appear with paired parallels in 2:22a,b; 3:10a,b (with *pas* in the first member but lacking exact parallelism), and 3:14–15 (with *pas* in the second member). In 3:24

only a single member appears, and cf. the variations found in 5:4, 5:5*a,b*. All these examples are judgmental, i.e., they lay down the judgment that certain actions and responses are or are not of God. The formula is used to make the judgments impressive and memorable. It can also exercise the related function of prescribing a course of action: in 4:21 a commandment is explicitly formulated in this way, and 3:3–4, 3:6*a,b*: 5:1*a,b* have paired members, one prescriptive and the other judgmental. The formula thus appears to be a teaching device used in the Johannine community, and its simple form naturally attracts additional comments.

The added comment in v. 10 is not carefully phrased: **in it** (*autō*) **there is no cause for stumbling**. *Autō* may indeed refer to the light (*RSV, NEB, JB*), but possibly to him (*AV, RV, NIV, GNB*) who loves his brother. If the latter, is the cause for stumbling something detrimental to himself or to others? The Greek *skandalon*, originally a trap or snare, has the transferred sense of anything that takes a person unawares and trips him up, an unexpected cause of injury, an obstruction that turns out to be an ambush. (The examples given by AGB, p. 760, s.v. *skandalon* 3, for stain or blemish (Bultmann) scarcely prove the point.) Since *skandalon* is not part of the Johannine vocabulary (though the corresponding verb is used in Jn 6:61; 16:1; see Stählin, *TWNT* VII, s.v. *skandalon*, C. IV), it is tempting to suggest that it reflects some part of the dispute with the dissidents. But it probably expresses little more than the devout sentiment of Ps. 119:165: 'Much peace have those who love thy law, and for them there is no hidden danger (*skandalon*)'. The comments added in v. 11 insist that being and walking in the darkness entail lack of direction and inability to see (cf. Jn 12:35, 40): the chief promises and benefits of gnosis are thus denied to him who hates his brother and walks in darkness. Their availability to him who walks in light is asserted in what follows.

TRANSITION FROM STATEMENT TO DEVELOPMENT
2:12–14

12–14. Three rhetorical clauses introduced by **I am writing** (*graphō*) are followed by three beginning with **I write** (*egrapsa*). The variation is formal. A Greek letter-writer, if conscious of his immediate activity of writing, could use the present *graphō*; or, if placing himself alongside the reader, could view his action as past and use the conventional letter-writer's aorist *egrapsa*, 'I have written'. (The presence of the epistolary aorist in *NT* is not undisputed; so BDF, sect. 334. The fullest discussion is in Robertson, pp. 845f.) In the

Epistle until v. 13, all references to 'write' are in the present; from v. 14 onwards they are in the aorist. It may be suggested that the formal variation marks the point in the Epistle where the writer ends his presentation of the 'agreed statement' of the sending group (see on 1:1–4) and begins his own treatment of some main features of the statement. Already in 2:1–2 and 2:7–8 he has interposed his own comments; now he picks up the themes which dominate vv. 7–8 and sets about developing them: the new age that is already dawning in 2:15–3:10, and the old commandment in the new age in 3:11–4:21. The close similarity though not identity of the *graphō*-series and the *egrapsa*-series perhaps indicates that the writer now permits himself his own didactic variation of the common agreement. Both series may be intended to be encouraging and conciliatory (cf. 2:21, 27), in view of the severity of verse 11 and much that is to come.

The readers are addressed first as **little children** (*teknia*, 12a) or children (*paidia*, 13e, Greek 14a). In the Epistle the two words are always in the vocative (hence they are a respected leader's name for those in his care) and they mean the same. *Teknia* is a favourite Johannine designation (rare elsewhere in ancient literature) 2:1, 12, 28; 3:7, 18; 4:4; 5:21; cf. Jn 13:33. It is varied by *paidia* in 2:13, 18; cf. Jn 21:5: this is a common word, found frequently in the Synoptic Gospels, including important sayings of Jesus, but never in the vocative. The vocative singular *paidion* occurs frequently in the solemn speeches of Tobit (especially in the Sinaitic text) and is no doubt a homely Jewish story-telling idiom which John mostly transferred to *teknion*. In the Epistle neither word has the concerns of actual children in mind; both refer to members of the community. It has been suggested that **children, fathers**, and **young men** set out in a rhetorical figure the range of qualities and experience in the community (Dodd, pp. 38f.), but such an intention would have been better served by changing the order. It is more likely that **fathers** and **young men** designate two groups within the community; not leaders of the community, such as elders and deacons (Houlden, p. 70), but groups somewhat in conflict or at variance. If so, the writer is not making general statements about different levels of experience within the community: he is simply stating—without at this stage giving or withholding approval—the claims which the two groups make, claims which subsequently he will criticise and qualify. He writes because they make these claims, which when pressed are not compatible.

The sixfold **because** translates the Greek *hoti*, which could also be translated 'that': the Epistle is written (a) because fathers and young men make their respective claims; and (b) to remind them that they are **children** whose sins are forgiven (cf. 1:9; 2:1) and who know the Father (cf. 2:3). According to the ancient conventions about human life and its stages (as reported by Philo, *On the Creation* 104f.), *paidion* is the name for a child up to seven years. He becomes a young man (*neaniskos*) in the period 21–28 years when his body reaches full development; thereafter he marries and fathers children and is a man in the prime of his life. Not till age 49 does he become a senior citizen (*presbytēs*). Obviously the writer is not using his terms with even conventional precision; but the point needs to be made that he is not necessarily referring to groups widely differing in age. **Fathers** are those members of the community who have the responsibility and firmness of family life; **young men** those unhindered by such responsibility and conscious of their developing strength.

Hence twice, without variation, it is said that the **fathers know him who is from the beginning** (see on 1:1). They look backwards to the beginning of the community (scarcely towards the beginning of creation); among the maturer members of the community that familiar change had already taken place (often requiring no more than thirty years) by which an originally innovative group becomes the guardian of its own past. They claim knowledge of him who disclosed himself at the beginning, though the writer is evasive about the identity of that being. In v. 12 the children's **sins are forgiven for his** name's sake: it is God who forgives (1:9) through the mediation of Jesus Christ (2:2; for **name** see on 3:23).

In 13a,b is the reference to God or Christ? After 13e,f where the children know the father, the reference in 14a,b must surely be to the Son; but why does the writer leave the answer open to debate unless for tactical reasons? He will shortly develop his case that acknowledgement of the Father is possible only if coupled with acknowledgement of the Son; but for the moment he leaves well alone and turns to the **young men** who have **overcome the evil one**, i.e., the devil. In a few *NT* passages we encounter the adjective *ponēros*, 'evil', with the masculine article as a name for the devil (an idiom exclusive to early Christianity; Harder, *TWNT* VI, pp. 558f.): in Mt.'s interpretation of the parable of the Sower where Mk has Satan and Lk. the devil (13:19; cf. 13:38); possibly Mt. 5:37; 6:13, where the neuter cannot be ruled out; Eph. 6:16; and 2 Th. 3:3. Whatever the origin of this usage, it occurs in picturesque accounts of conflict with the adversary of God. In the Epistle (cf. also Jn 17:15) it belongs to the writer's popular conception of a Christian community surrounded by and under attack from a *kosmos* hostile to God. The whole *kosmos* is in the power of the evil one, but God protects him who is born of God and the evil one does not touch him (5:18–19). Indeed, the Son of God appeared in order to destroy the works of the devil, who has no power over Christians unless they commit sin and give him power (3:8–10).

Hence the young men are right to claim that they have **overcome the evil one**. The theme of overcoming is prominent in Revelation: it refers to overcoming the pressures of the world, actual infliction of pain and more subtle attempts to undermine Christian faith and love. It is triumph through martyrdom (Rev. 12:11), just as Jesus overcame the world (Jn 16:33). In the Epistle there is no suggestion of martyrdom: it is faith which overcomes the world (5:4). The young men may have been confident that having overcome the evil one they need no longer concern themselves with what originates in the world and belongs to it. Apart from reminding them that **the word of God abides** in them, suggesting that not their strength but God's self-disclosure is the means of overcoming, the writer does not dissent from their claim.

The writer of the Epistle will work out more fully his deep suspicion of the world, but it is a pragmatic and not a theoretical suspicion. One of the shorter writings in the Nag Hammadi library, the *Authoritative Teaching*, expresses its own suspicion in the parable of the wicked fisherman (an image at least as old as Hab. 1:13–17): 'We exist in this world like fish. The adversary spies on us, lying in wait like a fisherman, wishing to seize us, rejoicing that he might swallow us. For [he places] many foods before our eyes, (things) which belong to this world. He wishes to make us desire one of them and to taste only a little, so that he may seize us with this hidden poison and bring us out of freedom and take us into slavery. For whenever he catches us with a single food, it is indeed necessary for [us] to desire the rest. Finally, then, such things become the food of death' (Meyer, p. 281; Ménard (1977), pp. 24, 55).

This lively parable, so much more appealing than the inconsequential solemnities of much gnostic writing, comes from a document that is not even overtly gnostic. Yet it goes much further than I Jn in its disapproval of the world. It is concerned with the soul and its predicament, whereas the Epistle is concerned with a community under threat. (In a similar way Qumran applied the fisherman parable to its own historic circumstances (Vermes, p. 238) before generalising it in the piety of 1QH 3.26 and 5.7–8; Vermes, pp. 159, 165.) Just as the Epistle is distinguishable from gnostic writings, when knowledge is the subject, by its practical concern for the commandments, so its view of the world is determined by social pressures and not by a cosmic theory.

THE ENDING OF THE OLD KOSMOS 2:15–3:10

15–17. Up to this point, the letter has dealt almost exclusively with concerns within the Christian community and with the symbolic opposition of light and darkness. When, however, the young men are introduced who have overcome the evil one, the symbolic darkness must be identified as **the world** (for the meaning of *kosmos*, see on 2:2). Although Christ atones for sins of the whole social community as well as for those of the Christian community, love cannot be extended to the *kosmos* and its characteristic features. Christians are under obligation to love one another and to love God; and because 'the whole world is in the power of the evil one' (5:19), they are under obligation not to love the world. Love for the *kosmos* and love for God (see on 2:5 and 3:11) are in opposition, not least because the *kosmos* is passing away, whereas **he who does the will of God abides for ever**. To set one's love on ambitions which arise from a society in process of dissolution is to give oneself to untruth (2:21, 27; and see on 1:6); to set one's love on the will of God, and to practise love within the Christian community is to be in relation with what is permanently valid (see on 2:6). The writer's conviction that the darkness (see on 2:8) and the *kosmos* are passing away (*paragetai*; cf. 1 C. 7:31, 'The form of this world is passing away') is based partly on the primitive Christian conviction that the end is near of society-as-we-know-it and partly on his assessment of society as he knew it. He describes it in three phases **the lust of the flesh and the lust of the eyes and the pride of life**, each of which merits examination.

Lust is a rendering of *epithymia*, uncommon in Johannine writing (of the devil's desires, in Jn 8:44), but familiar in the commonplace morality of the early church. As noun or verb it means desire or longing in various senses: neutral in Lk. 15:16; 16:21; Phil. 1:23; Heb. 6:11; Rev. 9:6; 18:14; approving in Mt. 13:17; Lk. 17:22; 22:15; 1 Th. 2:17; 1 Tim. 3:1; 1 Pet. 1:12; and disapproving everywhere else, e.g., Jas 4:2. In Rom. 1:24, and perhaps 1 Th. 4:5, *epithymia* refers to improper sexual desire, and the reference in Mt. 5:28 to 'everyone who looks at a woman to *desire* her' is reasonably close to **the lust of the eyes**. Compare the possibly contemporary *Didache* 3.3, 'Do not be foul-mouthed or give free reign to your eyes; for all these things beget adultery'. The **lust of the flesh** is accepted language in Pauline circles; e.g., Gal. 5:16f., 'Walk by the Spirit, and do not gratify the *desires* of the flesh. For the *desires* of the flesh are against the Spirit and the *desires* of the Spirit are against the flesh' (cf. 5:24; Rom. 6:12; 13:14; Eph. 2:3; 1 Pet. 2:11; 2 Pet. 2:10, 18). In these references the desire of the flesh may include but is not confined to sexual desires. *Epithymia* often expresses a longing for someone else's possessions (Mk 4:19; Ac. 20:33; Rom. 7:7f.; 13:9; 1 C. 10:6; 1 Tim. 6:9) and, more generally, is used of those desires that marked the life of Christians before their conversion, e.g., 1 Pet. 1:14, 'As obedient children, do not be conformed to the *passions* of your former ignorance' (cf. 4:2f.; 2 Pet. 1:4; Eph. 4:22; Col. 3:5f.; Tit. 2:12; 3:3). Unfortunately for this simple view, they were not absent from their lives after conversion, e.g., 2 Tim. 4:3, 'The time is coming when people will not endure sound teaching, but having itching ears they will accumulate for themselves teachers to suit their own *likings*'—a situation similar to that of the Johannine community (and cf. 2. Pet. 3:3; Jude 16, 18).

Flesh has only minimal theological significance in Johannine writings. In 1 Jn it is used only here and at 4:2 and 2 Jn 7, where, without emphasis, it indicates the actual human existence of Jesus. In the Gospel of John, according to Hebrew idiom, it means humanity (17:2), mere human existence and activity, contrasted with divine existence (3:6; 6:63; 8:15). In 1:14, 'the Word became flesh' sums up the activity described in 1:4–13 and means that the (divine) word became operative—providing illumination, receiving testimony, appealing to his own, experiencing rejection, and yet creating children of God—within human existence. Those who became children of God were not the offspring of blood relationships (that is, 'of the will of the flesh', i.e. sexual desire, or a father's desire for children), but of God. In 6:51–56 the same significance of flesh is present—indeed is essential to the interpretation of the passage—but is sharpened by the controversial background of the discourse. In 6:32–51 Jesus expounds the manna as life-giving food: those who eat it will not hunger or thirst, nor will they die. Eating this bread is a symbol for accepting and believing him as the one who has come down from heaven. For the Jews that is difficult, for he is Joseph's son and they know his father and mother (cf. 1:13). His birth is an obstacle, and so is his death—the giving of his flesh for the life of the world. The development in 6:52–56, where eating his flesh is joined to drinking his blood, derives from 'shall not hunger . . . shall never thirst' in 6:35. This violent imagery indicates the absolute condition for receiving eternal life: namely, complete acceptance of his actual human dying as the means by which life and light are given.

The word translated **pride** is *alazoneia*. Originally the pretention of a vagrant imposter, it was then used to describe the conceit of someone who boasted in more than he actually possessed. Then it moved into the company of such words as brashness and self-will,

conceit and contempt (Prov. 21:24). In Wis. 5:8 it is the arrogance
that comes from wealth, parallel to pride. In 2 Mac. 9:8 it is the
violent arrogance of Antiochus, in 15:6 the arrogance of Nicanor
who set himself up in rivalry to God. Philo writes thus of *alazoneia*:
'It is conspicuous in the great, who as I have said are amply provided
with the evil thing by riches and distinctions and high offices and
so charged with these, like men who have drunk deep of strong
wine, become intoxicated and vent their selfish rage on slave and
free alike and sometimes on whole cities' (*On the Virtues* 162).
Comparison of this passage with Theophrastus' description of the
alazōn in his *Characters* (Dodd, p. 42) shows how much the word
moved from humbug to violence in three hundred years.

In *NT* the adjective appears in two lists of vices: Rom. 1:30,
alongside 'insolent' and 'arrogant'; and 1 Tim. 3:2, between 'greedy'
and 'arrogant'. The noun appears elsewhere only in Jas 4:16 to
describe the arrogant self-confidence of the trader who makes his
plans without reference to God. Hence *alazoneia tou biou* means the
arrogance that comes from possessions (*bios* in the same sense in 1
Jn 3:17; see AGB). Neither the old translation **the pride of life**, an
archaic phrase for ostentatious living, nor *NEB*, 'the glamour of
life', catches the threat of self-assertive violence that the word
contains.

Hence **lust of the flesh** means such desires as are prompted by
the internal pressures of our human nature. **The lust of the eyes**
means the desire aroused in us by external objects or persons. **The
pride of life** indicates the arrogance that comes from possessions or
power. As the writer of 1 Jn looks at the world, he observes the
ruthless determination of human beings to use their strength to
satisfy the internal and external pressures which they normally experience. That is what the world is like, and love of the world leads
to that situation.

Such an estimate of this naughty world (as the *Book of Common
Prayer* called it) is modest and sober: it does not say the half of what
could be said about the corruption of our social existence. It is
neither exceptionally pessimistic or dualistic, but is drawn from the
popular morality of late antiquity. Within the *NT*, Paul's tirade in
Rom. 1:18–32 comes to mind, and among non-Christian exponents
of popular morality there is Plutarch, *c.* AD 50–100. 'On the whole,
Plutarch's morality is negative. He acknowledges that mankind and
society are "sick" internally in their souls as well as externally in
their behaviour. In his view health can only be restored by the
expulsion of both internal and external evils' (Betz, p. 7; for *epithymia* and *alazoneia*, see the discussion of *de cupiditate divitiarum*, pp.
289ff.).

It is, however, somewhat surprising to find popular morality of this kind turning up in the Johannine writings which seldom reflect on the personal causes of social shortcomings and, when they do, attribute them to evil influences (the evil one and the devils; see on 2:14). Moreover, the author's suspicion of the world is less surprising than his apparent confidence in the Christian community: 'anyone born of God does not sin . . . and the evil one does not touch him' (5:18). Even if 'does not' describes intention rather than practice, it is a very sanguine statement—as the writer himself knows (2:1; 3:6; 5:16). He is torn between what the community should be, indeed what properly speaking it is, and what it has recently shown itself to be, namely, a community broken by dissidence. Many false prophets and deceivers have gone out into the world (4:1; 2 Jn 7), just as Judas had gone out into the night (Jn 13:30). It was perhaps this shocking event which had persuaded the writer for a short time to abandon the safe shelter of euphemism (the evil one) and expose the ruthless self-seeking of the world and (as he thought) of those who had left the community to enter the world (cf. Vögtle, pp. 92-4).

CONTESTED CLAIMS TO ANOINTING 2:18-27

At this point the dissident group, which has already influenced much of what the author has written, is brought into the forefront with the name **antichrist**. The word is not found anywhere outside Christian circles and may have been invented by the author (presumably though not certainly before writing this letter) on the model of *antitheos*; cf. Philo, *On Dreams* 2.183, *tois enantiois ho theos kai ho antitheos nous euphrainetai, Pharaō* ('God and Pharaoh, the mind opposed to God, have pleasure in contrary matters'). MM, s.v., explain that in Greek anti-X can indicate either a claim to be X or opposition to, equivalence to, or substitution for X.

It is commonly said that this passage of the Epistle mentions 'the Antichrist' implying a well known and much dreaded figure. But *antichristos* lacks the definite article and could be taken as '*an* antichrist' or opponent of Christ. This suggestion is supported by its immediate change to the plural: 'you have heard that an opponent of Christ is coming: well, not only one opponent but many'. The article with *antichristos* in 2:22 and 4:3 clearly refers back to this mention, and in 2 Jn 7 it is generic, like the accompanying *ho planos*, 'the deceiver'. Whether a dreaded figure, not elsewhere called antichrist, was part of primitive Christian expectation, may be deferred for the moment: it is first necessary to discover what is actually implied by explicit references.

(i) It is part of the community's tradition, or at least something they had been told, that an opponent of Christ would come—presumably to their notice; but the expectation is vague.

(ii) It is more than fulfilled, however, in the **many antichrists** who have appeared. They were apparently members of the community (**of us**, *ex hēmōn*, in the partitive meaning of *ex* with the verb 'to be'; AGB, s.v. *ek*, p. 235, 4 a), but they had left it. In 4:1 the same dissidents are called 'false prophets', and in 2:26 and 2 Jn 7, 'deceivers'. Hence the nearest traditional warning is Mk 13:22: 'False christs and false prophets will arise and show signs and wonders, to lead astray, if possible the elect'; though the Johannine expectation scarcely includes signs and wonders. The parallel in 2 Pet. 2:1 is close: false teachers in the community, who are compared to the false prophets of Israel, 'bring in destructive heresies, even denying the Master who bought them'.

(iii) The very act of withdrawing from the community convinces the writer that the antichrists had not belonged to it. Indeed the withdrawal had taken place **that it might be plain that they all are not of us**. The words **they went out** are repeated in ET from the beginning of the verse; the Greek simply has **but that it might be plain**, a common Johannine trick of word omission; cf. BDF, section 448(7); unless this is a final *hina* equivalent to an imperative (MHT III, p. 95), which would translate 'but let it be plain'. The grammar of what follows is ambiguous: if **not** negatives the verb, translate 'all of them do not belong to us' (*RSV, JB*); but if **not** negatives **all**, translate 'not all (of the community) belong to us '(*AV, NEB*). To the writer it is unthinkable that a member of the community should not remain within the community. The very act of creating a new community distinguished from the world, as light is distinguished from darkness, carries the necessary implication that members of the community remain in the light (see on 2:6). From his reaction to the spiritual and social shock caused by the departure of the dissidents the author produces one of his strongest theological convictions; but its origin is not theological. It is no more than an example of the stock response of any marginal group when dissident members break away.

(iv) This is explained a little more fully when it is said that the false prophets have gone out into the world, that they are of the world and the world listens to them (4:1-5; 2 Jn 7). Since the world listened to the dissidents, it is to be presumed that they gained attention for their version of the Christian faith by removing unattractive features and perhaps adding pleasing ones. Their favourable reception by the world would disturb the parent community which lacked recognition from the world and experienced its hatred (3:1,

13). It would soothe their hurt if it could be thought that the dissidents were a part of the world that had intruded into the community. They had doubtless become members in all sincerity but had brought with them presuppositions which had remained unchanged in the transforming environment of the Christian community. When they found a development of Christian convictions which supported their original presuppositions, they adopted that development and made it out to be the only Christian truth.

(v) Presumably they claimed that they were **anointed by the Holy One**. Against the claim, the writer assures his readers that they too possess an anointing (v. 20, *kai hymeis*; cf. *NEB*, 'You, no less than they are among the initiated') by which they all have knowledge (which probably expresses the intended meaning of *oidate pantes* better than the oddly unfinished phrase **you all know**; the apparent lack of an object no doubt produced the change from *pantes* to the widely attested *panta*, which would translate 'you have all knowledge'). The dissidents claimed knowledge of the truth and asserted that other Christians spoke falsely (2:22, 27; see on 1:6).

(vi) They denied (wrongly as the author insists) that Jesus was the *Christos*, the Anointed One. That is why the name *antichrist* was given to them. The Greek of v. 23, if translated literally, would be: 'Who is the false person if not he who denies that Jesus is not the Christ'. The verb *arneomai* which expresses the negative idea of denying can be used with (as here) or without an accompanying negative which in English is unnecessary and confusing. But it is sensible enough if translated 'who makes the denial "Jesus is not the Christos" '.

It is not likely that the dissidents were interested in varieties of Jewish messianic expectation. Their denial is therefore not concerned with Jesus as the expected Jewish Messiah (even though the Gospel takes pains to relate *Messias* meaning *Christos* to Jewish and Samaritan expectation; Jn 1:41; 4:25). They deny that he possesses what they themselves possess: an anointing from the Holy One. Hence in the writer's judgment (or perhaps in their own explicit statements) they deny that Jesus is the Son of God (see on 1:3), and he uses the emphatic judgmental formula (see on 2:10) to give his ruling against the dissidents' view: **No one who denies the Son has the Father. He who confesses the Son has the Father also.** Hence the dissident **antichrist** denied both Father and Son though clearly he did not think so. He denied the significance given to Jesus by tradition in the Johannine community. His error, from the community's point of view, was not a heretical manner of describing the significance of Jesus but a denial that Jesus had much significance for communion with God.

(vii) Why they made that denial must be pieced together from other references in the letter, especially 4:1–4, where the dissidents are called false prophets. That very name indicates that they indeed possess a prophetic gift even though what they say is judged to be false. In their own estimation the spirit is from God, and possession by the spirit makes them those who belong to God. Since this spirit does not confess Jesus, they claim access to the Father without him. They are no longer interested in Jesus come in the flesh because they themselves possess the spirit—and of course God is spirit (Jn 4:24). See further, on 4:1–6; 5:6–12.

The antichrists are thus dissident members of the community, dissatisfied with the original teaching and inspired with a new confidence in their own anointing. Is it a satisfactory explanation of the name fastened on them by the writer of the letter that they deny Christ, or are they part of a mysterious evil conspiracy? In 2:13f., the young men have overcome the evil one; in 4:4, the community has overcome the antichrist. In 3:10, the children of God are distinguished from children of the devil, who no doubt belong to the world and to darkness. But is that anything more than customary polemic against religious opponents, as among the Qumran sectarians? They at least had a theology of the conflict and a plan for war between the sons of light and the sons of darkness.

As far as we know, the Johannine community had nothing of that kind, even in Revelation. Yet it is customary to say that the Johannine antichrist is simply one variant of a long-established, widespread expectation for the last times, namely, that an intensely evil, perhaps supernatural, being (conventionally called the Antichrist) would appear and launch an attack on God's truth and God's people. The first Christian writer to present the NT indications in a comprehensive manner was Irenaeus in A.H. 5.25ff. during the second half of the second century. At an earlier time, it was expectation of an imminent parousia that had been the organising principle of Christian apocalyptic. But when Christ's return was delayed, interest moved to the Antichrist and things associated with him (Vielhauer, in Hennecke II, p. 600; cf. his discussion of apocalyptic in early Christianity, pp. 608–42). It is more than likely that this speculation about an opponent of the Messiah was a purely Christian development (in Jewish writings the opponent always opposes God, not the Messiah), and the beginnings of it are to be found in 2 Th. 2; Mk 13; and Rev. 13 and 17.

It is of course true that many traces can be found in the Hebrew Scriptures and Jewish writings of the ancient myth of the dragon of chaos, the dreadful beast who opposes the creative deity. But the representation of the chaotic, God-denying experiences of life by a dragon, even by a dragon myth, does not imply that an actual dragon exists—just as the rebellion (against Moses) enshrined in a golden calf did not imply that the deity really was a calf or at least preferred to sit on a calf-shaped throne. Such imaginative symbols are devices for assessing experiences at more than their face value and bringing them into relation with our deepest understandings of reality.

The myth of the opponent of God seems to have been used in two ways: (1) to assess a major political threat to God's people, e.g., Antiochus Epiphanes (c. 165 BC), in Dan. 9:27, etc.; Pompey, with his invasion of Judaea in 63 BC, in *Ps. Sol.* 2:29, 'Delay not, O God, . . . to turn the pride of the dragon into dishonour'; Caligula, with his threat to the Holy Place (AD 40), possibly reflected in Mk 13; and Nero, with his attack on the Christians in AD 64, presumably indicated in the cryptic number of Rev. 13:11–18; (2) to discern a spiritual conflict arising within the community and to use the imaginative quality of the myth to provide a resolution of it: notable examples are 2 Th. 2, which combines with the standard images of political aggression the expectation of inner disruption from a demagogue and religious charlatan; and the *Testaments of the Twelve Patriarchs*, a kind of treatise on moral theology which frequently uses the name Beliar as a symbol of the self-destructive impulses of the community; *Test. Ben.* 7.2 (for Beliar in 2 C. 6:15 and in Qumran, see Fitzmyer, pp. 211–13). 'The adversaries of God in this final conflict were identified not so much with demonic or cosmic powers as with the unrighteous elements among men—the heathen and the recalcitrant who served the Prince of Darkness (Belial) and constituted his "army" ' (Gaster, pp. 257f.).

If the Johannine antichrist is indeed related to the mythical figure, it belongs not to the first usage (there is no trace of a political aggressor), but possibly to the second. Yet there are no imaginative embellishments and even those who confidently assert that the dissidents are attached to the Antichrist of the last days have to admit that the writer had nothing to teach about this figure (Rigaux, p. 386). Nor is it illuminating to say that the writer historicised (Bultmann, p. 36) or rationalised (Dodd, p. 49) the myth, for it is the nature of myths to have a bearing on historical changes and rationally developed conflicts. A myth is normally quiescent, preserved by cultic recitation and activity; it becomes activated and hence effective only when severe external or internal pressures are the stimulus. The writer of the Epistle may have wished to activate the myth; but he scarcely succeeded.

It is however conceivable that the Johannine community used the figure of Judas the betrayer as a symbol of the dissident group. The

Gospel makes use of traditional material about Judas: a muted
version of his part in the arrest of Jesus (18:1–5); a surprisingly
explicit version of his designation as betrayer at the supper (13:21–
30); and it introduces Judas into the traditional episode of the
anointing (12:3–8). In this way the actual business of betrayal is
played down so that the stress can fall on Judas' thievery and
demon-possession. The Gospel of John also brings Judas into material not present in the Synoptic Gospels: he provides a kind of
inclusio for the footwashing and is marked out as the demon-pos-
sessed betrayer, unclean, not chosen, the author of internal opposition as foreseen in Scripture (13:2, 10–11, 18). The saying that 'a
servant is not greater than his master' (13:16) may have a reference
to someone who thought he was. In the commentary attached to the
discourse on the Bread, reference is made to many disciples who
found unacceptable the teaching on eating the body and drinking
the blood of Jesus even though such words are spirit and life; and
it is said that Jesus 'knew from the first who those were that did not
believe and who it was that would betray him' (6:60–64). 'After this
many of his disciples drew back and no longer went about with
him'. Even the Twelve were not entirely sound: 'Did I not choose
you, and one of you is a devil?', namely Judas the son of Simon
Iscariot (6:66–71). In the final discourses, an intervention by Judas,
pointedly labelled 'not Iscariot', asks why Jesus discloses himself
only to disciples and not to the world. The answer seems indirect,
even evasive: 'if a man loves me he will keep my word, and my
Father will love him, and we will come to him and make our home
with him' (14:22ff.). The answer, however, would be apt if directed
against those who had gone out into the world because they no
longer honoured the word of Jesus and did not wish communion
with the Son as well as the Father. Finally, in 17:12, Jesus asserts
that he has safely guarded those that God gave him 'and none of
them is lost but the son of perdition', thus indicating Judas by one
description of the man of sin in 2 Th. 2:3. 'It seems probable that
John saw in Judas this eschatological character who must appear
before the manifestation of the glory of Christ (just as in 1 Jn 2:18,
22; 4:3 heretical teachers are represented as Antichrist)' (Barrett[2],
p. 508). It is not, of course, suggested that Judas, one of the Twelve,
devised the views of the dissidents, but simply that the community
scarcely needed a mythical antichrist when they could load the
repellent figure of Judas with demon-possession and moral failings.

So much for the dissidents. By contrast it is worth noting what
the author claims, perhaps under pressure from the dissidents, for
this understanding of the faith of the community: that you cannot
have access to the Father if you deny the Son, and that Jesus is the

essentially anointed one; that the community possesses its own anointing, which instructs them in the truth without the need of new
teaching—indeed they have known it from the beginning and must
continue in it if they are to receive the promised eternal life. Jesus
Christ is not only the mediator of their present access to the Father,
but equally of their approach to God if he appears and confronts
them.

18. This radical disruption of the community is evidence that **it
is the last hour**. It is difficult to know how to understand that
statement. Does the writer mean that his community has arrived at
the final moment for deciding its future or is he gazing apocalyp-
tically, at a water-clock no doubt, and realising that it shows an
hour to the end of the world? Has he abandoned his comforting
conviction that the darkness and the world are passing away and
the true light is already shining (2:8, 17) for a sudden panic about
the end of all things? There are few other signs in the Epistle of
apocalyptic nerves: even when he speaks of the divine appearing,
the reference is oddly tentative (2:28; 3:2). The phrase **last hour**
occurs only here in the Bible. It is commonly said to be equivalent
to 'the last days' and similar expressions in the Bible and *DSS*
(Schnackenburg, p. 142) and no doubt in the Gospel too. But there,
last is always joined with 'day', not **hour** (Jn 6:39f., 44, 54; 11:24)
and consistently refers to resurrection at the last day. In Jn 6 the
old eschatological language is revived and adapted as a symbolic
assertion that those who believe on the Son hold the conviction that
their approach to Jesus is prompted by the Father, and if they both
eat his body and drink his blood will find their existence given
ultimate significance in the new age.

The word **hour** also has some share in that symbolism: it is the
hour 'when the dead will hear the voice of the Son of God, and
those who hear will live' (5:25, 28), and it is the hour for the new
worship of the Father in spirit and in truth (4:21, 23). But above
all, it is the hour of Jesus, the hour for the Son to be glorified (2:4;
7:30; 8:20; 12:23, 27; 13:1; 17:1), and hence the hour for his
disciples to suffer (16:2–4). How is the striking use of hour in the
Gospel related to the **last hour** here? It may be suggested that the
writer of the Epistle made the stock response of a community leader
when the community is threatened by dissent and disruption. In
effect he says: 'We have tolerated these people so far, but this is the
final blow. It is now a question whether we continue to exist as a
community'. This sharp reaction gives vent to his own shock, justifies his condemnation of the dissidents (despite his advocacy of
love), and is intended to bring the community to his support. When
however the Gospel is being composed, the Johannine community

has come to terms with the disruption and has worked out a more adequate theological response: the decisive hour for the community was marked by the death and glorification of Jesus. The community's dismay is thereupon interpreted as part of the destiny of Jesus, and the teaching of the Epistle is brought to its proper conclusion. (The common insistence that **last hour** is naively eschatological perhaps arises from a too literal interpretation of **hour**; see therefore, LS and MM, s.v.; and also MM on *eschatos*, which supports the translation of *en chairō eschatō* in 1 Pet. 1:5 as 'in a season of extremity'.)

19. For **would have continued** (*memenēkeisan an*, an unaugmented pluperfect of *menō*, giving a then-clause following the if-clause, **if they had been** (*ei . . . ēsan*), which expresses an unfulfilled condition in past time), see on 1:6.

20. Attention is suddenly switched from the dissidents to **you**: **You have been anointed by the Holy One**; or, to translate more literally (noting the emphatic position of **you** in this polemical passage, and the pendent nominatives in vv. 24 and 27): 'you too have a *chrism* from the Holy One (or the Holy Place)'—implying 'just as much as they' (cf. *NEB*). We may infer that the dissidents justified their withdrawal by claiming a *chrism* which the community lacked. Since *chrisma* appears in *NT* only here and in v. 27 (even the verb is rare: three times in Lk.-Ac., once in Paul, once in Heb.), it is likely both that the term was introduced by the dissidents and that the significance they attached to it was not what the writer of the Epistle meant when he briefly adopted it.

Its meaning is scarcely to be derived from *OT* where *chrisma* means anointing oil (eight times in Exod.), glaze (once in Sir.), or an anointed sanctuary or prince (once in Dan.). The verb, except for a handful of references to the cosmetic or the preservative use of oil, is entirely cultic, referring to the anointing of kings and priests (and exceptionally of a prophet) in such a way that new life-power was mediated by the oil. The anointing conveyed priestly powers or kingly virtues. In a few early kingship stories these include spirit possession; and in Isa. 61:1 the prophetic speaker says: 'The Spirit of the Lord GOD is upon me, because the LORD has anointed me'. The word 'anoint' is here used in a transferred sense, 'to give full authorisation' (Westermann, p. 365), and the contents of the oracle are not directly relevant to the noun *chrisma* in the Epistle.

It is clear that the use of this passage from Isaiah in the synagogue sermon at Nazareth was intended by Luke to throw light on the designation *Christos* (Lk. 4:18). Something similar is suggested by the Melkizedek document from Qumran, where the messenger who brings good tidings in Isa. 52:7 is interpreted as 'the Anointed one of the spirit' by reference to the anointed prince of Dan. 9:25 and Isa. 61:2–3 (Vermes, p. 267; de Jonge, pp. 309–12; this association of spirit and anointing seems absent elsewhere in Qumran writings and other Jewish literature: *TWNT* IX, pp. 502–11). Luke uses it again in Ac. 10:38, where Peter says that 'God anointed Jesus of Nazareth with the Holy Spirit and power'; and Paul may intend it in 2 C. 1:21–22, where God has 'anointed us, set his seal of ownership upon us, and put his Spirit in our hearts as a deposit' (*NIV*).

Persuasive as this scanty evidence perhaps should be, it is noteworthy that the writer of the Epistle in fact says nothing about the Spirit in this passage; and his subsequent references are formal (3:24; 4:13) or polemical (4:1–6; 5:6–8), and are somewhat undeveloped theologically. It is therefore suggested that the dissidents not only introduced the word *chrisma* but also claimed that they, not the rest of the community, were anointed with the spirit (see, however, Marshall, pp. 153–5).

Where did the dissidents (or indeed anyone) find that idea? Did it originate not in Jewish but in hellenistic circles? Evidence for anointing in orthodox Christian practice is plentiful from the beginning of the third century, but earlier is lacking. Yet Irenaeus and Clement of Alexandria make reference to anointing rituals among second-century Valentinian gnostics (Mitchell; Lampe, PGL s.v.). In the recently discovered *Gospel of Philip*, chrism plays an important part alongside other rituals and the information provided by this document can be used with caution to identify some features in a religious milieu which may have influenced the dissidents. The *Gospel of Philip* is dated in the second century by Wilson, pp. 3–5, in the second half of the second century and placed near Antioch by Krause in Foerster II, p. 77; and in third-century Syria by Ménard (1967), p. 34. The *Gospel* is a collection of 'sayings', only loosely co-ordinated and not always consistent. The form in which we now read it is the result of considerable development.

The *Gospel of Philip* community possessed a set of linked rituals: 'The Lord has [done] everything in a mystery, a baptism and an anointing and a eucharist and a redemption and a bridal chamber' (68). Features of this apparently orderly scheme (soon lost in the confusion of other sayings) are found in Irenaeus' description of the various Marcosian practices: 'The baptism of (that is, instituted by) the visible Jesus took place for the remission of sins, but the redemption by the Christ who descended upon him for perfection. . . Some of them prepare a bridal chamber and perform a mystic rite, with certain innovations, for those who are being consecrated, and they claim that what they are effecting is a spiritual marriage'. Of another group: after the redemption 'they anoint the initiate with oil from the balsam tree. This oil is said to be a type of the sweet savour which is above all terrestrial things' (*A.H.* 1.21.2, 3).

In the *Philip* community the anointing is superior to the baptism. 'For from the anointing (chrism) we are called Christians, not because of the baptism. And Christ was called [so] because of the anointing, for the Father anointed the Son. But the Son anointed the apostles. And the apostles anointed us. He who has been anointed has the All. He has the resurrection, the light, the cross, the Holy Spirit. The Father gave him this in the bridal chamber, he received [it]' (95). This saying claims an esoteric tradition, superior to the Church's baptismal tradition, by which the believer who genuinely merits the name Christian is brought into being and possesses the totality—namely, the resurrection life, the necessary illumination, the power of the Cross which rends the veil separating this inferior world from the *plērōma* (to which the bridal chamber corresponds; cf. Saying 125), and the Holy Spirit which distinguishes spiritual from ordinary Christians.

Yet the *Philip* community did not rely exclusively on the anointing. 'Nobody will be able to see himself, neither in water nor in a mirror without light. Nor again will you be able to see in light without water and mirror. Therefore it is fitting to baptize in the two, in the light and the water. But the light is the anointing' (75). The conclusion that baptism and chrism are reciprocally essential for self-knowledge depends on the arguments that you become like the image you contemplate, and that the light (i.e., the anointing) must create the true image for contemplation. Hence the anointed gnostic is told, 'You saw Christ; you became Christ' (44); 'this one is no longer a Christian but a Christ' (67).

What that means can be discerned in a group of sayings which reinterpret *NT* resurrection teaching in gnostic terms. Since the soul is a precious thing in a despised body (22), flesh and blood (as Paul says) cannot inherit the Kingdom of God. What does inherit is the flesh of Jesus and his blood, since (as John says) 'He who will not eat my flesh and drink my blood has no life in him'. Then the gnostic interpretation of this gross language is given: 'His flesh is the logos and his blood is the Holy Spirit. He who has received these has food and has drink and has clothing' (23)—that is to say, the soul that has stripped off the flesh like a garment rises clothed in the flesh and blood of Christ, namely, logos and spirit. (This symbolic interpretation is as old as Ignatius, *Trall.* 8, where flesh means faith and blood means love; cf. *Rom.* 7). 'By water and fire the whole place is purified . . . There is water in water, there is fire in anointing' (25). In a related saying the writer explains that

'I do not speak of this fire that has no form, but of the other, whose form is white, which is beautiful light, and which gives beauty' (66). Hence he seems to mean that the water of baptism does what it obviously signifies—it cleanses; but that the anointing oil produces secret effects beyond anything it may signify—namely, the beautiful illumination which recreates the beauty of the soul.

Nobody would suppose that the *Gospel of Philip* describes the religion of the Johannine dissidents. Its formulation of teachings and practices is at least a century later than 1 Jn; but it may well help to identify the impulses that gave rise to dissidence. Some features of the *Gospel of Philip* are already known to us from the earlier remarks of Ignatius and Irenaeus, and there are discernible points of contact between this gnostic *Gospel* and notable features in the Epistle.

(i) The significant references to *chrism* in both documents, without satisfactory parallels elsewhere. Baptism and chrism are both accepted, but *chrism* in *Philip* far exceeds baptism and conveys the All. So perhaps the dissidents taught when they claimed the witness of water and spirit (5:6f.) and exercised prophetic powers (4;1).

(ii) The statements that the name Christian is given to those who have received the *chrism*, that contemplation of Christ turns the gnostic from a Christian into a Christ. This conviction allows no further role for Jesus once the *chrism* has been received. Moreover the gnostic view that Christ did not reveal himself as he really is but as each was able to see him (*Gospel of Philip* 26) perhaps implies that what was heard, seen, looked upon and touched (1 Jn 1:1) was not the true image for contemplation.

(iii) Contempt for bodily existence which requires the flesh and blood of Christ to be understood symbolically (cf. 1 Jn 4:2). Hence the following instruction to gnostics: 'You who are with the Son of God, do not love the world, but love the Lord, that those to whom you give birth shall not resemble the world but shall resemble the Lord' (*Philip* 112).

(iv) Both documents speak about love, and it must be admitted that *Philip* 45 does so with more moral insight: 'No-one will be able to give without love. Because of this, that we may receive we believe, but in order that we may give in truth, since if anyone does not give in love he has no profit from what he has given'.

(v) The gnostic conviction that 'he who has the knowledge of the truth is free' is complemented in *Philip* 110 by the statement that 'the free man does not sin, for he who sins is a slave of sin' (quoting Jn 8:34). This reproduces one strand of the Epistle's teaching (3:6, 9; 5:18), while the statement that even gnostics, the seed of the

Holy Spirit, are slaves of wickedness (*Philip* 125) reproduces the other (1:8; 5:16–17).

(vi) The description of gnostics as 'the seed of the Holy Spirit', and 'the seed of the Son of man . . . the true race . . . the children of the bridal chamber' (*Philip* 102), is one illustration of later developments of the seed metaphor (hidden by the *RSV* translation 'nature') in 1 Jn 3:9.

All these items correspond to views adopted or rebutted in the Epistle. They mark out roughly the same area of discourse. The community of the *Gospel of Philip* has remained Christian in a marginal fashion; the dissidents of the Epistle have moved sharply away from an orthodox christology but doubtless thought themselves to be in possession of a superior and more effective development of the Christian tradition. Although rather widely separated in time, both communities show the influence of popular gnostic conceptions though neither is supported by a well-developed gnostic speculative scheme.

In opposition to the dissidents, the writer asserts that his community does indeed possess a *chrism* from **the Holy One**. That may refer to God himself, or to Jesus (cf. Jn 6:69 'you are the Holy One of God'—but not perhaps if the phrase echoes the dissidents' claim since they deny that Jesus is the Christ, 2:22), or just possibly to the Holy Spirit which is not elsewhere so named in the Epistle. Indeed **holy** appears only here. It is therefore worth remarking that the *Gospel of Philip* uses a pictorial image (according to Ménard, p. 196, from Byzantine churches) in which the holy place is baptism, the holy of the holy is redemption, and the hoiy of the holies is the bridal chamber (*Philip* 76, 125). This elaborated imagery is unsuited to the Epistle, but the proper sense may be (if Jn is quoting opponents) 'an anointing from the Holy Place', i.e. the transcendent spiritual world.

What then does the writer of the Epistle oppose to the dissidents' *chrism*? It is something the community can know (vv. 20*b*, 21), a kind of truth to be distinguished from falsehood (21), something taught and accepted (27). There is a structural similarity between 27*a* and 24*a* which is plain in Greek and can be shown in English only by a word-for-word translation:

27*a* You/the chrism which you received/
       from him/remains in you.
24*a* You/what you heard/
       from the beginning/in you let it remain.

This suggests that the chrism is the original (? baptismal) tradition of the community. This is all they need; no further teaching is required if the promise of eternal life (25) is to be realised. As

against the gnostic claim to possess a secret tradition, they themselves have all the information.

This interpretation, strongly suggested by **his anointing teaches
you about everything** (27), therefore favours the reading 'you know
all things' in v. 20 instead of **you all know**.

The Greek is *oidate pantes* (you all know) or *oidate panta* (you
know all things). The two readings are equally old; but *panta* is
more widely supported (Metzger, p. 710). Either *pantes* is the original reading and is directed against the claim of a few dissidents to
possess superior knowledge, so that *panta* is a widespread scribal
correction to supply an object after *oidate*; or *panta* is the original
reading, editorially emended in Alexandria to produce a more modest assertion. Editors of the Greek text and translators mostly favour
pantes; commentators are divided. In recent years Dodd, Schnackenburg, Bultmann, Houlden and Marshall have decided for *pantes*,
whereas Windisch-Preisker, Nauck, O'Neill and Grundmann have
adopted *panta*. It cannot matter greatly.

Is it sufficient to identify the anointing with a body of teaching?
Does such a seemingly non-personal interpretation fit the verbs in
v. 27 (**as his anointing teaches you**)? Attention has been drawn
(Schnackenburg, p. 152) to the links between 2:20–27 and the
Paraclete sayings in the Gospel:

21 you know the truth—Spirit of truth (Jn 14:17; 15:26)
22 Jesus is the Christ—the Spirit of truth glorifies Jesus (Jn
    16:13f.)
24, 27 what you heard from the beginning and the anointing
        abides in the community—'the Spirit of truth . . . dwells
        with you and will be in you' (Jn 14:17)
27 his anointing teaches you about everything—'the Paraclete,
    the Holy Spirit. . .will teach you all things' (Jn 14:26); 'the
    Spirit of truth . . . will guide you into all truth' (Jn 16:13)

There is obviously some relation between the two sets of passages,
but it is not obvious that those of the Epistle can be glossed by the
Gospel references. The Epistle lacks any reference to 'the Holy
Spirit'; Paraclete is used (in the Epistle) of Jesus, not of the Spirit;
in this context there is no reference to the Spirit's testimony or its
work of convincing or convicting (*elenchein*). In the Gospel passages
the main verbs stress the giving, sending, going forth and coming
of the Spirit; the Epistle uses verbs of possessing and receiving the
chrism. Indeed, the presence or absence of the *chrism* is a matter of
confessing or denying that Jesus is the Christ—which could appropriately be attributed to the Spirit, but in John is not. It is tempting
to relate the *chrism* to baptism by means of Jn 3:5–8, 'born of water
and spirit', but in the Epistle the phrase is always 'born of God'.

Since the Epistle says, 'by this we know that he abides in us, by the
Spirit which he has given us' (3:24; 4:13), why then did the writer
not use that thought in the present passage? Presumably because
the dissidents also claimed the Spirit: supposed activities of the
Spirit had to be tested (in the writer's view) by confession of Jesus
and the love he commanded (3:23–4:3; 4:12–16). When therefore
he needed some distinct item to put in opposition to the dissidents'
chrism, he called on 'what you heard from the beginning'.

There is some parallel to this use of anointing language in the
second century. Ignatius (*Eph.* 17) warns against being anointed
(*aleiphō*) with the stinking teachings of the prince of this world.
Justin (*Dial.* 40.1) expounds the Passover lamb as a type of Christ,
'with whose blood, in proportion to their faith in him, they anoint
their houses, that is themselves, those who believe in him' (cf.
Apost. Trad. 37.3; Dix, p. 70). Clement of Alexandria (*The Instructor*
2:2) explains that 'the blood of the Lord is twofold. For there is the
blood of his flesh, by which we are redeemed from corruption; and
the spiritual, that by which we are anointed'. But the Epistle is
scarcely to be illustrated by these rhetorical devices; rather more by
Jn 6:63, 'the words I have spoken to you are spirit and life'. The
writer of the Epistle is convinced that the original tradition is a
living force within the community: 'the word of God abides in you'
(2:14). It is the word of life (1:1), and therefore has its own inherent
power to instruct. The old commandment which they heard at the
beginning becomes a new commandment when the darkness of
partial understanding gives way to the true light (2:7f.). The Epistle
is written not because its readers need to be told the truth, but to
persuade them that they know it already (2:21).

The links between this passage and the Paraclete components of
the Farewell Discourses can best be accounted for if the Epistle
preceded Jn 14–16. The Paraclete teachings would then be a sharp-
ening of the theological understanding of the Spirit, intended to
resolve the ambiguity disclosed in the community when both sides
claimed endowment with the Spirit. *Chrism*, it is suggested, was
introduced into the community by the dissidents. The writer of the
Epistle did not disclaim the word, but attached it to the original
(? baptismal) tradition. But was that anything but a first response?
If the dissidents said: 'Not only baptism but also an anointing which
is essential for true life', would it not be more convincing (especially
when the word of life was being set down in narrative form) if the
evangelist could point to a separate event and private disclosure? In
that case, perhaps the Footwashing would fill the bill. All the evan-
gelists inherited a tradition that Jesus had been anointed by a woman
and, despite protests, had accepted the action. In Mk and Mt. the

ointment is poured on the head; in Lk. and Jn on his feet. The protest in Mk, Mt. and Jn is against the waste of ointment when the money might have been given to the poor; and Jesus justifies his acceptance of the anointing by a cryptic reference to his burial. The protest in Lk. is against the character of the woman, and Jesus justifies her action as a sign of love. Jn attributes the protest to Judas and says it was hypocritical: 'not that he cared for the poor but because he was a thief' (Jn 12:6). He was in the movement for what he could get out of it, and pointedly refused to honour Jesus, especially in respect of his death. John's Anointing narrative is linked with the Footwashing by the verb *ekmassō* (to wipe; in Jn 11:2 and 12:3 of Mary's anointing, in 13:5 of Jesus' action at the Footwashing—elsewhere in *NT* only in Lk. 7:38 of the anointing in Simon's house). It is possible that the evangelist was prompted by the tradition of the Anointing and a saying like Lk. 22:27 ('I am among you as one who serves') to develop a narrative that could be expounded as an anointing of disciples. (The Anointing and the Footwashing are similar in structure: (i) in the course of a supper (*deipnon*), 12:2, 13:4; (ii) oil or water poured on feet which are then dried, 12:3; 13:5; (iii) protest, 12:4; 13:6ff.; (iv) justification which includes an oblique reference to the death of Jesus, 12:7; 13:10f.) The Footwashing is essential if disciples are to have a share in Jesus (13:8), but it is not to be understood as a cleansing (accepting the short reading in 13:10 with *NEB*, *JB*): 'He who has bathed does not need to wash'. Hence a baptised Christian needs no further cleansing, but he does need participation in Christ which he achieves by the example (13:15). The ritual action of footwashing is thus displayed as teaching about caring for one another, which is not far from the Epistle's love for fellow Christians. Judas is excluded from its benefits because of his refusal to honour Jesus, and is perhaps seen as a type of the dissident Christians.

21. Since they possess the **anointing** they **know the truth** (see on 1:6) and the author writes (see on 1:1–4) to warn them against attemps to stretch the truth or pervert it. The grammar of this sentence is cobbled together. The Greek *hoti* comes three times; in *RSV* translated twice as **because** and the third time as **that** (with the verb **know** added to make sense). But the first two could also be translated by 'that': **I write to you, not** (to say) that **you do not know the truth, but** (to say) that **you know it.** The meaning is clear enough.

No lie is of the truth. The contrast between truth and falsehood has already appeared at 1:6, 10 and 2:4. The strength of feeling behind it is shown by its present and later application to the controversy with the dissidents (2:21f., 27; 4:1, 20; 5:10). The *pseud-*root indicates lack of conformity to fact or truth. If the verb is used

actively of making erroneous statements, it may but need not necessarily imply that the facts or truth are known but are being inten-
tionally concealed, misrepresented or reversed. If the verb is used
passively of receiving erroneous statements, it may imply being
deceived by lies or simply being mistaken. The context determines
the meaning. When God says 'you have forgotten me and trusted
in lies' (Jer. 13:25) or when the people confess (Isa. 59:13) to
'denying the Lord, and turning away from following our God,
. . . conceiving and uttering from the heart lying words', they are
talking about disloyalty. The root occurs frequently in polemic
against pagan gods and against false prophets (as in 4:1; cf. therefore
the lying spirit of 1 Kg. 22:21–23: the writer of the Epistle strongly
insists that the spirit of error is not sent by God). In 1:10 and 5:10
certain assertions would make God a liar, that is would treat him as
a pagan god. In most references, however, truth and falsehood are
opposed ways of seeing one's situation in relation to God, and the
test is more practical than doctrinal: following the commandments,
doing what is right, loving one's fellow Christian. This suggests that
confession of Jesus is of the same kind.

22f. The whole matter, in the dispute with the dissidents, turns
on confessing or denying that Jesus is the Christ, that is, the one
who is anointed by God in such a sense that he is the Son without
whom it is impossible to have the Father (see above). **Confess**
translates the verb *homologeō*: its meaning stretches from 'promise'
to 'admit' (as John Baptist admitted that he was not the Christ, in
Jn 1:20) and so 'confess' sin (1 Jn 1:9); and then to 'declare publicly,
acknowledge': hence in this passage acknowledging the Son,
acknowledging that Jesus Christ has come in the flesh (4:2; 2 Jn 7)
and acknowledging Jesus as Son of God (4:15). The acknowledgement takes place in face of a denial from within the original community (in Jn 9:22 the acknowledgement is made against threats
from the synagogue leaders). In the Epistle, the *homologia* has not
yet become a formal element of community life such as is suggested
by Rom. 10:9f. and Heb. 3:1; 4:14; 10:23. The exact expression
has the Father (cf. 2 Jn 9) occurs only in the Johannine Epistles.
To judge from the Jewish parallels cited (2 Mac. 8:36; 11:10; 3
Mac. 7:16; *Test. Iss.* 7; *Test. Dan* 5; Hanse, *TWNT* II, pp 822–3),
the meaning is to have the help of God. No doubt the dissidents
used it in the sense implied by 3:9, 'the divine seed remains in him'
(*NEB*).

24. For **what you have heard from the beginning**, see on 1:1.
For **abide in**, see on 2:6. The sentence begins with an emphasis
missed in *RSV*: You then—**let what you heard**. Cf. v. 27.

25. The Greek runs thus: **And this is** the promise which **he**

(emphatic Johannine *autos*, presumably referring to Jesus) **has promised us**. The noun and verb 'promise' occur only here in Johannine writings though they are reasonably familiar in Acts, Paul, and Hebrews. It may be suggested that the writer has borrowed them from the dissidents who relied perhaps on the promise of the Spirit (cf. Lk. 24:49; Ac. 1:4; 2:33, 39; Gal. 3:14; 4:28f.; Eph. 1:13), whereas the writer gave primary significance to eternal life (accusative case in Greek, instead of the expected nominative, by attraction into the case of 'which', *hēn*). For him, the Spirit had an important function in relation to the new life of the Christian (see on 3:24ff.); but it did not add a new component, or replace an old component, or even lead to a stage beyond earlier stages; for eternal life was nothing more nor less than abiding in the Son and in the Father (see also on 1:2).

It may be noted that the Paraclete passages in the Farewell Discourses of the Gospel contain promises that Jesus will give or cause God to give the Spirit, and that these passages have the appearance of being additions to an earlier draft. The main body of the Gospel is less explicit, but takes pains to show the dependence of the Spirit on the words and glorification of Jesus. By contrast, in Jn 1–12 Jesus is everywhere and without reservation the embodiment of eternal life. The writer of the Epistle relies on that tradition; the composers of the Gospel had to make room for both traditions, even if they adapted the Spirit sayings to their belief in the primacy of Jesus.

26. The dissidents are **those who would deceive you** (so 2 Jn 7; and cf. 3:7; 4:6), although the Greek verb *planaō* could be translated 'mislead', without any necessary suggestion of deliberate deception. The false christs and false prophets of Mk 13:22 may possibly lead astray the elect. The idea has apocalyptic currency, e.g., 2 Th. 2:11, 'God sends upon them a strong delusion (*plane*), to make them believe what is false'; and when the apocalyptic imagination gets into its stride in Revelation, the dragon leads astray the whole world (Rev. 12:9; 13:11ff.; 18:23; 19:20; 20:3, 8, 10): a symbolical representation of the Roman imperium as the conspiracy against God. At times of radical social change, finding the right way is difficult and mistaken social judgments are easy. It is commonplace to excuse blunders by pleading conspiracy and deception. The community for whom the Epistle was written were scarcely in the apocalyptic mood, but the writer borrowed the apocalyptic word *plane* to express their dismayed confusion.

27. This repeats and summarises what has gone before. As at v. 24, the sentence begins with an idiom natural to spoken emphasis: 'And as for you—**the anointing which you received**'. The second half of the verse can be taken in several ways, since (i) *menete* can

be indicative ('remains') or imperative ('let it remain'); (ii) *hōs*, **as,**
may be taken up by *kathōs*, **just as,** and a parenthesis **and is true
and is no lie;** hence translate: **as his anointing teaches you . . .
just as it has taught you, abide in him,** *RSV*; or (iii) translate 'but
as his anointing teaches you . . .. so (*kai*) **it is true and is no lie.**
And **as it taught you,** (you) **remain in him'** (*en autō* could stand
for *en toutō* and mean 'in it', i.e., the anointing; but the *en autō* of
v. 29, which must mean 'in him', is doubtless already in mind; see
Schnackenburg, pp. 161f.). This general looseness of expression,
which suggests dictation, is no great matter in a rhetorical summary.

CONTESTED CLAIMS TO BE CHILDREN OF GOD **2:28–3:10**

The next stage of the campaign against the dissidents is more difficult. When it was a question of the *object* of faith—what significance was proper to Jesus—the author could rely on the tradition
of the community; but when it was a question of the *activity* of
faith—what morality was proper to Christians—he had to find his
way more experimentally.

No doubt all Christians, compliant and dissident Christians alike,
agreed that sinful human activities are to be avoided and rejected.
They differed on the interpretation of sin. In the most general terms
a sin may be described as an activity, individual or social, intentional
or unintentional, which makes it difficult to believe in the goodness
and presence of God. From this, two possibilities arise: either God
sees to it that those who possess his anointing constantly demonstrate his goodness and presence, in which case they are of course
without sin (see on 1:8); or God provides a standard of goodness
which his people are expected to reach, and a remedy for their
failures. The tradition of the community embodied the latter possibility: the 'agreed statement' refers to keeping commandments, a
means of cleansing from sin, and (the writer added) a sponsor for
sinners (1:7; 2:1–3).

But the dissidents were captivated by the former possibility: to
be born of God was to become incapable of sinning (3:9). That
enticing conviction, however, is ambiguous: it could mean that those
born of God always keep the commandments (which is unlikely), or
that they can, indeed should, ignore the commandments because
their spontaneous born-of-God activity always demonstrates the
goodness and presence of God (which is delusory and quickly becomes divisive).

For this reason the dissidents had separated from the community,
and the case against them is the more difficult to work out because
the writer of the Epistle really agrees with them that a person born

of God cannot sin—though by 'cannot' he means 'must not' rather than 'does not'. To check those who think that sin does not matter, he must say that a Christian cannot sin; and to deflate those who think themselves sinless, he must offer a remedy for sinning. Yet he may have been aware and, if so, uneasily aware, that Jewish tradition spoke of the patriarchs as sinless (*Prayer of Manasseh* 8; *Test. Iss.* 7; *Test. Zeb.* 1); and that a Pharisee like Paul could claim that as a Jew he was blameless as regards the Law, and as a Christian had nothing on his conscience (Phil. 3:6; 1 C. 4:4). The writer finds his way through these difficulties by broaching the present character of the children of God (2:28–3:3) which is then defined negatively by the absence of sin (3:4–11) and positively by the practice of love—when he feels much more at home.

In so doing, he makes liberal use of his favourite teaching device (see on 2:10–11), namely, paired statements beginning 'everyone who' or 'he who', which are used to give definitive judgments or instructions. The pair of statements in 2:29 and 3:9 (the latter repeated with minor variation in 5:18) form an *inclusio* for this part of the argument:

2:29 Everyone who does right is born of him.

3:9 No one born of God commits sin.

The former is judgmental, the latter is prescriptive. That is, the former expresses or defines the community's judgment about the status 'born of God'; whereas the latter tells those born of God what they should not do. (It is a statement like 'No experienced teacher strikes a child'—not stating what is the case but what ought to be.) The other paired statements similarly vary in their function.

3:3 Everyone who thus hopes in him purifies himself
    as he is pure (prescriptive).

3:4 Everyone who commits sin is guilty of lawlessness
                                              (judgmental).

3:6a No one who abides in him sins (prescriptive);
  6b No one who sins has either seen him or known him
                                              (judgmental).

3:7 He who does right is righteous, as he is righteous
    (the judgmental first clause is converted into a
    prescriptive statement by the addition of the second
    clause, i.e., 'should be righteous as he is').

3:8 He who commits sin is of the devil (judgmental).

The argument ends by repeating 2:29 in an equivalent form: 'whoever does not do right is not of God', and by adding 'nor he who does not love his brother' to make a transition to the next theme.

28. The encouragement to **abide in him** may refer to God (2:6;

3:24; 4:13, 16), or to Father and Son (2:24), or to the Son (3:6).
Perhaps the writer is deliberately ambiguous; but if a choice has to
be made it turns on whose appearing and **coming** is expected. It is
commonly taken for granted that Christ's appearing is intended
(questioned by O'Neill, pp. 32–6). But why should the writer decide
to use that thought, which is alien to his other teaching, is introduced by a tentative 'if' (not *when* as in the usual translation; see
immediately below), and is not obviously demanded by the argument? The answer would be clear if the **coming** of God had been
promised by the dissidents to those who received their kind of
anointing and denied to the rest of the community, who would
shrink from him in shame (*aischynthōmen ap' autou*, a pregnant
construction: to be ashamed in a Jewish context means to be embarrassed, humiliated and rejected—not necessarily associated with
moral distress).

In reply the writer reassures the community that they, no less
than the dissidents, would have **confidence**, not embarrassment, in
the presence of God (cf. 3:21; 4:17; 5:14; Greek *parrhēsia*—in the
Gospel always in the dative, meaning 'publicly'; not so in the Epistle
where it may be a dissident usage). Both 'presence' and 'coming'
can represent the Greek *parousia*, which has become a technical
expression for the return of Christ. It appears nowhere else in
Johannine writings, but it is used explicitly of Christ in 1C. 15:23,
six times in 1 and 2 Th. (and once of 'the lawless one'); of the
coming of the Lord in Jas 5:7, 8; and of Christ and of the day of
God in 2 Pet. 1:16; 3:4, 12. But in Jewish writings it could equally
be used of God's self-disclosure to Moses and Elijah (Jos. *Ant.* 3.80,
203; 9.55) or of God's expected arrival to establish his earthly
kingdom: the dominant conception in the *Testaments of the Twelve
Patriarchs*, after obvious Christian glosses have been excluded (see
Test. Sim. 6.5; *Test. Levi* 2.11; 5.2; 8.11; *Test. Jud.* 22.2, 'until the
parousia of the God of righteousness'; *Test. Zeb.* 9.8; *Test Naph.*
8.3; *Test. Ash.* 7.3). In late antiquity *parousia* took on the special
meaning of a royal visit, or of the coming of a hidden divinity (AGB,
s.v.). It would be much in line with the thought of hellenistic
Judaism if the dissidents spread the conviction that their anointing
alone would lead to a *parousia* of God—and if they could promise
the Father, why did they need the Son?

The writer of the Epistle, in order to contain the dissidents, is
willing to concede the possibility of a future disclosure of the divine
person. He twice says (here and at 3:2), 'if he is disclosed' (*ean
phanerōthē*; cf. *RV*, *JB*). Commentators and translators in general
agree that 'if' is equivalent to **when**, and they hasten to explain that
no doubt is implied. 'The use of *ean*, "if", does not place the *fact*

of the coming in doubt, but merely its time and circumstance'
(Marshall, p. 165). But if **when** was intended, why not use *hotan*,
as at 5:2 (and often in the Gospel; cf. esp. Jn 4:25; 7:27, 31; 15:26;
16:4)?

According to AGB (s.v. *ean* 1.d), at times the meaning closely
approaches that of *hotan*, whenever, or when; but the instances
given are weak. Isa. 24:13 and Am. 7:2 translate Hebrew *'im* with
the perfect, when it is idiomatically nearly equivalent to 'when', and
are scarcely illuminating. In Tob. 4:3 (BA) *ean apothanō* means
'when I die'; and in Tob. 6:17 the BA text has *ean*, the S text *hotan*,
'when you approach her'. These are more to the point, but may still
be examples of Hebrew idiom. *NT* specimens are of variable quality.
Jn. 12:32 ('if I am lifted up') can be pressed into service only if the
evangelist's knowledge of the death of Jesus is attributed to Jesus
himself; in any case the logion means not that Jesus will draw all
men *when* he is lifted up, but on condition that he is lifted up. So
also Jn 14:3 means 'I will return on condition that I first go'. Heb.
3:7, 'if only you will listen', is irrelevant. The 'if someone comes'
clauses in 1 C. 16:10; 2 C. 13:2; Col. 4:10 express a genuine element
of doubt about the expected arrival; but in 2 C. 5:1 *ean* genuinely
approximates to 'when'. The problem can be solved by analysing
the uses of *ean* in the Epistle. They fall into three groups:

(i) Conditions which may or may not be fulfilled, though they are
very likely to be: 'if anyone sins', 2:1; 'if our hearts do not condemn
us' (on one construction of this clause), 3:20; and 'if anyone sees
his brother sinning', 5:16. We take these to mean: 'when this happens, if it does'.

(ii) Conditions which at times are fulfilled, at times are not: 'if we
keep his commandments', 2:3; 'if we ask anything', 5:14. We take
these to mean 'when(ever) it happens'.

(iii) Conditions which some do, some do not fulfil: 'if anyone
loves the world' (= anyone who loves), 2:15; 'if you know' (= you
who know), 2:29; 'if we love one another' (= those of us who love),
4:12; 'if we know', 5:15. This group includes a number of polemical
passages where use of the conditional (and indeed of the first person
plural) softens but does not conceal the polemic: 'if we say . . . if
we walk in the light', implying 'those who assert . . . but we who
walk', 1:6–7; and similarly 1:8–10; 'if what you heard from the
beginning abides in you', 2:24, implying 'since the original tradition
persists among you, as it does not among others . . .'; 'if anyone
says', 4:20, implying that someone does make this untrue statement.

Returning now to 'if he is disclosed': it could fall under (i), not
under (ii), since it is not a repeatable possibility, and most probably

under (iii)—a polemical statement: 'if, as some suggest, he is disclosed'.

More important, however, than the grammatical discussion are considerations drawn from Johannine teaching. At the beginning of the Epistle, the new life has already been disclosed (1:2). Indeed all other occurrences of the verb *phaneroō* are in the past tense: Christ was disclosed to take away sins, to destroy the activities of the devil, and to demonstrate the love of God (3:5, 8; 4:9). 'The Son of God has come and has given us understanding' (5:20). It is already possible to say of Christians that if they have the Son they have life (5:12). What more could be added by a *parousia* of the Son? It is true that the writer looks confidently towards the day of judgment: but there is no hint that Christ plays a part in the judgment different from the part he already plays (4:17). Moreover, if we turn to the Gospel, this impression is confirmed: the Son already exercises judgment—he who believes on him has already passed from death to life (cf. 1 Jn 3:14). The hour is coming and now is when the final judgment is carried out (Jn 5:22–29; cf. 12:31). Jesus has come down from heaven to gather those who have been given to him by God, after which he returns to heaven and raises up his own at the last day (Jn 6:39–43). Unlike the manna, which the fathers ate yet still died, Jesus is the bread which when eaten gives life for ever (6:48–51). If that is so, any further intervention is pointless. Indeed, in Jn 17 Jesus prepares his return to the Father by handing back his responsibility for the world and by praying that those whom God has given him may be where he is and may behold his glory. True, in 14:3 Jesus says, 'I will come again and will take you to myself, that where I am you may be also'. The coming again is in a little while: 'because I live, you will live also' (14:19). Presumably, therefore, the return is neither at the *parousia* nor at the individual believer's death but at his own resurrection. 'If a man loves me, he will keep my word, and my Father will love him, and we will come to him and make our home with him' (14:23). That indeed is the teaching of the Epistle against the dissidents.

29. The writer now shows his doubtless polemical determination to elucidate the Christian condition in terms of doing **right** (see on 1:9). If God is intended by **he** and **him**, the reference is to God's benevolence. If Jesus is intended in the first clause, what would it mean to say that he was known to be **righteous**? Not that he was a strictly law-abiding Jew; but, either that his death was for the rescue and benefit of sinners (2:1–2), or that he invariably did the will of his Father (Jn 5:19). The former sense is confirmed by 3:5–7: 'You know that he appeared to take away sins. . . He who does right is righteous, as he is righteous'. It is indeed the business of a

Christian to be like Christ in taking away sins (5:14–17); if he acts in this manner—that is, if he loves his brother—he is right as *he* is right. 'Whoever does not do right is not of God, namely, he who does not love his brother' (3:10).

Even if Jesus is intended by **he** in the first clause, God must be intended by **him** in the second, since 'born of God' is the exclusive meaning elsewhere (3:9; 4:7; 5:1, 4, 18). It soon becomes plain that this is one of the expressions under debate between the writer and the dissidents. The thought of rebirth or birth from God is scarcely to be found in *OT* and little represented in *NT*. Heb. 1:5; 5:5 quote Ps. 2:7, 'You are my son, today I have begotten you'; so also Ac. 13:33 and the D text of Lk. 3:22—with reference to Christ. I Peter describes Christians as 'born anew to a living hope by the resurrection of Jesus Christ', as born anew, 'not of perishable seed but of imperishable, through the living and abiding word of God', and as 'newborn babes' (I Pet. 1:3, 23; 2:2). Tit. 3:5 says that Christians are saved 'by the washing of regeneration and renewal in the Holy Spirit'. The prologue to John's Gospel speaks of children of God who are born 'not of blood nor of the will of the flesh nor of the will of man, but of God' (1:12f.); and the conversation with Nicodemus begins with the repeated assertion that no one can see or enter the kingdom of God unless he is born anew (or from above), that is, unless he is born of water and the Spirit (3:3–8).

The symbolism of rebirth, therefore, was known within the early Church, but it played a significant part only in the Johannine community and at the time of conflict with the dissidents. It must have been picked up from non-Jewish sources, where its general meaning must be sought. Philo makes free use of the symbolism. Our bodies, he says, are moulded from human seeds, but our souls spring from divine seeds and so their stock is akin to God (*Life of Moses* 279). It is the peculiar task of God to sow and beget what is excellent (*Allegorical Interpretation* 3.180). In allegorical vein, Leah received the seed of wisdom and brought forth beautiful ideas worthy of the Father who begat them (*Posterity of Cain* 135). In *On the Cherubim* 42ff. he purposes to speak of the conception and birth pangs of the virtues, which is a divine mystery and its lesson is for the initiated; and he continues with an allegorical treatment of God's visiting Sarah and fathering her offspring—which, being interpreted means that generic virtue presents joy to him who attains to piety.

Philo is in fact preoccupied with the perplexing human combination of soul and body, such that it is impossible to establish ethical harmony from the powers within our nature. The higher mind of *logos* or *pneuma* must conquer and control the lower nature. When we die, our immaterial part joins 'the immaterial' in a rebirth (*On the Cherubim* 113f.). By the mystery of the divine begetting that rebirth can be anticipated while we are still in the body. Even though Philo's undoubted use of mystery terminology may be interpreted more or less seriously, there can be no doubt that he is intensely serious in putting forward the conviction that the soul can be miraculously elevated through its assimilation of and by 'the immaterial' (Goodenough (1962), p. 138); though he can be less intense when using the related expression 'sons of God'. Commenting on Dt. 14:1 he says in one place, 'they who live in the knowledge of the One are rightly called sons of God', and in another, that the passage has the clear meaning that God will protect and provide for them as would a father (*Confusion of Tongues* 145; *Special Laws* 1.318). Whatever the range of meaning, 'born of God' was a recognisable and persuasive possiblity in late antiquity.

It appeared also in tractate XIII of the Hermetic writings, composed within a hundred years of AD 200 and providing instruction in the form of a dialogue about the rule 'no one can be saved before rebirth'. The seeker for rebirth is told: 'withdraw into yourself, and it will come: will, and it happens. Suspend the perceptions of the body, and there will be the generation of divinity. Cleanse yourself from the reasonless punishments of matter'. And so the twelve punishments—ignorance, grief, incontinence, and so on—are driven out by the ten divine powers: knowledge, joy, self control, and so on—and the postulant is cleansed; cf. 1 Jn 3:10. 'Know you not that you are a god and a son of the One?' (*CH* XIII.1, 7f., 14; Grese). Teaching of this kind was, of course, irresistible to the Christian gnostics: to take one significant example, Irenaeus (*A.H.* 1.21) describes a variety of gnostic views of redemption: 'They affirm that it is necessary for those who have attained to perfect knowledge that they may be regenerated into the power which is above all. Otherwise it is impossible to enter into the Pleroma, for it is this (redemption) which leads them down into the profundities of Bythos (the Depth). For the baptism of the visible Jesus took place for the remission of sins, but the redemption by the Christ that descended upon him for perfection'. That has perhaps some similarity to the views of the dissidents and, in general, exploration of the evidences of hellenistic religion helps to define an area within which discussion of rebirth took place.

In contrast to these ambitious conceptions, whether they are profound or pretentious, the writer of the Epistle confines his understanding within narrow limits. Anyone born of God does what is right and overcomes the world (5:4). Stated negatively, he does no sin (3:9; 5:18); stated positively, he loves God and those who are born of God, namely, his fellow Christians and the Son of God (4:7;

5:1). Finally, the connexion of thought in vv. 28–29 is to be noted. When God makes his *parousia*, he comes to acknowledge his own, to the dismay of those who are not his own; but everyone who does right is born of him and will be acknowledged.

3:1. Yet if we are **called** (i.e. acknowledged as) **children of God**, it is in virtue of his exceptional love (**what** feebly represents the Greek *potapēn*, properly meaning 'of what kind?' but often used in the sense 'how great!'; **that** translates an explanatory *hina* and subjunctive), not in virtue of our success in doing what is right. God's initiative in exercising his love is stressed in the Epistle: cf. 4:16, 'the love God has for us'; 4:9f., God's love is shown in the sending of his Son into the world that we might live through him and that he might be the expiation of our sins; cf. 3:16. The designation is **children** (*tekna*) **of God**, in all the Johannine references in the Epistle and Jn 1:12; 11:52, not 'sons' as in Matthew and Paul (but note that Paul uses 'children' and 'sons' indiscriminately in Rom. 8:14–21). In *OT*, Israel is called God's first-born son, God acts towards them as a father would, and the Israelites are often compared to dutiful or rebellious children; but the expression 'children of God' is confined to Dt. 14:1 (cf. Hos. 1:10). At a later period it began to appear in wisdom literature where the righteous man, to the derision of his opponents, 'professes to have knowledge of God and calls himself a child (*pais*) of the Lord' and 'boasts that God is his father'. The opponents who once said, 'Why has he been numbered among the sons (*huioi*) of God?' finally capitulate and admit their error, for the Lord covers the righteous with his right hand and shields him with his arm (Wis. 5:5, 16). Thus the traditional presentation of God as the protective father is complemented by the righteous son who claims knowledge of God, and is also given a theological grounding in the statement that 'God created man for immortality, and made him the image of his own eternal self' (Wis. 2:23, *NEB*). The distance between that usage and what is found in the Epistle is not great; and wisdom teaching is a more likely origin of the Johannine 'children of God' than *Ps. Sol.* 17:30, 40, where the Lord Messiah recognises that the holy people are all sons of God, though he too blesses them with wisdom and gladness.

The **children of God**, not recognised by the world (see on 2:2), are marked out by doing what is right and so are sharply distinguished from children of the devil (3:10), who doubtless include the antichrists (4:4). When the author has claimed for his community the status of **children of God**, he adds, with polemical intention, **and so we are** (*kai esmen*; omitted by later manuscripts, perhaps because the rhetorical point was no longer perceived). The following sentence begins in Greek with *dia touto* ('for this reason') which may refer to what has gone before (that we are certainly children of God), or to the statement introduced by *hoti*, 'that it did not know him'. The construction beginning with *dia touto* and continuing with *hoti* occurs several times in the Gospel: fairly clearly it both refers to what has gone before and provides a confirmation in the *hoti* clause.

2. Beloved (see on 2:7) serves the rhetorical purpose of calling attention to an emphatic development of what has just been said: **we are God's children now**, in contrast to our status in the future. What future is in mind? As the Greek text is now punctuated and translated, it is the future disclosure of God (or Christ). Hence the meaning is: 'we are already sons of God—what we shall become if (or when) he is disclosed is unknown, except that we shall be like him'. If that indeed is the writer's meaning, he is admitting that members of his community possess a lower status which will be advanced to a higher status—thus seriously weakening his case against the dissidents, who claimed to possess the higher status in virtue of the anointing and the begetting by God. It is possible that the writer ineptly concedes the dissidents' case, or that he wishes to indicate that advancement is possible beyond any status that can now be claimed; but a different punctuation and translation of the Greek (as *NEB* mg.) would make his argument less vulnerable. **It does not yet appear** represents *kai oupō ephanerōthē*, which could also be translated 'though he has not yet appeared' (AGB, s.v. *kai*, I.2g). The indirect question **what we shall be** is then more suitably attached to **we know**; **but** (not in the Greek) disappears, and **that** (representing *hoti*) becomes 'for'. The argument proceeds thus: 'we are already children of God, though he has not yet appeared. We know what we shall be, for if he does appear we shall be like him, for we shall see him as he is'. When God appears to claim his own, their likeness to him will also be apparent. This will be their confidence before God if, or when, he appears (see on 2:28). A coherent meaning is given to the whole verse, despite the objection of Schnackenburg, p. 170, that the changed punctuation disturbs the parallelism; in fact the flow of the verse is much improved.

We shall be like him (namely, God) expresses a dominant theme in the religion of late antiquity. In Jewish teaching it was founded on Lev. 19:2, 'You shall be holy, for I the LORD your God am holy', a commandment adopted by Jesus in the form 'You, therefore, must be perfect, as your heavenly Father is perfect' (Mt. 5:48; 'Be merciful, even as your Father is merciful' in Lk. 6:36). Rabbinic teachers developed the theme; e.g., 'How can a man be called by the name of God? (referring to Jl 2:32). As God is called merciful, you too must be merciful. The Holy One, blessed be He, is called gracious, so you too must be gracious . . . and give presents freely. God is called righteous . . . so you too must be righteous. God is called *ḥāsîd* (loving, devoted) . . . so you too must be *ḥāsîd*' (*Sifre* on Dt. 11:22(49), cited by Vermes (1981), p. 43 and see n. 82). That of course refers to the moral imitation of God. Is it possible that believers might become like God in some more substantial sense? The Johannine tradition itself contains a hint that it might. Jn 10:34f. offers the surprising argument that Jesus cannot rightly be accused of blasphemy in calling himself Son of God since the Jewish law contains the words 'I said, you are gods' (Ps. 82:6), and applies them to human beings to whom the word of God came. The stock Jewish explanation was that Israelites were called gods in virtue of possessing the Law, and hence were like God in that respect; and the psalm in fact equates 'gods' and 'sons of the Most High' (see SB II, p. 543).

It has to be remembered that hellenistic religion used the word 'god' more freely and generally than either the main Jewish or Christian tradition. But then Irenaeus allows himself to say: 'None other is called God by the Scriptures, but only the Father of all, and the Son, and those who have the adoption (*A.H.* iv. introd.)— so that all sons of God may be called God in virtue of their adoption by the Father of all. The language seems extravagant; the intention is likely to have been conventionally modest. A later parallel may perhaps be found in the *Sentences of Sextus*, a collection of pagan moral maxims, edited, revised and modified by a Christian compiler, probably about AD 180–210 (Chadwick, pp. 138, 159). The maxims reveal great moral earnestness and urge ascetical renunciation of the world in order to pursue the aim of being made like God. 'There is no living the life according to God apart from acting with prudence, goodness and rightness (*dikaiōs*)' (399)—which is no more than commonplace; but it comes into better focus in the maxim: 'A man pure (*hagnos*, cf. 3:3) and stainless has freedom with God as a son of God' (60). Its distinctive form is found in maxims dealing with likeness to God: 'It is sufficient for complete happiness to have the knowledge and the likeness of God' (148). 'He best honours God who makes his mind as far as possible like God' (381). Clement of Alexandria quotes that or a similar maxim in a chapter expounding what he takes to be Plato's view, and bases it on the ancient saying that 'like will be dear to like' (*Strom.* 2.22)—a widespread belief in late antiquity; cf. Philo, *On the Giants* 9: angelic souls 'must be apprehended by the mind, that like may be discerned by like'.

If only a being who is like God can have communion with God there are various possibilities. (1) Some may already be like God in their inmost nature though unaware of the truth and unable to exploit it. They need to discover their identity and be called to the exercise of it. That is the gnostic solution which is scarcely evident in the Epistle. (2) Some may be transformable into the likeness of God by initiation and anointing and insemination. That appears to be the dissidents' solution, and it is not wholly unacceptable to the writer of the Epistle (though their rejection of the Son is). (3) All the initiated are sons of God and therefore practise the moral imitation of God; but they perceive and are related to the Father by means of the Son, the Anointed One. 'The Son of God has come and has given us understanding, to know him who is true; and we are in him who is true, in his Son Jesus Christ' (5:20). That is the solution insisted on by the writer of the Epistle: less simple than the other two, and perhaps less constricted by the assumption that only like perceives like.

Biblical writings are reserved in their use of language about 'seeing God'. The stock conviction that no one can see God and live (Exod. 33:20) is set aside only in a few exceptional references to Moses (e.g., Exod. 33:11), and in a few imaginative prophetic oracles with strong cultic associations (1 Kg. 22:19; Isa. 6:1, Am. 7:7; 9:1). A cultic reference also lies behind the more general promises in the Psalms: 'the upright shall behold his face' (Ps. 11:7; cf. 17:15), since 'to behold the face of God' was used as a technical term for visiting the sanctuary (Weiser, pp. 39f., 72f.). The beatitude 'Blessed are the pure in heart, for they shall see God' (Mt. 5:8) was a consciously archaic form of the same kind. Philo is prepared to say that the Existent can be perceived and known, not only through the ears, but with the eyes of the understanding, though when we say that the Existent is visible we are not using words in their literal sense, for it is impossible that the Existent should be perceived at all by created things (*Posterity of Cain* 167f.). This discretion is absent from hellenistic religion. In Hermetic Tractate XIII the disciple Tat becomes a god in the course of his instruction by Hermes and exults in what has happened to him by regeneration: he is now able to see God, *to pan horō* (*CH* XIII. 13).

Paul has a few indications: 'Now we see in a mirror dimly, but then face to face' (1 C. 13:12); and, 'we all with unveiled face, beholding the glory of the Lord, are being changed into his likeness from one degree of glory to another: for this comes from the Lord who is the Spirit' (2 C. 3:18; cf. 4:6).

The Epistle is far less speculative than these writers: indeed, its argument is purposely prosaic to counter the speculative flights of the dissidents. If God is indeed disclosed **we shall see him as he is**— namely, *dikaios*, the source and upholder of what is right. If he appears, we shall see that he is *dikaios* as we know him to be (2:29), and that will simply confirm what from the beginning we have seen with our eyes (see on 1:1). As it is, we cannot see God, but we can see the brother who needs our love (4:20).

3. Hope and being **pure** are not Johannine themes. The verse is simply a transition to v. 4 with which it is paired (see introduction above). **Hope** *(elpis)* would better be translated 'expectation': it refers to the dissident belief that God would appear for those possessing their anointing (so taking **him** to mean 'God': *NEB* regards *autō* as a true dative of the person interested, and translates 'has this hope before him'). **Pure** *(hagnos)* was originally a cultic term, the stock word in Greek religion for 'holy' (rather than *hagios* which was favoured in Jewish and Christian writings); but it followed a familiar path and became an ethical word. Clement of Alexandria defined it as 'having' nothing bad on one's conscience' *(Strom. 7.27.2)*. **Him** represents *autō*, and **he** represents *ekeinos*, namely, Jesus (see on 2:6). Therefore the thrust of this verse may be suggested by a paraphrase: anyone who expects God to appear must purify himself as Jesus (whom the dissidents disregard) is pure— that is, without sin.

4-7. Sin is first presented as **lawlessness** *(anomia)*. The word is not elsewhere used in Johannine writings and is not common in *NT*. Its meaning depends on the social circumstances in which it is used. It can be a general equivalent of **sin** (in an *OT* quotation in Rom. 4:7), or the opposite of what is **right** *(dikaiosynē* in v. 7). It might express the not very perceptive view that all wrongdoing is direct disobedience of the divine law (as Dodd, p. 80, thought was true of LXX); or it could suggest lawless disorder in a disintegrating society, and hence social subversion (see the apocalyptic passage 2 Th. 2:3-7; and Mt. 24:11f., where many false prophets arise and lead many astray; wickedness *(anomia)* is multiplied and most men's love grows cold). In that case **everyone who commits sin is guilty of** (or rather 'is committing', since guilty is an *RSV* interpretation) a disruptive act.

Since the writer of the Epistle appears indifferent to disorder in the world, it is unlikely that he intends that sense of *anomia*; and it is plain that his moral instruction is not framed against disobedience to the Torah and its commandments, with the single exception of the commandment of love. Hence he uses *anomia* here to mark sin as a wrong act, wilfully done. It is doing what is prohibited and omitting what is commanded, in contrast to a different view in v. 8; and his chief concern is with the activity of sinning. Previous references to sin in the Epistle have spoken about averting the consequences of sinning: by cleansing, confession, atonement, and the name—see on 1:7, 9; 2:2, repeated in 4:10; 2:12); and in 5:16f.

the damage done by particular sins is dealt with by intercession. But here attention is turned to the habit of sinning, and again in 5:18. By disclosure of him in whom **there is no sin,** by abiding in him, by seeing and knowing him the habit of sinning is ended. The will to do what is right is released by that kind of illumination, and it cannot be said (as no doubt the dissidents did deceptively say, v. 7) that the anointed Christian has no need to choose and to do what is right by a deliberate act of the will. The writer would not perhaps have objected to the way it was later presented in *Gospel of Philip* 110.20f.: 'Those to whom it is not permitted to sin, the knowledge of the truth lifts up the hearts, which means it makes them free, and makes them be lifted up above the whole place . . . But he who has become free through the knowledge is a slave for love's sake to those who have not yet been able to take up the freedom of the knowledge'.

In composing this section the writer has given his own interpretation to the traditional expression **to take away sins** which reappears in Jn 1:29: 'the Lamb of God who takes away the sin of the world'. It occurs twice in *OT* (representing Heb. *nāśā'*, 1 Sam. 15:25; 25:28) in petitions, in one case to God, in the other to David, that acts of disobedience or incivility might be forgiven. Here, however, the writer presses it into a new meaning: removing not the consequences of sins but the choosing of sinful actions. For **appeared,** see on 1:2; for **abides in him,** see on 2:6; for **seen,** see on 1:1; and for **known,** see on 2:3.

8-10. When sin is a wrong act wilfully done, the view is simple but superficial; for many of the most destructive and most obstinate sins are seemingly neither willed nor intended. The writer therefore uses his teaching formula (see introduction above) in vv. 7 and 8 to move over to a different, perhaps complementary, view of sin. Acting sinfully is the inherent activity of those who belong to the devil's family, just as doing what is right is the inherent activity of those who belong to God's family. The fact that some people commit sin, not by choice but because they are what they are, removes them (in the thought of late antiquity) from the category of blame, but not from the category of guilt. They are destructive and bear the consequences of their destructive actions. Correspondingly, those who are **born of God** can claim no credit for doing what is right: **they cannot sin.** This extraordinary, artificial division of mankind into those who are bound to sin and those who cannot sin must be regarded as a debater's device against his opponents. It was no doubt the dissidents who first made the claim that their anointing released them from the normal standards of what is right for, whatever they did, they could not sin. Their critics were bound to sin and would be ashamed before God at his coming (2:28). The Epistle reverses the claim and insists that those who are born of God show what they are by doing what is right.

The writer introduces **the devil** partly to strengthen his polemic (equivalent to 'the evil one'; see on 2:13f.): this was a familiar denunciation of religious opponents who seemed to threaten the safety of the community, e.g. Judas is called a *diabolos* in Jn 6:70; cf. 13:2, 27 (Satan); the Jewish false prophet and magician is called 'a son of the devil', Ac. 13:10; and various rivals in Asia Minor were associates of Satan (Rev. 2:9, 13, 24). But the Gospel and the Epistles lack all interest in demon-possession: their use of the terms devil, evil one, Satan, and prince of this world is symbolic. What the symbols refer to is a series of dismaying threats from the world outside and from traitors within the community. The symbols identify these threats as more than the contingent misfortunes of the existing community: they are only the most recent manifestation of the dark threat to God and the things of God. To say that **the devil has sinned from the beginning** (cf. 'He was a murderer from the beginning', Jn 8:44) presents him as the archetype of sinning.

In the confrontation between **the children of God** and **the children of the devil**, freedom from sinning derives from the disclosure of **the Son of God to destroy the works of the devil** (works is an archaism favoured by translators, though they use 'deeds' in v. 12; 'actions' or 'activities' would be more suitable). The devil's activities and the practice of sinning are one and the same. The Son of God destroys them by being disclosed, for his disclosure is the means of birth from God and insemination with the divine seed—if indeed that is the meaning of v. 9*b*. The Greek, literally translated, says 'because his seed (*sperma*) remains in him'. The writer's habit of composing memorable slogans again produces ambiguity: *sperma* may either be used in the collective sense 'children' (Abraham's seed, Jn 8:33, 37) and **him** refers to God, whence *RSV* mg. 'the offspring of God abide in him', cf. v. 6; or **him** refers to **one born of God** and 'his seed' (*sperma autou*) means a seed of the divine, interpreted in *RSV* text as **God's nature**. The former possibility simplifies the expositor's task but is doubtful because the expected article is missing, and *sperma* is not elsewhere used of God's children. The latter possibility is adopted in modern translations and requires an interpretation of 'seed'.

The metaphorical use is absent from pharisaic Judaism and Qumran but is common in hellenistic religion (Schulz, *TWNT* VII, p. 545). Philo is a plentiful source: God 'has set for himself in the soul seeds far-shining, radiant, full charged with meaning, as he has set the stars in heaven' (*Allegorical Interpretation* 3.40). 'God sows in souls nothing futile, but seeds so successful and perfect in every case that each one immediately yields the full crop of the fruits appropriate to it' (*Posterity of Cain* 171). The later gnostic writers could scarcely resist the metaphor: the *Gospel of Truth* ends thus: 'It is those who are truly manifest who are in the true and eternal life and speak about the light that is perfect and full of the seed of the Father, and that is in his heart and in the Pleroma, while his Spirit rejoices in him and glorifies him in whom he was; for he is good and his children are perfect and worthy of his name, for the Father loves such children' (*EV* 43.10–20).

The symbol indeed is highly useful: it suggests that spiritual growth can be as powerful and productive as physical growth, and that a barren life can be transformed by divine action, as barren land is transformed by the sowing of seed. It is a hellenistic commonplace and not esoteric. Its most familiar biblical occurrence comes in the interpretation of the Parable of the Sower: 'the seed is the word of God' (Lk 8:11); cf., therefore, 1 Jn 2:14, and the indwelling word or words of Jesus, Jn 5:38; 15:7; 'born anew, not of perishable seed but of imperishable, through the living and abiding word of God', 1 Pet. 1:23. The Johannine tradition is consciously aware of the generative power of words lodged in the mind and experience of Christians, and regards the word of God as a projection of the divine being—very similar indeed to the wisdom of God in Jewish tradition; cf. 'And then there shall be bestowed on the elect wisdom, and they shall all live and never again sin' (*1 Enoch* 5:8f.).

Schnackenburg, p. 191, wishes to identify the seed with the Holy Spirit, partly because rebirth corresponds to the prophetic promise of a new heart and a new spirit, partly because rebirth is associated in primitive Christian tradition with baptism and the gift of the Spirit (Jn 3:5–7; Tit. 3:5). It is clear that the gift of the Spirit was a matter of dispute between the community and the dissidents (4:1ff.), and it is possible that the writer of the Epistle was claiming the seed (understood as Spirit) for his own adherents and denying it to the others. But since the Spirit is an ambiguous witness, needing to be tested, it is more likely that the seed is the word which they heard from the beginning (2:24), which, by means of the transitional final clause of v. 10, is now restated as **the message which you heard from the beginning** and developed as the commandment of love in vv. 11–18.

THE OLD COMMANDMENT IN THE NEW KOSMOS
3:11–4:21

THE MORAL TRADITION 3:11–18

There is now a sharp change from repudiation of sinning to advocacy of loving. Most of the language is already familiar. 'Love of God' in the agreed statement (2:5) has already been interpreted as 'love of the brother' (2:10f.) and is now driven home, it would seem by deliberate repetitions and contrasts, which in turn recall 2:14–17. Yet the section is not merely a reworking of themes already announced, for the writer adds precision to the stock contrast between love and hatred by adding lack of compassion (**closes his heart against him**, 3:17). For the first time he explicitly introduces the contrast between **life** and **death**, with *thanatos* ('death') making its first appearance in the Epistle, 'murder' (*sphazō*) its only *NT* appearance outside Revelation, and *psychēn tithenai* showing its exclusively Johannine meaning, 'to lay down one's life'. Here for the first time the death of Christ is explicitly mentioned, though with a reserve that is also characteristic of the Gospel.

11. In 1:5 **the message** is that 'God is light'; here, **that we should love one another** (cf. Jn 13:34f.; 15:12). Compare the implication of 2:7–11 that the commandment which is both old and new is love for the brother; the statement of the double commandment in 3:23 as faith in the name of Jesus Christ and love for one another, or alternatively in 4:21 as love for God and the brother; and the association of love with commandments in 5:2f. In the Epistles the verb 'to love' (*agapaō*) most frequently refers to human love for people and things and sometimes for God, and three times to God's love for us (to which can be added the six uses of 'beloved'). The noun *agapē*, especially when used absolutely or in the phrase 'the love of God', is sometimes ambiguous: either God's love or love for God (see on 2:5). It can also indicate human love for people or describe God as love. The majority of contexts where love occurs are argumentative: commanding love and urging reasons for it, rejecting its opposite, or repudiating particular statements about it, e.g. 4:10, 20. The author is opposing some who assert their love for God; not that he denies love for God but he is determined to qualify it by the commandment 'that he who loves God should love his brother also' (4:21; cf. Mk 12:29–31). He supports the commandment with reasons: if you love someone who has brought children to birth, you must of course love his offspring (5:1). Since Christians are God's children, and we know what love he has shown us in calling us his children (3:1), then if we claim to love God we must clearly love one another (4:11). In fact, since God is invisible, we can display our love for him only by loving the brethren we can see (4:12, 20). We have a choice of *saying* that we love or of actually loving—and no doubt it is implied that the dissidents have made the wrong choice.

From these arguments it might be inferred that love is a possibility freely open to everyone. We can choose to love or not to love, or we can choose between loving the world and the love of God (2:15). The inference is rejected in 4:19 with the statement: 'We love, because he first loved us'. The decisive exposition comes in 4:7–12. Love comes from God, in the sense that everyone who loves has been brought into being by God and shares the characteristic awareness of God. A person who does not love lacks awareness of God, 'for God is love' (4:8, 16). Thus the mutual love of Christians is rooted in God himself, not by contemplation of the divine being but by perception of the loving action of God in sending his Son into the world that we might live through him, and that the Son might make amends for our sins (4:9f.). In another aspect 'God is love' means that the divine indwelling is experienced by the Christian community as mutual love: 'If we love one another, God abides in us and his love is perfected in us' (4:12; expressed individually in 4:16). Thus love for the brother belongs to the world of light, to doing what is right, and to the experience of life. Christians who are beloved of God (it is notable how aptly the writer uses the address 'beloved') already belong to the divine world.

Once this comprehensive estimate of practical loving is grasped, it is easier to understand why 'the love of God' is ambiguous. We can read it as indicating God's love with more or less confidence in 3:1; 4:9, 10, 12, 16–18. For a less certain decision, see on 2:5; and also 2:15, a polemical passage, where the author hints that the dissidents' claim to love the Father is denied by their love of the world (so *RSV*), unless he means that the divine love has no place within a man given to wordly love (as *NEB*). Even more nicely balanced are the thoughts in 3:16f.: **By this we know love, that he laid down his life for us; and we ought to lay down our lives for the brethren.** It is implied that we know genuine love from the model displayed by Christ, and that we ought to behave in a comparable fashion. But if what Christ did was God's act, as 4:9f. will later suggest, then from his self-giving we also know God's love. Further, if someone can help his brother in need but does not, **how does the love of God abide in him?** That could mean: how does the divine love as displayed in Christ, *or* how does that love for God which the dissidents claim, abide in him? The latter meaning must be intended in 5:3, as the previous verse shows: 'to love God is to keep his commandments' (*NEB*). None of these passages, it may be supposed, was written with careless imprecision. Each of them uses the flexibility of 'the love of God' to correct and reshape the dissidents' assertions about Christian love.

The verse begins with **For**, representing the Greek *hoti* which can operate as a co-ordinating conjunction; and the second clause begins with **that**, representing *hina* with subjunctive, explaining **this**.

12-13. The citation of **Cain** is abruptly introduced in compressed phrasing (the addition of *hos* after Cain would improve the syntax) and it provides the only explicit *OT* reference in the Epistle (perhaps for a combination of reasons: the Johannine school lacked interest in Torah; the author was averse to the apocalyptic imagery exploited in Revelation, or had not yet seen how to exploit *OT* symbols in favour of Christ). Even so there are few coincidences in language with Gen. 4:1-16. **His brother** appears in Gen. 4:2, 8, but Abel is always named; Cain's **deeds** (*erga*) may be suggested by his working (*ergazomenos*) the land; but LXX lacks **evil** and the violent verb **murdered** (*sphazō*), often a technical word for sacrificial killing but also used of human slaughter (in Revelation for the slaughter of the lamb, the faithful, and one of the bestial heads). At first sight Cain seems to be introduced as a stock example in the style of Jewish exegesis where Cain is wicked and Abel godly (Kuhn, *TWNT* I, s.v. *Abel*, pp. 6-9). Thus in *Jub.* 4:2-5 and *1 Enoch* 22:7 the two appear conventionally, and in *1 Enoch* 85:3-5 Cain represents sin and Abel martyrdom. In Wis. 10:3 the wicked Cain fell away from wisdom by being angry; in *Test. Benj.* 7.5 he is a type of envy and hatred of brothers; in *Apoc. Mos.* 3:1 he is a son of wrath. In the elaboration of the story in Philo's *Sacrifices of Abel and Cain*, Cain represents love of self and Abel love of God, with the moral that the worse attacks the better. Josephus (*Ant.* 1.53-59) thinks that the sacrifices of Abel, who had respect for justice and paid heed to virtue, were more acceptable to God because they grew spontaneously and were not forced from nature by the ingenuity of grasping man; whereas Cain was depraved (*ponērotatos*) with an eye for gain, the first to think of ploughing the soil.

In all these mentions, from a period of perhaps three centuries, there is nothing that goes beyond treating Cain as a moral warning. The same must be said of 'the blood of righteous Abel' in Mt. 23:35, and the conviction in Heb. 11:4 that the preference of Abel's offering to Cain's shows that the former was righteous. There is a hint of something different, however, in Jude 11, which includes, in a steady denunciation of those who have fallen into error, the statement that 'they walk in the way of Cain, and abandon themselves for the sake of gain to Balaam's error, and perish in Korah's rebellion'. These people 'pervert the grace of God into licentiousness and deny our only Master and Lord, Jesus Christ', and they set up divisions (Jude 4, 19)—perhaps distinguishing *psychics* from *pneumatics* (Kelly).

When we look again at the Epistle, it is clear that Cain may have begun as a moral warning but he has become something more. He represents the world which kills, or threatens to kill, Christians as well as being an example of hatred which produces murder. He appears in contrast to Jesus who gave his life for us, whom therefore we must follow in giving our lives for the brethren. Cain and Jesus illustrate the division of mankind in the great conflict for life and truth.

That is different from the old Jewish exegesis, and the nearest analogy (except the hint in Jude) is in Valentinian views described by Irenaeus, *A.H.* 1.7.5: 'They assume three types of men: the spiritual, the choic, and the psychic, corresponding to Cain, Abel and Seth, in order that they may represent the three natures, not with reference to an individual, but with reference to kinds of men'. With the help of *Exc. Theod.* 54 this somewhat muddled statement can be disentangled: Cain is the irrational nature, created of dust, ending in corruption; Abel the rational and just nature, made of dust but endowed with soul which has a choice of destinies; and Seth is the spiritual nature which receives training for perfection. Whoever composed that scheme lacked all moral interest in Cain's homicide, and was simply using the three names as a pretext for dividing mankind into classes with different natures. In *A.H.* 31.1-2 Irenaeus says that there were some who regarded Cain as originating from the superior power, together with Esau, Korah and the Sodomites who were attacked, though in fact ineffectively, by the inferior creator. In most recent times Judas 'alone of all the apostles recognised the truth and accomplished the mystery of the betrayal, by which everything earthly and heavenly is dissolved'. This veneration of Judas is perhaps the third stage of some such process as the following: (i) dissidents are regarded as betrayers of Christ; (ii) Judas as their antitype is written into the gospel narratives; (iii) dissidents turn the reputation of Judas to their own advantage. Thus the odd Cainite form of antinomianism may well have had its origins in the kind of conflict reflected in Jude and the Epistles of John.

Why (*charin tinos: charis* used as a preposition with the genitive, 'for the sake of what?') **did he murder him**? Because his actions were bad and his brother's good, that is his were unacceptable and Abel's were acceptable to God. The impulse for murder was resentment—a simple and familiar thought. In Jewish wisdom and piety, the good man is too often the victim of resentful malice.

Hence a reference to the world (see on 2:2) and its hatred is not surprising as a consequence of v. 12 and a preparation for v. 17 (cf. Jn 15:18–20). **Do not wonder. . . .that** (*NEB* has 'if'; Greek *ei*) **the world hates you**: verbs of emotion are sometimes followed by *ei* instead of *hoti* 'that'; AGB, s.v. *ei* II.

14–15. Against the world's hostility, the writer builds up Christian confidence (cf. vv. 19 and 24): **we know that we have passed out of death into life**; we know it **because we love the brethren**. It would be possible to attach **because** to the second verb: 'we know that our passage from death to life was a consequence of our love'—which is not wholly untrue to the writer's thought for it now equates life and love. To enter life is to be enlightened (see on 1:7), not as a reward for loving but as an experience and practice of loving. In the Gospel 'he who hears my word, and believes him who sent me, has eternal life; he does not come into judgment (cf. on 2:28), but has passed from death to life' (Jn 5:24). The Gospel has much to say about love, especially about loving Jesus; but the expression 'passing from death to life' is firmly attached to believing. Here it is attached to loving the brethren. Language which is appropriate to the final judgment, also no doubt to the end of individual life, is transferred to a corporate experience of moving from hatred to love. In characteristic style the author formulates paired judgmental clauses (see on 2:10):

He who does not love abides in death.
Anyone who hates his brother is a murderer.

The uncommon word *anthrōpoktonos* for **murderer** occurs in the Greek Bible only here and at Jn 8:44: the devil 'was a murderer from the beginning', because he robbed Adam of immortality (Barrett). The commoner word is *phoneus*, and its verb appears in the Synoptic saying which associates murder with anger (Mt. 5:21); but in the Epistle murder is linked with hatred. If life, light and love belong together, so do death, darkness and hatred. In biblical usage the verbs in Hebrew and Greek conventionally translated 'to hate' have a wide range of meaning, more or less emotionally coloured: they may indicate regarding someone with disfavour, or dealing with someone to his disadvantage, or rejecting his claim to a place in society, or treating him with malice and cruelty (see on 2:9). Since in this passage hatred is associated with murder, the most emotional sense is intended. A minority group which feels itself at a disadvantage in a hostile world often interprets the attitude of outsiders as hatred (v. 13), and sometimes is tempted to use the psychological mechanism of hatred to generate energy and increase its powers of resistance. The author of the Epistle assigns the world's hatred for the community to the devil whose activities have been dealt with by the Son of God (3:8). Hence he has no need to promote hatred of the world and he can forbid hatred of the brethren and its destructive consequences.

Despite the saying of Jesus recorded in Mt. 5:43 ('You have heard that it was said, "You shall love your neighbour and hate your enemy" '), and the ritual demand of the Qumran sectarians 'to love all the sons of light . . . and hate all the sons of darkness' (1QS1.9; Leaney, pp. 120f.), the Epistle is in agreement with a prominent strand of ancient Jewish teaching. Hatred of brethren is forbidden by Lev. 19:17 and by rabbinic tradition. 'The evil eye and the evil nature and hatred of mankind put a man out of the world' (*Aboth* 12.11). Johanan b. Torta (*c.* AD 120) said that the Second Temple was destroyed because people loved money and hated one another: 'so learn that hate of man for his fellow man is a sure sin before God, and weighs as heavily as idolatry and unchastity and murder' (*Rabb. Anth.*, p. 463). In *Test. Gad* 2–5 the patriarch confesses to hatred of Joseph and warns against the undiscriminating malice of hatred, its willingness to cause death, and its alliance with envy, lying and slander. 'As love would quicken even the dead, and would call back them that are condemned to die, so hatred would slay the living, and those that had sinned venially it would not suffer to live. The spirit of hatred works together with Satan'. The author's formulation of such thoughts is that **no murderer has eternal life abiding in him** (see on 2:6).

16. Love is recognised by the activity of loving, specifically the action of Jesus (*ekeinos*; see on 2:6) when **he laid down his life for us.** This is a common early Christian statement about the death of Christ though formulated in a manner peculiar to Johannine writings. 'To lay down one's life' represents *tithenai psychēn*, found elsewhere only in Jn 10:11–18; 13:37–38; and 15:13. In John the verb *tithēmi*, 'to put, to place', has the meaning 'to put aside, to lay down' one's life, the purpose being expressed by *hyper* 'for the benefit of' someone, found as early as 1 Th. 5:10. In Jn 10:11 the good shepherd lays down his life for the sheep; that is, to protect them. In 13:37 Peter offers to die to save Jesus from death. In 15:13 Jesus utters the maxim that 'Greater love has no man than this, that a man lay down his life for his friends'. This therefore is self-sacrifice for the benefit of the community, a thought rare in ancient Israel though familiar to the Greeks (Hengel, pp. 9–15). The death of Jesus is the paradigm which is valid for all members of the community who must lay down their lives for the brethren.

17. From such a heroic demand there is a sudden drop to this reproachful argument for social care. It can perhaps be defended by supplying a suppressed stage of the argument: if each member may be called on to surrender his life for the benefit of the community, how much more must he be willing to surrender his property to help a needy brother. **The world's goods** may imply wealth, but need not; they represent *bios tou kosmou*, i.e., property, or livelihood, in the existing society ('if a man has enough to live on', *NEB*). **Closes his heart against** renders *kleisē ta splanchna autou apo*, and is not found elsewhere: its meaning comes from a Jewish idiom which locates generous feelings in the bowels, and might be translated 'witholds his compassion from him'. The unprepared introduction of this subject and the emotional tone of the appeal suggest that someone who does claim the love of God is being indicted. Perhaps the rift in the community involved money as well as faith and morals. The sentiment in itself is, of course, unexceptionable. Charity was constantly urged and practised in Judaism (*Rabb. Anth.*, ch. xvi), commended by Jesus (Mt. 6:2–4; Lk. 12:33), and practised in the early church (Ac. 2:44f.). Jas 2:15–16 makes a somewhat similar appeal to those who say they have faith. But the implication here might well be that the departure of the dissidents had reduced the community's funds.

18. The appeal ends with a rhetorical flourish: they are to show their love not (only) **in word or speech but** (also) **in deed and in truth** (which may be a hendiadys, 'in genuine activity'). **Word** is *logos* and **speech** is *glōssa* ('tongue'—here only, in the Gospel and Epistles); reversing the words, the modern translation might be 'talk and statements'. This depreciation of speech is unusual in the Johannine writings which are devoted to exploring the power of speech.

THE THEOLOGICAL TRADITION 3:19–24

The previous section ended with a reproach, intended to create some sense of guilt in readers or in people known to them. The natural continuation is in v. 21: **Beloved,** (only) **if our hearts do not condemn us,** do **we have confidence before God.** If others (the dissidents, no doubt) confidently claim fellowship with God, the claim can be true only if their conscience (Hebraically disguised as their heart) does not condemn them. The condition for having a good conscience is doing what is pleasing to God; the benefits are mutual indwelling and participation in the Spirit.

19–21. That clear argument, however, is obscured by two verses which, as they stand in Greek, are difficult to translate. *RSV* forces its way to a rendering which may or may not be meaningful; *NEB* offers three possible translations. The problem can be displayed by the following wooden translation:

19a [And] by this we shall know that (*hoti*) we are of the truth,
19b and before him we shall persuade our heart,
20a that/because (*hoti*) if our heart condemns us,
20b that/because (*hoti*) God is greater than our heart
20c and knows all things.

The sentence is marred by too many appearances of *hoti*, whose meaning is ambiguous, and by the uncertainty of the words 'by this', which may point backwards or forwards (see on 2:3). There is even a further possibility that the second *hoti* in 20a should not be regarded as the conjunction meaning 'that' or 'because' but the neuter accusative relative pronoun from *hostis*; in which case it would be joined with 'if' as *ho ti ean*, meaning 'in respect of whatever matter'. That is an escape from one confusion to another.

Leaving aside for a moment the syntax, what could be the meaning of 20b: **God is greater than our heart**? Either that God is a stricter judge than our conscience and knows faults which our conscience is disinclined to admit; or that God is a more generous judge than our conscience and knows grounds for mercy which our conscience cannot admit. Commentators are overwhelmingly in favour of the latter interpretation: the whole Epistle presents a loving God in such a way as to dismiss fear (Schnackenburg, p. 203), a God who exercises magnanimity (Bultmann, p. 57), who overrules our doubts and knows who really belong to him (Houlden, p. 101). Calvin's view that the phrase indicates 'the greater severity of God's judgment, compared with our standards, is quite inappropriate in the present context' (Marshall, p. 198).

By contrast, however, it must be argued that the view of God's greater severity is the only one appropriate to this passage. If the reproach of vv. 17–18 is intended to activate a guilty conscience, then v. 20 is a simple argument from less to greater; if our conscience condemns us, how much more will God. If the commentators are right, the argument would run thus: even if our conscience condemns us, God knows that we are really his and overrules our conscience. By that argument the writer would have fallen into the dissidents' trap. They no doubt justified their rejection of Jesus and their unwillingness to be bound by commandments by arguing that they had fellowship with God. Any painful promptings of conscience had been overruled by God himself. The writer of the Epistle has indeed composed a clumsy sentence, perhaps because he realised how easily he could damage his case; but he must be allowed to know what he was doing, and the severe interpretation is to be preferred.

If the general presentation of a loving and magnanimous God is thought to exclude the judgment of God, why is the writer so anxious to establish grounds of confidence **before him**? Verse 20 is something of an afterthought to explain **reassure our hearts before him**, and can be most simply mended by adding 'we know' before the third *hoti* (making three uses of 'know' in a sentence which illustrates the maxim: Don't add afterthoughts: begin again). There is some question about the correctness of **reassure**, since the Greek *peithō* means to convince or persuade—in certain circumstances to persuade with money (2 Mac. 4:45; 10:20; Jos. *Ant.* 14.281, 490). In Mt. 28:14 it is rendered by 'satisfy' in the promise: 'If this comes to the governor's ears we will satisfy him and keep you out of trouble'. In *Mart. Polyc.* 10.2 the proconsul says to Polycarp: *peison ton dēmon*, perhaps 'conciliate the people', echoing a phrase from Xenophon. That may be near enough to **reassure our hearts**, and other meanings make little sense in this passage. The writer's intention seems to have been to follow his appeal for practical expressions of love by saying: in that way we shall know that we belong to the truth and we shall reassure our conscience—remembering that if our conscience condemns us, so does God who is superior to our conscience and knows all about us. Only if our conscience does not condemn us can we boldly approach God.

22. From passages in the Gospels it is clear that the early Christians were convinced that God would hear their requests and grant them. The Q saying in Mt. 7:7–8 expresses that conviction in its absolute form: 'Everyone who asks receives, and he who seeks finds, and to him who knocks it will be opened'. The accompanying 'parables' put forward the argument that if a father will satisfy his hungry son with food, all the more will the heavenly Father satisfy his children with good things. Not surprisingly, this conviction attracts qualifications, partly about what God will give (the corresponding saying in Lk. 11:13 specifies the Holy Spirit) but chiefly about the conditions for granting requests. Mk 11:23–24 requires faith in God, namely, a firm belief that the request will be or has been granted; and the following verse specifies the willingness to forgive as necessary for receiving God's forgiveness. Mt. 18:19–20 requires the agreement of two persons about any request and, significantly, goes on to assert the presence of Jesus with an assenting two or three. There is a similar condition in *Gospel of Thomas* 48: 'If two make peace with each other in the same house, they shall say to the mountain, Be removed! and it will be removed'. Later in the Epistle **whatever we ask** is qualified by 'according to his will'.

In the present verse the open promise is made conditional on keeping his commandments and doing what pleases him. It must be regarded as probable that the dissidents claimed unrestricted fulfilment of God's promise: because they had fellowship with the

Father, they had unrestricted access to his bounty. The writer of the Epistle sets up a moral condition; the writer of the Gospel, on the other hand, sets up a theological condition. The promise of God's answer to prayer comes three times in the Farewell Discourses (14:12–14; 15:7; and 16:23–24): all three insist that the granting of requests is entirely dependent on Jesus. To take only the first passage, placed immediately before the first promise of the Paraclete: 'Truly, truly, I say to you, he who believes *in me* will also do the works that *I do*, because *I go* to the Father. Whatever you ask *in my name, I will do it*, that the Father may be glorified *in the Son*'. The insistence on the Son is intended to combat the dissidents' rejection of him. There is even a variant of the saying in 14:14 which reads: 'If you ask *me* anything in my name, *I* will do it'. Between the writing of the Epistle and the composition of the Farewell Discourses it had become necessary to stress the theological rather than the moral qualification of the promise. Both are mentioned in v. 23.

23. For **commandment**, see on 2:4ff. **That we should believe** in Greek is *hina* with explanatory subjunctive; and the verb **believe** (*pisteuō*) has the normal Greek construction with the dative, meaning 'trust, or have confidence, in his name' (cf. 4:1 'Do not trust every spirit', *panti pneumati*). But it may be intended to have the same meaning as the characteristic Johannine construction with the preposition *eis* (as in 5:13, 'you who believe in the name', *eis to onoma*) which implies a pledge of loyalty beyond ritual or intellectual assent. This is the first appearance of 'believing' in the Epistle. In 4:16 with the accusative (like 4:1 with the dative) it means 'have confidence in'. In 5:1 and 5 it is used of believing *that* Jesus is the Christ and the Son of God; cf. 5:4, which contains the only occurrence of the noun *pistis* in the Gospels and Epistles. In 5:10 and 13 the verb is used with the accusative of believing in the Son of God and in his name. In the body of the Epistle therefore the thought of 'believing' does not play the dominant role which is notable in the Gospel; though the final chapter, in a rather formal way, comes closer to the usage of the Gospel. If it is asked why 'believing' should be introduced at this point in the Epistle, it may be suggested that having confidence in **the name of his Son Jesus Christ** is part of the confidence that a Christian may have before God. In biblical usage, the **name** commonly signifies a person's standing, authority and power. In 2:12 our sins are forgiven 'for his name's sake', that is, because of Jesus' standing with God. Here and in 5:13, believers put their confidence in the authority of Jesus and pledge their loyalty to it. See also on 2:22; 4:2f.

24. For **abide**, see on 2:6. The section ends, as it began in v. 19,

with a statement of what the Christian can know, this time using
the judgmental teaching formula (see on 2:10):
**All who keep his commandments
abide in him, and he in them.**

By this (looking forward: see on 2:3) is somewhat awkwardly taken
up by *ek tou pneumatos*, 'from the Spirit' (*ek toutou* would have been
easier as in 4:6); and the relative pronoun **which**, logically accusative, has been attracted into the genitive case of **Spirit** to which it
refers. This sentence neatly moves on to the next subject and, almost
in passing, stakes a claim for the community's possession of the
Spirit. Since the gift of the Spirit was probaby in dispute between
the community and the dissidents, the writer of the Epistle presumably decided not to deal with the subject until he had prepared a
firm foundation for his argument.

THE SPIRITS **4:1-6**

Although this section at first may seem to be an isolated unit, further
examination suggests that it has been carefully placed in this position. In 3:23 God's twofold command is stated: (A) that we should
believe in the name of his Son Jesus Christ, and (B) that we should
love one another. In 3:24 the reward for obedience is the characteristically Johannine mutual indwelling: (X) we abide in him, and he
in us. The next section 4:1-6 takes up the link-word **spirit** and
discusses it in relation to theme A; and is followed by 4:7-12 which
develops theme B without abandoning theme A. Then in quick
succession the Johannine X theme is joined to a renewed mention
of the Spirit, and to themes A and B (4:13-16). This looks like a
planned scheme, carefully carried out. Apart from references to
spirit little new is added: the writer is not giving further development to his argument but pressing it home by repetition and wider
application.

   1. Spirit (*pneuma*) means an apparently inspired utterance which
may or may not come from God, spoken by persons who seem to
be or claim to be **prophets**. (The subject is recently discussed with
some reference to this passage in Hill (1979), pp. 146-52.) *Pneuma*
is not used in that sense in the Gospel, nor indeed frequently in the
rest of the *NT* (cf. 1 Tim. 4:1, 'deceitful spirits and doctrines of
demons'). The utterances are to be scrutinised (scrutiny is a familiar
requirement in the Pauline writings) to detect their origin, **whether
they are** (*ei* in an indirect question) **of God**, or the misleading
utterances of **false prophets** who have gone out into the world. The
reference is to the dissidents (see on 2:19, where they are called

antichrists); the term itself belongs to old Jewish tradition, e.g., the conflict between Jeremiah and his rivals (Jer. 28), and hence the need to distinguish between genuine and false prophets (Dt. 13:1–5).

The early Christians were equally aware of the ambiguity of inspired utterance whether in relation to magical practitioners (Ac. 13:6), false teachers within the community (Mt. 7:15; 2 Pet. 2:1; cf. Ac. 20:30), or the secular power (Rev. 16:13; 19:20). At times, both the Christian community and the surrounding culture seemed to contain powerful and desirable energies which could not easily be distinguished; and yet, as Paul said: 'We have received not the spirit of the world, but the spirit which is from God' (1 C. 2:12); or, as the Epistle has it, **the spirit of truth and the spirit of error** (v. 6). That expression is absent from the Gospel (for **error**, see on 2:26), but the Farewell Discourses refer to the Spirit of truth (Jn 16:13; also 14:17 and 15:26, where 'Paraclete' is added) and the Samaritan Discourse mentions worship in spirit and truth (Jn 4:23f.; cf. 1 Jn 5:7, 'the Spirit is the truth').

There are verbal parallels to the Epistle's two spirits in Jewish writings. *Test. Jud.* 20.1 discloses 'that two spirits wait upon man—the spirit of truth and the spirit of deceit', so that everyone may choose whichever he will. That however is nothing more than the stock 'good and evil inclinations' of Jewish teaching (*Test. Asher* 1.5), which also appear in the *Community Rule* of Qumran: God has appointed for mankind 'two spirits in which to walk until the time of his visitation, the spirits of truth and falsehood'. The Qumran community, in a somewhat different way from the Johannine community, was in conflict with fellow members of the same religion. This conflict may have prompted them to adapt a conventional statement about the two spirits as characteristic of everyman and use it to divide mankind into those who walk according to the spirit of light and those who walk according to the spirit of darkness (1QS 3.18–21). Unlike Qumran, however, the Epistle's aim is not didactic but polemical. It is less concerned with the created nature of everyman, or even with the distinction between true believers and false believers; but rather with countering the dissidents' claim that they are prophets who alone possess the Spirit which gives direct access to God. For such a claim Qumran provides a good precedent: 'It is through the spirit of true counsel concerning the ways of man that all his sins shall be expiated that he may contemplate the light of life. He shall be cleansed from all his sins by the spirit of holiness uniting him to his truth, and his iniquity shall be expiated by the spirit of uprightness and humility. And when his flesh is sprinkled with purifying water and sanctified with cleansing water, it shall be made clean by the humble submission of his soul to walk perfectly in all the precepts of God' (1QS 3.6–9; Vermes, p. 75; cf. discussion of this purification in Riches, p. 126). Those concluding words show that Qumran gives a precedent but not a parallel, for the dissidents asked no allegiance to the commandments of God. Possession of the Spirit, they thought, in itself showed them what to do and made all necessary expiation for their sins. The writer of the Epistle does his best to claim a gift of the Spirit which was compatible with keeping the commandments and with the expiatory role of Jesus Christ.

2–3. The test of genuine inspiration is acknowledgement of Jesus Christ (for **by this**, see on 2:3; for **confess**, see on 2:23); denial of him is the very meaning of **antichrist** (see on 2:18). The verb **confess** is followed by a double accusative, namely, **Jesus Christ** and **come in the flesh**. It is not immediately clear how the two are related. *RSV* gives one possibility: **confesses that Jesus Christ has come in the flesh**; but **confesses Jesus Christ** as having **come in the flesh** is equally possible. Somewhat less likely is: **confesses Jesus** as **Christ** (i.e., Messiah) **come in the flesh** (Moffatt). The parallel clauses require consideration:

2*b* Every spirit which acknowledges Jesus Christ come in the
flesh
  c is of God, and
3*a* every spirit which does not acknowledge Jesus
  b is not of God

The textual tradition supplements the solitary **Jesus** in 3*a* by a variety of additions which are fairly obvious echoes of 2*b* in the interests of symmetry and confessional explicitness. The shortest reading is satisfactorily supported by early and good witnesses (cf. Metzger). The clauses are therefore exactly balanced except for the words **come in the flesh** which are absent from the second clause.

The earliest witness to this passage is Polycarp (*Ep.* 7) who uses only the negative clause: 'For everyone who shall not confess Jesus Christ having come in the flesh is antichrist, and whoever shall not confess the testimony of the cross is of the devil'. This comprises (i) a reference to v. 3*a* (though *NTAF* rates the probability no more than grade C and says that Polycarp's quotations have the appearance of being made from memory; pp. 100, 84) with a supplement from v. 2*b* to convert a test for true inspiration into a denunciation of heretics; (ii) a rewriting of v. 3*b* on the model of 2.22 or 2 Jn 7; (iii) a second negative clause on denying the testimony of the cross, without verbal reminiscence of the Epistle; and (iv) a reference to 3:8. Polycarp's formulation is not reliable testimony for the original

text of the Epistle, but shows that Johannine language could be
adapted to fighting views such as those of Cerinthus who taught that
Christ descended on Jesus at his baptism but left him before the
cross (Irenaeus, *A.H.* 1.26.1).

The Epistle's stress on **come in the flesh** must be carefully defined. Although repetition is the writer's preferred method of emphasis, he fails to repeat the phrase in the second clause and the
word **flesh** does not occur again in the Epistle. The first mention of
repudiating Christ in 2:22 makes no use of the idea, nor does the
subsequent mention of devotion to Christ in 5:1. The implied contrast is not between a Christ who came in the flesh and a Christ
who was present in appearance only, but between accepting Jesus
as both Christ and Son of God and discarding Jesus for the benefits
of the Spirit. There is tension between flesh and Spirit, and it
appears again in two awkward intrusions in Jn 3:6 and 6:63. In this
passage of the Epistle the emphasis lies on acknowledging Jesus, in
giving the utmost priority and finality to the person who had human
existence and was called Jesus—which name indeed defined once
and for all the meaning of the designation Christ.

Hence it is misleading to think of the dissidents as 'denying the
incarnation' (a complex and perhaps anachronistic denial). It has
been remarked that 'the writer never says why it is a matter of such
importance to his faith that Jesus came in the flesh' (Houlden,
p. 107); which is true enough if the writer was defending some such
conviction as that the pre-existent Jesus Christ 'was truly united
with human flesh rather than that he merely came into a human
body and indwelt it' (Marshall, p. 205). But his reason is sufficiently
plain if he was trying to preserve an attachment to Jesus Christ,
including his teaching and demonstration of love, which some were
abandoning.

This dispute within the Johannine community appears again in
the Gospel, in a partially resolved form, especially clearly in the
Paraclete passages where acceptance of the gift of the Spirit is
accompanied by an anxious determination to make the Spirit always
dependent on Jesus. To regard the reference to **come in the flesh**
as an attack on docetic christology is unhelpful, for the word 'docetism' jumbles together varieties of thinking arising in popular
magical religion, gnostic imaginings, and even spiritual exegesis (cf.
Ignatius, *Trall.* 8–10, where the writer defends his own spiritual
exegesis, that faith is the Lord's flesh and love is the blood of Jesus
Christ, from the suspicion that he believed that 'he suffered only in
semblance').

The Epistle is written in more austere and less imaginative fashion
than any of these (whatever may be true of the Gospel) and simply

defends adherence to Jesus against those who would abandon or
pass beyond him. The presence of such people elsewhere in the
primitive church is suggested by those who said 'Jesus be cursed',
in 1 C. 12:3 (at the beginning of a passage which deals with the
gifts of the Spirit); by the 'enemies of the cross of Christ', in Phil.
3:18; and those who 'profaned the blood of the covenant . . . and
outraged the Spirit of grace', in Heb. 10:29. (see also on 2.22f., and
the introduction.)

In v. 3 **every spirit which does not confess** is grammatically and
textually odd: the indicative verb has the negative *mē* instead of the
regular *ouk*, and *mē homologei* is replaced by *luei* in the margin of
1739, a tenth-century Greek manuscript; and by *solvit* in the Old
Latin version and the Vulgate, with support in some Greek and
Latin patristic texts. The verb *luō* (used at 3:8 in 'destroy the works
of the devil') can mean to unloose, set free, do away with, abolish
or destroy. The Latin *solvo* presumably means to separate or detach;
Knox, rendering the Vulgate, translates 'would disunite Jesus', and
adds: 'apparently in the sense that it would deny the identity of the
human Jesus with the divine Christ; but the phrase might have a
more general sense of 'destroying' Jesus' (Knox, p. 555). The arguments for this textual variant are insufficient to make it the original
reading (with Metzger, p. 714 and Marshall, p. 207f., and against
Bultmann, p. 62, Schnackenburg, p. 222, and Brown (1979), p.
111); but even if it were original, it would neither strengthen nor
weaken the interpretation here proposed.

In the second sentence **This is the spirit of the antichrist** is
obtained by supplying the word *pneuma* after *to* in the phrase *to tou
antichristou* which, however, may mean something more general like
'the event of the antichrist', taken up by the neuter *ho*. For **antichrist**, see on 2:18; for **world**, see on 2:2.

4–6. In preparation for a renewed appeal for love within the
community, the writer now increases their consciousness of being
a community separate from the world. **You** who **are of** (i.e., 'have
your origin from') **God** are set over against them who have their
origin from **the world**, who are prompted in what they say by the
world, and hence are listened to by the world. Their awareness of
being a minority group within the larger society is balanced by the
assertion that **he who is in you is greater than he who is in the
world**. At long last the writer takes up his previous agreement that
the young men have overcome the evil one (see on 2:12–14), and
tells the whole community that they **have overcome them**, i.e., the
dissidents. He agrees that to talk of having overcome (as the young
men do) is entirely proper, but he redefines the object of the verb:
not simply the evil one, or even the world (as in 5:4f.) but the

dissidents. It is, however, obvious from the attack on the dissidents in 2:18–23 and from the instruction to test the spirits in 4:1–3 that the dissidents have not been overcome and are still a threat to the community, or at least an attraction to some members of it. Hence the statement that they have overcome the dissidents is really an appeal to reject their influence. Finally, the writer changes from **you** and **they** to **we**: that is, he returns to the authoritative position of the we-group which validated the 'agreed statement' (see on 1:1–4) and he formulates the prescriptive-judgmental couplet:

Whoever knows God listens to us,
and he who is not of God does not listen to us.

For the final clause, see on vv. 1–2.

THE TRADITIONS REPEATED 4:7–21

Having separated the community from the world, the writer now returns to his insistence on love within the community. In 2:29 he dropped a couple of markers for the future course of his argument: (i) 'righteous', which gave rise to the discussion of sinning, and to the requirement of love established by the contrasted examples of Cain and Christ; and (ii) 'born of him', which now initiates the fuller exploration of love, and the requirement that we should **love one another**.

7–8. The phrase **born of God** was introduced at 3:9, and appears again at 5:1, 4, 18—a person so described does not sin, acts lovingly, believes that Jesus is the Christ, and overcomes the world. He is a member of the Christian community by the generative power of God. The same thought is presented by the statements that **we** (or **you**) **are of God** (4:4, 6) in contrast to them who **are of the world**, i.e., they have become what they are by the corrupting influence of the world. Compare 5:19, 'We know that we are of God, and the whole world is in the power of the evil one'. When, however, the writer adopts the simpler presentation (replacing the verb 'to be born' by the verb 'to be'), he can include more than persons in his description. So in 4:1–3 'spirits' may or may not be of God, for 'spirit' is an ambiguous term; but **love** is unambiguous (despite the repudiation of loving the world in 2:15): **love is of God**. That form of statement might be misleading: the writer does not mean that love in general, love of any kind, derives from the generative power of God. He makes his meaning plainer in a teaching couplet:

He who loves is born of God and knows God.
He who does not love does not know God.

To be **born of God** is not necessarily to know God; indeed in some gnostic forms of religion it is precisely those who belong to the highest deity who are not aware of their proper nature and therefore lack knowledge of that wherein their origin lies (see on 2:3).

That awareness, according to the Epistle, is achieved and demonstrated by loving; **he who loves knows** (the aorist *egnō*, 'has come to know', and so 'knows'). The discussion of love is directed towards love within the community (4:7, 12, 20, 21): community love is doubtless intended even when the writer attaches no object to the verb. Even if the use of 'love' without an object is deliberate, and is intended to turn the mind towards the nature of loving rather than to its object, it must be remembered that the writer has carefully separated the community, where love is practised (or should be), from the world which receives little approval in the Epistle and fares not much better in the Gospel. The writer is not so foolish as to suppose that love is unknown in the world and unpractised there: his repeated appeal for brotherly love in the community springs from his conviction that their religious awareness should at least reach the level of mutual caring known to Jews and Greeks. But his deepest concern is to advocate a loving which leads to knowledge of God and expresses the meaning of being born of God.

To strengthen his thrust he adds: **for God is love**, a deceptively simple statement which is difficult to analyse. If it were said, as it is by Philo, that God is mind (*nous*) it would mean that God is not corporeal as human beings are (and so it would be saying something about God's nature); or it would mean that God operates by processes akin to human thought (and so would be saying something about his actions). It is difficult to see how God's nature can be described by **love**; easier to see that his actions are being described as loving actions, as indeed they are in vv. 9–10. Nevertheless, it must be argued that **God is love** does not function mainly as describing God's activity but as defining the condition on which God may be known. Compare the Jewish *Shema* in Dt. 6:4, which does not exist to provide information about the unity of God but sets down the condition on which God will benefit his people: 'The Lord is our God, the Lord alone'. Therefore his people must not divert some portion of their energies to another deity but must love the Lord with all their heart, soul and might. The statement about God implies a demand.

So, earlier in the Epistle, when it is said that 'God is light', there

follows a demand that Christians should walk in the light. On this
the writer and the dissidents agreed; they diverged on its consequences. The dissidents took it to imply that they must cultivate
the Spirit, the writer that they must practise love. Hence his definition **God is love** is in some tension with what looks like their
definition 'God is spirit'. That definition can very properly be defended, and it is included in the Gospel (Jn 4:24) in the Samaritan
dialogue, though somewhat cautiously confined to worship. The
Epistle has something yet to say about Spirit (in 4:13 and 5:6–8)
but nothing corresponding to the spontaneous unpredictability of
Spirit that appears in Jn 3:8. When **God is love** is repeated in v.
16, it introduces a renewed demand for love within the community.

9–10. To safeguard the dominant emphasis on the love to be
displayed by the community two complementary statements are now
made, one revelatory, the other expiatory. Both begin **in this** (see
on 2:3), pointing to the disclosure (*ephanerōthē*; see on 2:28—*RSV*
uses the archaic translation **manifest**) of love, and to love's effective
work of **expiation** (*hilasmos*; see on 2:2). Both say that **God sent
his Son** (as also in v. 14, but not elsewhere in the Epistle). In the
NT the verb 'to send' admirably represents the Jewish institution
of agency (Derrett (1970), pp. 52f.; (1973), p. 76; Harvey (1976),
pp. 88–92; 106f., 115ff.; (1982), pp. 161f.) by which one person
sends another as his agent, to act fully with the authority and under
the instructions of the person who sent him. In the Gospel, Jesus
repeatedly asserts that he is sent by God, marks the end of his
commission by reporting that the disciples have come to believe
that God sent him, and in turn sends them into the world to bring
it to the same belief (Jn 17:8, 18, 21). Moreover, when the Paraclete,
the spirit of truth, is promised to disciples, Jesus explicitly says: 'I
will send him to you' (Jn 15:26; 16:7). If Jesus came as the agent
of God, the Spirit comes as the agent of Jesus; and that clearly has
a bearing on the dissidents' claim to possess the Spirit without
recourse to Jesus. Hence the choice of sending language in this
passage is both traditional and deliberate.

God discloses his own love by sending **his only Son into the
world**; cf. the close parallel in Jn 3:17. **Only** correctly represents the
Greek *monogenēs* (cf. the widow's only son, in Lk. 7:12) which can
also mean 'unique', though some prefer 'only begotten' (*AV*), because of the Johannine emphasis on being born of God. If the
dissidents are in mind, the word is used to suggest the priority of
the Son to the Spirit. If vv. 9 and 14 are taken together there is an
even closer agreement in thought, namely, that the Son was sent
into the world (i) to give life to those who believe, and (ii) to save
the world. In 9, however, the disclosure of God's love takes place

among us (Greek *en hēmin*, possibly 'to us', 'in our case'), **that we might live through him**. The community is in view, rather than the world, just as in Jn 17:9 Jesus says 'I am not praying for the world but for those whom thou hast given me, for they are thine'. In v. 10, the Son is an **expiation for our sins**, and the writer at this point does not echo what he wrote earlier: 'not for ours only but also for the sins of the whole world' (2:2). He limits himself to those who have been singled out by God's love for them (cf. Jesus' words in Jn 15:16, 19; 'You did not choose me, but I chose you': and, 'I chose you out of the world'). He allows only a responsive, not a creative value to our love for God; and so no doubt turns aside the dissidents' claim of exceptional devotion to God.

11. **If** (*ei* with the indicative, meaning, 'since') **God so** (as in Jn 3:16: 'in that manner'; or, 'so greatly') **loved us, we ought to love one another**. The logic of the demand appears faulty unless a missing step is supplied. That can easily be done from the foregoing argument. Either: God loves in such a manner, and we are born of God which means that we are like God—therefore we must love the others who are born of God (cf. 5:1). Or: since like recognises like, we can know God who loves in such a manner only if we love those whom God loves.

12. This verse both rounds off the argument for community love and makes a transition to the summary in vv. 13–16a. For **God abides in us**, see on 2:6; and for **perfected**, cf. 4:17f., and see on 2:5. **His love** presumably means the kind of love displayed by God, brought to full expression by its extension in community love. So far so good, but the verse begins with a seemingly alien remark, recalling indeed the first words of Jn 1:18, but unexpected at this point in the Epistle—**No man has ever seen God**. The Greek begins abruptly with *theon* without an article, in notable contrast to the frequent use of *theos* with the article in the surrounding verses; suggesting perhaps 'God in any form' or 'God as God' (Westcott, p. 151, who translates 'God hath no man ever beheld'). **Seen** is *tetheatai*, taken up by *tetheametha* in v. 14, perhaps harking back to the same verb in 1:1 and to the hope of seeing God (a different verb) in 3:2 (see the note there).

It may well be that the dissidents claimed that they had seen or had means of seeing God. The John who composed the Revelation was caught up by the Spirit, entered heaven, and saw the divine being and his entourage (Rev. 4:2ff.) which included 'a lamb standing, as though it had been slain'. The numerous references in Revelation to Jesus Christ would not have suited the dissidents, but there are sufficient precedents for heavenly journeying and visions of God in Jewish apocalyptic literature, e.g., in *1 Enoch* 71 where

Enoch makes the same journey as John and discovers that he himself is the Son of man; in 2 *Enoch* 22 where Enoch reaches the tenth heaven after a more extended journey and sees the divine face; and in *Test. Levi* 5 where the patriarch reaches the highest heaven and sees the Most High on a throne of glory. Against all such claims, the writer of the Epistle reasserts the older Jewish tradition that God can be heard but not seen (e.g., Dt. 4:12).

13–16a. For the functon of these verses, see the introductory comment on 4:1–6. Verse 13 repeats 3:24*b* with modest variations, and includes the mutual indwelling of 3:24*a*. Verses 15 and 16*a* contain nothing new except for phrasing. The pronoun in **we know** is emphatic (*hēmeis*), as it is in v. 14 **we have seen and testify**, implying 'we at least, even if they do not'. The first two verbs in v. 16*a* are perfects: 'we have come to know and believe'; or, since 'to believe the love' (*pisteuō* with an unusual accusative, no doubt decided by the verb 'know') is an odd idea, perhaps we should translate by 'put our faith in' (*JB*). **The love God has for us** is literally 'in us' (*en hēmin*), as in 4:9. Only v. 14 contributes a new thought, and even this has the appearance of old tradition.

The formulation **we have seen** takes up the words **no man has ever seen** of 4:12; but also **we have seen and testify** harks back to the beginning of the Epistle (see on 1:2; and cf. 5:6–10). It is also the Epistle's third and final statement that God **sent his Son** (see on vv. 9–10), though at this point his sending, with a wider reference than the community, is **as the Saviour of the world** (double accusative). The same designation is bestowed on Jesus by the Samaritans in Jn 4:42 (suggesting a possible source for this component of Johannine theology; Brown (1979), p. 37) and is supported by a few other statements in the Gospel. It raises two questions. (1) What does it imply? The word **saviour** is not found in Johannine writings beyond these two passages, though the verb occurs five times (note particularly Jn 3:17, 'that the world might be saved through him'; and 12:47, 'I did not come to judge the world but to save the world'). In the rest of the *NT* 'saviour' is a common designation for both God (as in LXX) and Jesus chiefly in the later writings, especially in the Pastoral Epistles and 2 Peter; but nowhere else is a **saviour of the world** mentioned.

In late antiquity, however, it was very much at home in the adulatory language of inscriptions recording the benefits of the Ptolemies and the Roman emperors. Evidence for the exact expression is first known for Hadrian (AD 117–138), but equivalent expressions and the idea itself are much earlier. They reach back to the time of Augustus and celebrate his achievement in bringing peace to the Roman world and re-establishing law and order (Foerster, *TWNT*

VII, pp. 1009–12). Thus in designating the Son of God as **saviour of the world**, this tradition is portraying him not as the redeemer of individuals but as the renewer of the social fabric (for this meaning of **world**, see on 2:2). (2) How can the writer of the Epistle endorse such a designation? He believes that the world is passing away, that it is in the power of the evil one and so opposed to God, that it hates and repudiates the community, is corrupt and not to be loved (2:15–17; 3:13; 4:4; 5:19). And yet he can write that God **sent his Son as the Saviour of the world**, and that he is the expiation for the sins of the whole world (2:2).

A similar dilemma appears in the Gospel. (i) The Prologue asserts that the world came into being through the Logos but, when visited by the Light-Logos failed to recognise the source of its existence.

(ii) In Jn 1–12, the world is indeed visited by the light but men prefer darkness; yet those who follow the light of the world will have the light of life (3:19; 8:12). Is it implied that some are saved from a world which is to be abandoned to its fate? The concluding part of this section of the Gospel moves in that direction, though not without diversions. In 12:25 Jesus says: 'He who loves his life loses it, and he who hates his life *in this world* will keep it for eternal life'. Yet a little later 'Now is the judgment of *this world*, now shall the ruler of *this world* be cast out; and I, when I am lifted up from the earth will draw *all men* to myself' (12:31f.). Yet in the end, 'I have come as light into *the world*, that whoever believes on me may not remain in darkness. . . .I did not come to judge *the world* (contrast 9:39) but to save *the world*. He who rejects me and does not receive my sayings has a judge; the word that I have spoken will be his judge on the last day' (12:46f.—a very apt judgment on the dissidents!).

The implication seems to be that the world is subjected to judgment, namely, a process of discrimination. The ruler of this world loses his control of mankind who are then drawn to Jesus to be judged by his words: those who accept his words enter the light; those who do not accept remain in darkness. And yet earlier in the Gospel, Jesus has been introduced by John Baptist as 'the Lamb of God, who takes away the sin of *the world*' (1:29), has been designated by the Samaritans as Saviour of the world, and has himself said 'the bread which I shall give for the life of *the world* is my flesh' (6:51).

(iii) In the Farewell Discourses, Jesus, having entered *the world* which knows not God (17:25), now returns to the Father (13:1; 16:28; 17:13). He leaves his disciples behind in *the world* (17:11) which hates them and causes them hardship (15:18; 16:33; 17:14). When the promised Spirit of truth comes to them, *the world* cannot receive him; indeed the Paraclete will convict *the world* on various charges (14:17; 16:8–11). The disciples in fact have been chosen out of *the world* and do not belong to it, as Jesus does not (15:19; 17:6, 14). Finally, as the Father sent Jesus into *the world*, so Jesus sends his disciples that *the world* may know that the Father had sent his Son and that the Father loved the disciples as he loved the Son (17:18, 21, 23).

(iv) In the Passion Narrative, Jesus says to Pilate: 'My kingship is not of this *world*. . . .For this I was born, and for this I have come into the *world* to bear witness to the truth' (18:36f.).

Thus in the Gospel it is not easy to discover a coherent understanding of the world or of the community's relation to it. The community could not withdraw and ignore the world. Although it valued its separation, it was forced at the very least to endure the world. It was prepared to rescue from the world some others who belonged to God. It must have thought that the world was still within the rule of God, if the words of Jesus were to judge it and the Paraclete was to convict it; and it remembered some old traditions that Jesus was the Saviour of the world and gave his flesh for its life. They therefore made the uncomfortable admission that Jesus sent his disciples into the world to bear witness to the truth—and there their responsibility ended. The truth took over to do whatever the truth would do. The world was not their responsibility if they left it to the truth.

According to the writer of the Epistle 'many false prophets have gone out into the world' (4:1). If that judgment is rephrased in a less partisan fashion, it might be put in such a form as this: 'Many members of the community, inspired by the Spirit, have been sent out into the world as witnesses to the truth'. That would be a proper initiative, within the range of the community's understanding of the world, except for the envoy's damaging decision not to confess **that Jesus is the Son of God**. When therefore the writer insists that **we have seen and testify that the Father has sent his Son as the Saviour of the world,** the emphasis falls on **his Son**. He is not providing information about the Son; but saying that, if there is to be a saviour of the world, it is the Son of God, namely, Jesus—and not some spirit-filled people who deny him.

16b forms an *inclusio* with v. 8 and thus ends that phase of the discussion of love. Before the writer leaves the subject, however, there is one further connexion to be exposed, namely, between love and **confidence**.

17. Confidence (*parrhēsia*) has already appeared at 2:28 and 3:21, and will appear again at 5:14. This repetition suggests lack of confidence on the part of the readers, either because of their own perplexities or because the dissidents' religious browbeating is having an effect. What can give us confidence when we hear not only our own self-reproaches but much more God's reproach (see on 3:20)? The fact that we keep his commandments and do what is pleasing to him (3:22). Hence **love** has its full development (**is perfected,** *teteleiōtai*; see on 2:5) **with us** (*meth hēmōn*, perhaps a Semitic variant of 'in us' in vv. 9, 16; or 'among us'; AGB, s.v. *meta*. AI) when it gives us **confidence for the day of judgment.** To love one another is to keep God's commandments: that community love is most fully effective when it is presented confidently before the divine love (v. 19).

Day of judgment is not otherwise a Johannine expression: indeed it is uncommon in the *NT* (Mt. four times, 2 Pet. twice, and Rev. once). In the Gospel, judgment is a frequent theme but it is not attached to a **day of judgment** except in the sense that 'now is the judgment of this world' (12:31). The old mythology of a Great Assize is replaced by the entry of light into the world (3:19), and by the passage from death to life as a consequence of hearing the words of Jesus and believing him who sent him (5:24; for the Epistle's treatment of this theme, see on 3:14). Indeed the Gospel is insistent that, in so far as judgment is a proper description of Jesus' task, judgment has been firmly delegated to Jesus by the Father (5:22, 27; 8:16) and is decided by the reception of Jesus' words (12:47–48). Even if some function in the judgment (of the world) is reserved to the Paraclete (16:8–11), it is to be performed in subordination to Jesus. By the time the material of the Gospel had been assembled in its present form, the judgment had been so firmly attached to Jesus that the expression **day of judgment** was no longer usable. Even when the Epistle was written it was already an archaic expression, and may probably be attributed to the dissidents for it accords with their warnings about the divine *parousia* (see on 3:2).

The syntax of the verse is not unambiguous. **In this** (see on 2:3) may refer to what has gone before; but, if 16*b* is part of an *inclusio*, it points forward: **love is perfected with us in this** respect, namely, (taking *hina* with subjunctive as explanatory) **that we may have confidence.** Then follows a clause beginning with *hoti*: **because** (or perhaps, more loosely, 'for')

> **as he is** (*kathōs ekeinos estin*)
> **so are we**
> **in this world.**

For *ekeinos*, see on 2:6. Without doubt it refers to Jesus. Commentators have objected that the present state of Jesus can scarcely affect our fate at the day of judgment; and, that if the earthly example of Jesus were intended, the verb would not be **is** but 'was' (Houlden, pp. 117ff.; Bultmann, pp. 72f.). The problem has been unnecessarily magnified. The phrasing has already become familiar in 2:6: we ought to walk as he (*kathōs ekeinos*) walked (past tense); in 3:3, we must purify ourselves as he (*kathōs ekeinos*) is pure; and in 3:7, we should be righteous as he (*kathōs ekeinos*) is righteous. The present passage means: As Jesus is an exemplar of love, so are we in this world. The example of Jesus was present to the writer of the Epistle, as it was present to the compilers of the Gospel. That was what he meant by having come in the flesh (4:2), namely, that Jesus, in word and deed, was available in the community tradition. He could not resist an epigrammatic statement, somewhat loosely attached, in his steady polemic against the dissidents. At judgment day we shall no doubt see God as he is (*kathōs estin*, 3:2); in this world, however, we are patterned upon that person (*ekeinos*), namely, Jesus. Compare Jn 13:15, 'I have given you an example, that you should also do as I have done to you'.

18–21. In the writer's argument, **fear** is the opposite of confidence. He is not making some over-simple comments on the psychology of fear and love (if he were he could be faulted for ignoring their close association), but repudiating the suggestion that members of the community should fear the divine parousia. The truth of the matter is that **he first loved us** (by sending his Son, v. 14); therefore we approach him not with **fear** but with **love**. **There is no fear in love** (*phobos* without an article, introducing the general thought of fear, followed by *ton phobon*, *ho phobos* referring to the thought already introduced) must include the double idea that God's **love** does not prompt any element of **fear**, and that love when fully expressed in community love (**perfect love**) excludes **fear** of God. Anyone who experiences such **fear** and expects **punishment** (i.e., reproof or injury) from God has not been **perfected in love**, has stopped short of the full development (v. 17) of community love, which is again commended by argument in v. 20 and commanded in v. 21. The writer is not discussing a theoretical possibility: there is somebody who claims to love God while hating his brother— presumably a fellow-member of the community with whom he is in disagreement. No doubt he objects to the brother ('hatred' is the writer's chosen word) because the brother has not seen God and, by implication, he himself has (see on v. 12). The writer is convinced, however, that no-one has seen God; he briskly dismisses the claim to have seen God and to love him **for he who does not love his brother whom he has seen cannot love God whom he has not seen.**

It may seem that the writer treats the convictions of the dissidents

with scant respect. In a measure he does, though he is prepared to
make room for some things they rightly perceive and emphasise, as
for example in the following section on the witness of the Spirit.
But he takes his stand against them when they try, on the pretext
of superior knowledge of God, to shake the confidence of traditional
believers and to put them in a state of fear. Wilfully to make people
afraid, to make them fear that God will curse them and injure them
is to be the agent of a destructive lie. It will not do to say that those
who have done wrong ought to be afraid of God; first, because what
is amended through fear is but insecurely remedied, and secondly,
because fear is much more the cause of wickedness than its consequence. The writer does not view human life as a network of
relationships marked by the exercise of power and controlled by
fear, but as a community of love. God is love and light, and the
only **commandment we have from him** is the double commandment
of love, conveyed and demonstrated by his Son, and expressed here
in the characteristic prescriptive teaching formula (introduced with
explanatory *hina* and subjunctive):

he who loves God should love his brother also.

TESTIMONY OF THE SPIRIT AND FAITH IN THE SON
5:1–13

1. The previous section has been neatly rounded off by a teaching
formula. This new section begins with such a formula:

> 1a **Every one who believes**
>   b **that Jesus is the Christ**
>   c **is a child of God** [lit. is born (*gegenētai*) of God]
>   d **and every one who loves the parent** [i.e., *ton gennēsanta*,
>   him who fathered the birth]
>   e **loves the child** [lit. the one born (*gegennēmenon*) from him]

The writer engages in a word-play on the verb *gennaō*, to beget
or bear a child, which has already been used at 2:29, 3:9, and 4:7
in describing those who do what is right and do not sin as 'born of
God', especially those who practise community love. The word-play
continues in v. 4 and it is tempting to suggest (with Bultmann, p.
76) that vv. 2 and 3 are an intrusion into an earlier text. Verse 1a
reappears in 4d, 5b; 1b in an equivalent form in 5c; and 1c in 4a.
But it also happens that 1d is taken up by 2c, 3a; and 1e in 2b.
Moreover, 2d and 3b,c introduce **commandments**, which are not

present in v. 1, and 4*b*,*c*, 5*a* stress **victory that overcomes the world**, which is equally unrepresented in v. 1. None of these themes is novel; but they are ingeniously woven together and brought into relation with the acknowledgement of Jesus as Christ and Son of God. Being born of God, loving God, loving the children of God, keeping the commandments and overcoming the world are the writer's main concerns, and for him they depend on the primacy of Jesus. This section, therefore, is not a continuation of the previous section but a free-standing summary which prepares the way for the writer's final argumentative encounter with the dissidents. Moreover, since the summary appears to have been derived by expansion of the teaching couplet in v. 1, the manner of its composition may to some extent account for the problems of detailed exegesis.

2. By this (*en toutō*; see on 2:3) may look backwards to the principle stated in 1*d*,*e*; or forwards to **when we love God** (with the more natural 'that' clause replaced by a **when** clause, because it would follow **that we love** too closely). Whichever is preferred, it is not easy to grasp the exact logic of what is being said: 2*b*,*c* can be read as suggesting that love for God is proof of love for the children of God, although the writer otherwise uses the converse argument that love for God's children is proof of our love for God (as suggested by 1*d*,*e* and expressed more plainly in 4:20f.). The problem can perhaps be solved by a paraphrase: If we act according to the principle **every one who loves the parent loves the child**, we know that we are indeed loving **the children of God when we** not only **love God** but also carry out **his commandments**. ('Carry out', instead of *RSV* **obey**, represents *poiōmen* in the text of B, etc., against the normal *tērōmen* in the text of ℵ , etc.; 'carrying out commandments' does not appear elsewhere in *NT*, but it is similar to 'carrying out the will of God' in 2:17.) The sentence is directed against those who claim to love God but reject commandments because they know by inspiration what to do.

3-5. It is a characteristically Johannine conviction that to love God (the genitive in **the love of God** is objective, and **that** represents explanatory *hina* with subjunctive) is to keep his commandments (cf. 2:4f.; 2 Jn 6; Jn 14:15, 21). It is, of course, one of the typical forms of Jewish piety as evidenced in the Psalms, Qumran and the rabbis; though the writer's confidence that the **commandments are not burdensome** (cf. Dt. 30:11) is dependent on his reduction of them to the two commandments of love. *RSV* punctuates the final words of v. 3 as an independent sentence: but *NEB*, *JB* more plausibly regard them as the beginning of 4*a*: **His commandments are not burdensome** because **whatever** (neuter for masculine, presumably a more general form of statement without significant difference of meaning, cf. Jn 6:37; 17:2) **is born of God overcomes the world**. For **world**, see on 2:2, 15–17. The world, undergoing dissolution, hates the community (3:13) but listens to the dissidents (4:5). But the community is stronger than the dissidents, and has overcome them by virtue of him who is in the community (4:4), and who is also, despite all appearances, God's agent as saviour of the world (4:14). All this brings back an echo of the young men of 2:13f. who 'have overcome the evil one', which is to be expected of any one **born of God**. But they must be reminded that the means of **victory** (the meaning here of *nikē*; AGB s.v.) **that overcomes the world** is their **faith** (the only appearance of the noun *pistis* in the Gospel and Epistles). The first use of **overcomes** in v. 4 translates the present tense of the verb *nikaō*. The second use translates the aorist *nikēsasa* which could be an equivalent of the perfect or even the present, but probably advances beyond the habitual victories proper to any one born of God and refers to total victory. Since it refers to the believer's practice of faith, it is not in the first place a reference to Christ's victory (Jn 16:33) but to each person's confession of Jesus as Son of God, such confession being part of the assault which inflicts defeat on the world (the constative aorist being used to express the idea of the infliction of defeat). The paragraph ends in 4a and 5 with a teaching couplet on victory and faith. For believing, see on 3:23.

5:6–13 The point has now been reached when the writer should make a direct attack on the dissidents' conviction that by possessing the spirit they can dispense with Jesus. But his approach is far from direct. No doubt his first readers were more comprehending than most subsequent readers have been: for they would quickly feel the controversial implications of **witness**, and would be familiar with a community debate in which **water, blood**, and **spirit** had already played a part. But the writer takes an uncomfortable route to his final conclusion, which comes in v. 11:

> **This is the testimony**
> **that God gave us eternal life,**
> **and this life is in his Son.**

It recalls the very opening words of the Epistle, when the we-group laid down their testimony to eternal life from the Father and insisted that their fellowship was with the Father and the Son (1:1–3). This conclusion is supported with a simple teaching couplet in v. 12 (the last of all) which asserts that adherence to the Son is the absolute precondition for possession of the divinely-given life. In this conclusion there is no word about **spirit**. It must be concluded that **spirit** played an ambiguous or even minor role in the writer's theology. If one collects all the teaching couplets, a good impression emerges of the teaching which the writer wished to drive home and fix in the habitual responses of his readers—and the **spirit** is not included. There is one defensive reference in 4:2–3 to spirits (i.e., inspired utterances) which do or do not confess Jesus Christ, a test for distinguishing the spirit of truth from the spirit of falsehood; but nothing more. The writer can say, rather formally, that God 'has given us of his own spirit', but it is clear that **spirit** does not play the same dominating part in his thought as **God** and **his Son**. (The same could be said of the writer who composed Jn 17.) But he could not deny that at least some former members of the community possessed the spirit and were inspired persons—even if they were false prophets (4:1). He must either deny inspiration a place in the community, or with some hesitation claim it for the community and firmly control it by subjecting it to Jesus Christ (cf. the Paraclete sayings in the Gospel).

His approach, however, is so allusive that later copyists felt more than usually free to introduce emendations (on which, see Metzger, pp. 715–18). In 5:6 **came by water and blood** is read by B (4th cent.), the Old Latin, the Peshitto Syriac, and the majority text, and was known to Tertullian (3rd cent); whereas 'by water and blood and (holy) spirit' is read by ℵ (4th cent), A (5th cent.), other Greek MSS, Syriac (ʰ), Coptic, and was known to Origen (3rd cent.). The longer text conforms the shorter text to the threefold pattern of vv. 7–8. Both readings were known to Cyril (5th cent.) who, with Ambrose (4th cent.) and three Greek MSS, also knew the form 'came by water and spirit' which conforms the text to Jn 3:5 and the dissidents' position. Finally, there is the reading 'by water and spirit and blood' in P (6th cent.) and other Greek MSS, which is not a very thoughtful attempt to combine the memory of Jn 3:5 with the original text. **Came by water and blood** preserves the writer's sharp polemical intention which the other readings fail to recognise.

In v. 7 (using the verse numeration of *RSV*, which here does not coincide with that of standard Greek texts), instead of **the Spirit is the truth** the Vulgate and one Greek MS has 'Christ is the truth'—not original but equally not remote from the writer's intention.

Next, there is the spurious addition to v. 8 (familiar from *AV*): after **witnesses** the addition has 'in heaven, the Father, the Word, and the Holy Spirit; and these three are one. And there are three witnesses on earth, the spirit, the water and the blood'. The addition was unknown to the Greek Fathers, and first appears in a fourth century Latin treatise; it is absent from all but four late Greek MSS, from the earliest Latin version and Jerome's Vulgate, and from the other ancient versions. It is not relevant to the argument of the verses into which it was interpolated, and merely illustrates the danger of trying to make theological capital of what the reader does not understand.

Finally, v. 10 caused some uncertainties. In the phrase **the testimony in himself**, the Greek word translated **himself** is uncertain: the witnesses vary between *heautō* or its contracted form *hautō*; but if suitable the *autō* form could be translated 'in him'. Further, **he who does not believe God** is very strongly supported in the Greek MS tradition, but God is replaced by 'the Son' in some Greek MSS and the Latin version. This is probably no more than an attempt to make the second clause of the teaching formula like the first clause.

6–7. Jesus Christ came by (*dia* with genitive of accompanying circumstances) or **with** (*en* with dative of things which accompany— the constructions are equivalent, and the variation is stylistic) **water and blood, not with the water only**, as some apparently insist, but with both. The community and the dissidents were at one in accepting the association of Jesus with **water**, and perhaps they shared the symbolic meanings of **water**. In the Gospel **water** first appears in John Baptist's explanation of his own baptising activity, and it is easy to remember the cleansing effect and symbolism of water (cf. Jn 2:6; 13:5, 10) and its suitability for initiation. But it is also suitable for renewal (cf. the healing waters, Jn 5:1–8) and is forcefully associated with the gift of new life. John baptises in order to disclose to Israel the coming one who will baptise with spirit (Jn 1:26, 31, 34); and when Jesus requests water from a Samaritan woman, he talks to her of living water, the water which becomes an inner source of eternal life (Jn 4:10–14; cf. 7:38f.).

Water is therefore a symbol of revelation and expresses the possibility of sharing the life of God. Hence, being 'born of water and the spirit' is a satisfactory symbolic description of being born anew (Jn 3:5, 7). It was promised by John Baptist, effective during the ministry of Jesus, and makes no call on **blood** and its associations. Indeed, apart from the book of Revelation, where blood frequently stands for martyrdom and vengeance, the Johannine writings make scanty use of the symbolism of blood: in the Epistles, apart from the present passage, a single reference in 1 Jn 1:7 to the blood of Jesus which cleanses from sin; in the Gospel, only the additions to or development of the discourse on the bread when 'drinking blood' surprisingly appears in Jn 6:53–56, and in the emphatic testimony in Jn 19:34 that 'there came out blood and water' from the pierced side of Jesus. This prodigy ought to be related in some way to the Epistle's insistence that Jesus **came by water and blood**, but it is difficult to know what response is expected. Cautious statements by medical authorities that the effusion is physiologically possible are irrelevant: the evangelist is not merely reporting medical information.

The succeeding verse looks like a secondary attempt to add support by mentioning an eyewitness who is sure he is telling the truth 'that you (? the readers) may also believe'. This may indeed have been directed to the dissidents, who accepted the implications of water but rejected the implications of blood; though a gruesome episode after the death of Jesus would scarcely incline them to better doctrine. Some have thought that the evangelist is symbolically indicating the two gospel sacraments, or thinking of Moses striking the rock in the wilderness and remembering his ability to turn water into blood (Num. 20:11; Exod. 4:9), or picturing an excessive fulfilment of the promise in Jn 7:38. But these are desperate expedients and reinforce the impression that blood symbolism consorts uneasily with Johannine teaching.

Something much simpler is required. Since water is associated with life, illumination and truth, and blood is a biblical symbol for violence, suffering and sacrifice, the Johannine image may mean that the violence endured by Jesus is accompanied by life and light to those who have seen and borne witness; or even that the benefits symbolised by water cannot be had apart from the sufferings symbolised by blood.

None of these considerations can prevail against the fact that the Gospel records the passion of Jesus in distinctive detail and pattern, and that the central chapters 5–8 report that Jesus did his work under constant threat of death. Even so, there are few explicit reflections on his death (it is like the death of a shepherd for his sheep, or the death of a hostage for his people, or the sowing of seed as a precondition of the harvest; Jn 10:11, 15, 17, 18; 11:50; 12:24), and some oblique references (e.g., 'my hour', and presumably 'the Lamb of God who takes away the sin of the world'), and metaphorical ones (lifting up, glorification; Jn 3:14–16; 8:28; 12:23). In a sense it is easy to give primary importance to life rather than death when Jesus says 'I am the resurrection and the life' (Jn 11:25).

Nevertheless, the death of Jesus is a constant preoccupation of the Gospel, and old language about blood is part of the tradition which the leaders of the community must pass on, indeed are unwilling to abandon. In their dispute with the dissidents they mark out their uncompromising position by using the old language in order to force the issue. For the position of the dissidents, see on 4:2–3. They were interested in the symbolism of water as representing new life and preparing for the Spirit, but once the Spirit was received (no doubt thanks to Jesus), what further benefit could be alleged in his death?

Their position was somewhat similar to that of Qumran: 'It is
through the spirit of true counsel concerning the ways of man that
all his sins shall be expiated that he may contemplate the light of
life. He shall be cleansed from all his sins by the spirit of holiness
uniting him to his truth, and his iniquity shall be expiated by the
spirit of uprightness and humility' (1QS 3.6–8; Vermes, p. 75). The
sectarian Jews at once added submission to the precepts of God; the
Johannine dissidents took it for granted that the Spirit guaranteed
the correctness of their conduct. For them **the Spirit is the truth**,
which can be regarded as a catchword of the dissident group.

The writer accepts the implication of the catchword because he
has just said that it is indeed the spirit that bears witness (*to mar-
tyroun*) to the water and the blood. In that case, what does he mean
by **spirit**? Presumably he means here what he means in 4:1, namely,
an inspired prophetic utterance. In the Gospel, witness or testimony
is a frequent theme: it is disputed whether Jesus should or should
not testify to himself and whether he could call as witness his own
actions, Scripture and the Father himself (e.g., Jn 5:31–39). But
the Gospel begins with John Baptist who came to bear witness to
the light, who indeed bore witness to his successor, saw the Spirit
descending on him as a dove—not only descending but also remaining on him—and acclaimed him as Son of God (Jn 1:7, 8, 15, 32–
34). That prophetic testimony is repeated and extended in the affirmations of the we-group in 1:2. Hence by the spirit the writer
means the inspired statements of the community leadership controlled by the tradition. In agreement with such a view is the
statement in Jn 15:26 that the Spirit, like the disciples, bears witness
to Jesus.

8–9. The next stage in the writer's presentation (for argument it
can scarcely be called) brings in the Jewish rule that the agreeing
testimony of two or three witnesses is required for reasonable proof
(Dt. 17:6; 19:15; cf. Jn 8:17): **There are three witnesses, the
Spirit, the water and the blood; and these three agree.** (In Greek
the sentence begins with *hoti* 'for', loosely used to link the additional
thought of this verse with the foregoing; and the sentence ends with
eis to hen eisin 'are [directed] towards the one', perhaps a vernacular
idiom under Semitic influence; cf. Brooke, p. 137; MHT II, p. 462;
III, p. 254.) It is logically odd that the spirit, which was first
introduced as a witness to the water and the blood, is now one of
three agreeing witnesses alongside the water and the blood. This
shift has taken place by one of two possible changes: either 'water
and blood' in v. 8 differ in meaning from the same words in v. 6;
or 'spirit' in v. 8 has a different function from 'spirit' in v. 7. If
'water and blood' have changed their meaning from (say) the bap-

tism and crucifixion of Christ in v. 6 to the sacraments of Baptism
and Lord's Supper in v. 8 (Bultmann, p. 80, who detects the hand
of an ecclesiastical editor), then it would be necessary to ask how
this intrusion of sacramental references would strengthen the case
against the dissidents with their reliance on the spirit. It would also
be necessary to ask why 'water' should signify Christ's baptism,
which the Gospel avoids mentioning, and why 'blood' should signify
the Lord's Supper, for which 'the breaking of bread' is the common
shortened form, and which is also not directly described in the
Gospel.

A straightforward sacramental interpretation can be made to work
only if some generous allowances are given to these difficulties; and
the situation is scarcely improved by the attempt, first of Manson
and then of Nauck, to show that the three terms, spirit, water, and
blood, refer to a single rite of initiation, preserved in the Syriac
church, that began with anointing and continued with baptism and
eucharist (Nauck, pp. 147–82).

Apart from the evidence of Syriac Christianity, it is well known
that the gift of the Spirit was received before baptism in the episode
of Ac. 10:44–48; and it is suggested that parallels are provided by
the section on 'the spirit of true counsel' in the *Community Rule* of
Qumran (quoted above), in consecration to the priesthood in *Test.
Levi* 8.4f. ('The first anointed me with holy oil, and gave me the
staff of judgment. The second washed me with pure water, and fed
me with bread and wine'; cf. Gen. 14:18), and in the initiation of
the Jewish proselyte in *Joseph and Asenath* (see Philonenko, pp. 89–
98: in some MSS of 8.11 God is to renew Asenath by his spirit that
she may eat the bread of life and drink the cup of blessing; but in
the initiatory passage (15.4) she is to eat the bread of life, drink the
cup of immortality, and be anointed with the incorruptible anointing—the order of the cult is either not fixed or unimportant).

These so-called parallels may be relevant to the Syriac rite but
scarcely to the Johannine community (cf. Schnackenburg, p. 263;
Marshall, p. 239). If the Johannine community possessed a rite of
initiation which began with an anointing and the reception of the
Spirit, the Spirit would not be such a hesitating component of the
writer's convictions. It is the dissidents who put spirit in the forefront, not the writer of the Epistle.

It is therefore necessary to abandon the suggestion that 'water
and blood' have changed their meaning, and to consider the converse: that 'spirit' has changed its function. In v. 7 **spirit** is a witness
that water and blood belong essentially to proper recognition of
Jesus Christ. Now in Jewish social disputes, the witnesses are often
the accusers (e.g., 1 Kg. 21:10; Sus. 28–41 when God is witness

against his people, he brings charges: Mic. 1:2; Mal. 3:5). So here, **the spirit** becomes an accusing witness, together with **the water and the blood**; the three are joined in bringing a case against those who do not believe that Jesus is Son of God. In any dispute it is proper to accept human testimony; how much more is it necessary to accept the divine testimony which God has borne to his Son—namely, in the inspired interpretation of the tradition about water and blood. Just as the Epistle began with a delicate threat (see on 1:1–4), so it ends with the suggestion that the dissidents stand accused before God.

10–13. The author now turns back (perhaps with some relief at having disposed of the spirit) to what engages his chief attention, namely, believing in the Father and the Son. He contrives two final teaching couplets (vv. 10 and 12): the first links **the testimony** with belief in God and is followed by emphatic statements which move from **testimony** to **eternal life**; and the second asserts that **eternal life** is exclusively available to him **who has the Son**. The Epistle ends (apart from the appendix) as it begins, with 'the word of life' (1:1), and that was the author's intention in writing. Verse 13 is written with rather special emphasis which is clear in the Greek: 'These things **I write** (*egrapsa*, recalling 2:14) **to you that you may know that you have life eternal** (*hoti zōēn echete aiōnion*), **to you who believe in the name of the Son of God**. It does not introduce any of the matters referred to in vv. 14–21, and may appropriately be regarded as a summary of the whole Epistle, rather than of the immediately preceding section.

Only v. 10 requires further comment. On the characteristic Johannine construction 'believing in' (here and v. 13—*pisteuō eis*, instead of *pisteuō* with dative), see on 3:23. The problem of the verse is the meaning and translation of *autō* or *heautō* (see above). *RSV* translates **He who believes in the Son of God has the testimony in himself**, following the tradition of *AV*; *JB* has 'inside himself'; *NEB* and others 'in his own heart'. This suggests (and suggested to all the scribes who wrote *heautō* for *autō*) an inward work of the Spirit in the believer which confirms outward kinds of evidence. If a person believes in the Son of God, he experiences or develops an inner conviction that what he believes is verified in practice. Such a conviction, though open to self-deceit, may indeed be true; but why it should be introduced at this point in the Epistle is not comprehensible. What purpose could it serve to persuade or controvert the dissidents who were inwardly convinced, and by the inspiration of the Spirit, that their belief was both true and effective? Moreover, this interpretation overlooks the deliberate parallel within the teaching couplet:

**He who believes in the Son of God has the testimony in him
(RV)
He who does not believe God has made him a liar.**

Why should anyone believe in Jesus as Son of God? Because God
has so testified to him. To refuse God's testimony is to treat God as
a deceiver and therefore to undermine the dissidents' firm belief in
God. At this point the writer's case is at its weakest for the dissidents
must have thought that God had testified (by giving them the Spirit)
to the truth of their position. In what sense did the writer suppose
that God had testified to Jesus as his Son? Presumably he refers to
traditions preserved by the we-group which, if they were guardians
of the Synoptic tradition would include the baptism of Jesus (Mk
1:11 and parallels) and his transfiguration (Mk 9:7 and parallels).
Yet the Gospel of John neither records the words 'Thou art my
beloved Son' nor describes the two episodes. Either the Johannine
circle did not know them (though themes from baptism and transfiguration appear in the Gospel); or it abandoned them when it
discovered that voices from heaven are credible only to those who
already believe what the heavenly voice says. Instead it transferred
the testimony to John Baptist: 'I have seen and have borne witness
that this is the Son of God' (1:34). This acknowledgement is made
on the direct instruction of God himself, and therefore is God's
testimony to his Son. Later in the Gospel the testimony of John is
supplemented and enriched by the evidence of Moses and the divine
origin of Jesus' actions (Jn 5:31–47). The Johannine circle could
have adopted the position taken in the Q saying that 'no one knows
the Son except the Father, and no one knows the Father except the
Son and anyone to whom the Son chooses to reveal him' (Mt. 11:27
and parallel): that is, there is no valid witness to the Son's relation
with the Father outside the circle of initiates. But that would have
put them dangerously in the power of the dissidents, and they
refused the temptation. Instead they developed, as it were, a college
of witnesses and displayed them in the great trial scenes of the
pre-Passion narrative. For the weakness of the Epistle's ending they
substituted strength.

POSTSCRIPT 5:14–21

The concluding section of the Epistle gives the impression of im-
provisation and rhetorical haste. Verses 14–17 are a casuistical gloss
on v. 18 which offers the first of three summarising statements
about the believer's self-awareness and awareness of God described

(in reverse order) as the true God and eternal life. Verse 21 seems an extraordinarily offhand ending.

14–17. If a community has persuaded itself that anyone who belongs to it **does not sin**, indeed cannot sin (3:9), how should it deal with someone who is observed sinning a sin (as the Greek has it in v. 16, using a cognate accusative)? Already in 2:1–2 the writer has set out to persuade them not to sin, but, in case anyone does, Jesus Christ is his sponsor with the Father and the expiation of their sins. But how should a member of the community act if he discovers a fellow member sinning? Should he (to preserve the purity of the community) denounce him as no true Christian, or rebuke him and demand a penance in the style of Qumran? Cf. CD12: 'Every man who preaches apostasy under the dominion of the spirits of Satan should be judged according to the law relating to those possessed by a ghost or familiar spirit (viz. condemned to stoning; Lev. 20:27). But no man who strays so as to profane the Sabbath and the feasts shall be put to death; it shall fall to men to keep him in custody. And if he is healed of his error, they shall keep him in custody for seven years and he shall afterwards approach the Assembly' (Vermes, pp. 114f., Rabin, pp. 59f.)

Not so in the Johannine community: the discoverer should act as the sinner's sponsor and ask **God** to **give him life** (*RSV* is surely right, despite the careless phrasing, to indicate that the subject of *dōsei*, 'he will give', in v. 16 is God and not the petitioner). But will God readily grant such a request? Yes, because **if we ask anything according to his will, he hears us**. The writer refers back to the confidence already established in 3:22, 'we receive from him whatever we ask'—with a prudent qualifying phrase: here, **according to** the **will** of him who is 'faithful and just, and will forgive our sins and cleanse us from all unrighteousness' (1:9). Moreover, **if we know** (*ean* used incorrectly with the indicative *oidamen*, perhaps colloquially halfway between 'if we know' and 'since we know') **that he hears us in whatever we ask, we know that we have obtained the requests made of him** (presumably because we, unlike the sinful brother, 'Keep his commandments and do what pleases him'; 3:22). Thus, by the simple, generous intercession of its members, a community which in principle expects to be sinless is prevented from becoming censorious and painfully rigorous.

Unfortunately another qualification is now required. **All wrongdoing is sin** (see on 3:4), and some kinds of sinning go too far to be remedied by intercession. The writer distinguishes between **sin which is mortal** and **sin which is not mortal**. This translation, perhaps unintentionally, recalls the distinction well known in Catholic moral theology between mortal and venial sins. Mortal sin is 'a

deliberate act of turning away from God as man's last end by seeking
his satisfaction in a creature'; it involves the loss of sanctifying grace
and eternal damnation, though confession to a priest (or the desire
to confess) and an act of contrition are sufficient for obtaining God's
pardon. Venial sin disposes the soul to death but does not wholly
deprive it of sanctifying grace and, according to the theology of
Penance, there is no obligation to confess venial sins when resorting
to the Sacrament (*ODCC*, pp. 942, 1431). The Fathers based their
distinction on 1 Jn 5:16; Aquinas was the chief author of the modern
distinction.

Even if the Epistle's thought is remote from such teaching, the
writer's failure to explain his own distinction, and indeed to make
up his mind about sinning and sinlessness, made it necessary for
others to provide a suitable casuistry. He uses the phrases *hamartia
pros thanaton* and *hamartia mē pros thanaton* (*ou* instead of *mē* in v.
17, unless *ou* should be omitted, with a few Greek cursives and
some Latin, Syriac, and Coptic witnesses: *mē* was perhaps suggested by the author's sense of style after *ean tis idē*, and there can
be no difference of meaning between *mē* and *ou*). Some translations
talk unhelpfully of 'deadly sin' (*NEB*, *JB*); others of 'sin that leads
to death' (*GNB*, *NIV*). It is always a matter of conjecture what the
writer thought he was saying. By 'sin leading to death', did he
mean: (i) wrongdoing that ended in death, such as in the case of
Ananias and Sapphira (Ac. 5:1–11), or the deaths of those who
misused the Lord's Supper (1 C. 11:30)? or (ii) defiant rejection of
God's commandments (contrasted with accidental disobedience)
which is met with expulsion and presumably death (Num. 15:30f.;
Dt. 17:12) cf. Heb. 10:26f., which can offer no expiation but only
threats of death for those who 'sin deliberately after receiving the
knowledge of the truth'? or (iii) the Qumran adaptation of deliberate
and negligent transgressions of the Law of Moses, such that negli-
gence required temporary exclusion from the community and deliberate sin resulted in permanent exclusion (1QS 7.20–9.2; Vermes,
p. 86)? or (iv) a specially horrifying sin, suggested by the exaggerated revulsion from incest in *Jub.* 33:13, 18: 'it is unclean, and
there is no atonement for ever to atone for the man who has com-
mitted it, but he is to be put to death' (cf. 1 C. 5:1–5)? or (v) the
sin against the Holy Spirit which in Mk 3:29 and Lk. 12:10 is
attributed to the opponents of Jesus, but in Mt. 12:32, when understood in terms of Mt. 12:18–21, could well be a disastrous misjudgment by his adherents? or (vi) apostasy, as in Heb. 6:4–6, where
some have been enlightened, have tasted the heavenly gift and have
become partakers of the Holy Spirit, but crucify the Son of God on
their own account and hold him up to contempt?

Only the last of these comes near the situation of the Johannine community. Possibility (i) has no support in either Epistle or Gospel; (ii) is too archaic even for first-century Judaism, let alone a Christian group; (iii) is ruled out by the writer's commendation of intercession; (iv) cannot be attached to a Johannine obsession; and (v) could be held rather against the writer of the Epistle than against the dissidents who, if anything, overstressed the Holy Spirit. Possibility (vi) does not fit the Johannine community's situation but it comes closest to it. The dissident group, who rejected Jesus as Son of God and allowed no significance to his blood, had sinned a sin leading to death and therefore were excluded from the promise that a petition in their favour would at once be granted by God. It is not necessarily implied that they were beyond all recovery, but nothing is said about conditions on which they could return. Their sin led them to death, that is, it took them back into the world of darkness and hatred from which the community had been rescued by love of the brethren (3:14). Thus the writer's formula is intended to preserve the fallible existence of a non-sinning community without compromising his acute opposition to the dissidents.

The promise that God will grant the requests of believers plays a prominent part in the Farewell Discourses of the Gospel (see on 1 Jn 3:22). Its most absolute statement is found in Jn 16:24, 'Ask and you will receive', which has close affinities with Mt. 7:7f. It is a rash promise and invites numerous qualifications, as here (**if we ask anything according to his will**), and in 3:22: if we perform his commandments and do what pleases him. It is significant, however, that all the qualifications in the Gospel are attached to Jesus: 'whatever you ask the Father *in my name*' (15:16); 'if you abide in *me* and *I* in you, ask whatever you will, and it shall be done for you' (15:7). The references in Jn 16:23f., 26, suppose that the disciples have hitherto made their requests to Jesus but henceforth will make them *in the name of Jesus* directly to the Father. Even though their situation is changed by the departure of Jesus and the gift of the Spirit, God's willingness to grant requests is as much dependent on Jesus as it was before. Indeed, in 14:13f., when Jesus goes to the Father, 'whatever you ask in my name, *I will do it*, that the Father may be glorified in the Son; if you ask anything in my name, *I will do it*'. It is right to comment that 'Jesus is still the agent of the Father's will, even after his departure from the world' (Lindars, p. 476); but it is equally necessary to observe that the primacy of Jesus is being asserted against the important but secondary benefits of the Holy Spirit.

18–19. Verses 18–19*a* are a variant of 3:9. In the earlier statement, members of the community are preserved from sinning by the presence within them of the divine seed; but seeds do not always germinate and seedlings can be frail. So here the writer turns to external protection which he presents again in a memorable but ambiguous phrase: **any one born** (*gegennēmenos*) **of God does not sin, but He who was born** (*gennētheis*) **of God keeps him**. The aorist participle *gennētheis* could be a stylistic variant for the perfect participle *gegennēmenos*: if so, the statement would mean that someone born of God does not sin, but keeps himself (reading *auton*, 'him', as *hauton* or *heauton*, as in a long list of Greek manuscripts and some Fathers; Metzger, p. 719)—presumably keeps himself free from sin, or keeps hold of God (Houlden, p. 133). But that is precisely what, according to the preceding verses, the community member may fail to do. The writer is more likely to have meant that the community member, if he is true to his profession, does not sin inasmuch as the Son, who more eminently is born of God, keeps him from harmful contact with the Evil One (or with what is evil). A subtle shift has taken place from the inward disposition for sin to the external pressure of evil. The whole *kosmos* (see on 2:2), that is, the structure of human society, under the domination of evil (or the Evil One; see on 2:15f.) is set in opposition to the community comprising those born of God.

20–21. The community, having been separated from the world, is now distanced from the dissidents who claim that they truly know God without acknowledging Jesus Christ as his Son. **We know that the Son of God has come** (Greek *hēkei*, a verb with both perfect and present senses; here only in the Epistle, four times in the Gospel, especially Jn 8:42, 'I proceeded and came forth (*hēkō*) from God'). The consequences are twofold: (i) **he has given us understanding** (*dianoia*, only here in Johannine writings, may indicate insight or perception, though in LXX it frequently renders the Hebrew 'heart') **to know** (*hina* with the indicative in the Greek text of UBS, though subjunctive in Nestle-Aland, possibly no more than the identity in pronunciation of long and short *o*; but possibly the indicative suggests 'that we may indeed know'; cf. Marshall, p. 253, n. 44) **him who is true** (Greek *ton alēthinon*, to which a number of witnesses add *theon* to make sure that the reference is to God; and other witnesses change to *to alēthinon*, 'what is true'; Metzger, p. 719). The Son of God is portrayed as the revealer of the true God, or the genuine God in contrast to idols (cf. the 'true light' of 2:8 and Jn 1:9). This is to be read with a touch of defiance and polemic, as in Jn 17:3: 'this is eternal life, that they know thee the only true God, and Jesus Christ whom thou hast sent' (cf. Jn 7:28). For the important influence of 'knowing' in the Epistle, see on 2:3;

though it is nowhere else said or implied that the Son of God came
to provide knowledge.

Statements about the coming of the Son of God and the consequences of his coming are not easily reducible to a coherent pattern.
(i) In addition to 5:20 it is said that Jesus Christ *came* in the flesh
and *came* by water and blood (4:2 and 5:6, using respectively the
perfect and aorist of *erchomai*), but that describes the nature of his
coming (in opposition to dissident views) and says nothing directly
about its purpose or consequences. (ii) It is said that God *sent* his
Son into the world (a) that 'we should live by him', (b) to be 'the
expiation of our sins', and (c) to be 'the Saviour of the world' (4:9,
10, 14). With (a) may be associated the statement that 'eternal life
is in the Son' (5:11). With (b) and (c) belongs the statement that
'he is the expiation for our sins and not for ours only but also for
the sins of the whole world' (2:2), and presumably also 'the blood
of Jesus his Son cleanses us from all sin' (1:7). (iii) It is said that
the Son of God *was disclosed* to destroy the activities of the devil
(3:8), with which can be associated 'He who was born of God keeps
him, and the evil one does not touch him' (5:18).

In these three groups of statements the Son is introduced by a
verb in the past tense: he came, God sent him, he was disclosed,
though it is usually presupposed that there are present consequences
of the past action. (iv) So also there are in the statement that 'he
laid down his life for us' in 3:16, for that action is a model of how
we should behave towards the brethren. (v) Two further statements,
nominally translated by past tenses, refer to Jesus as born of God
(see on 5:1), and say that God has borne witness to the Son (see on
5:9). The perfect tense of the verbs indicates a continuing condition:
the Son is always related to the Father, and the inspired interpretation of the tradition bears testimony to him. (vi) Finally, there are
a few statements cast wholly in the present tense: 'we have an
advocate with the Father, Jesus Christ the righteous', 'Jesus is the
Christ', and 'you know that he is righteous' (2:1, 22, 29; 3:7). See
on 2:28 and 3:2 for the argument that the expected appearing and
coming refer to the Father, not the Son.

All these statements are polemical, i.e., they are used to develop
the writer's case against the dissidents. He is deeply disturbed that
they dismiss him who came in the flesh in favour of their experience
of the Spirit. If Jesus' example is to be discarded (see on 2:6), then
his death is no longer understandable as a re-definition of Christian
loving (statement iv). Hence he insists on the flesh and blood of
Jesus (statement i) and activates old cultic tradition about expiation
by blood (statement ii). Jesus is therefore the helper of the hard-
pressed sinner, his sponsor before God (statement vi)—Jesus, be it

noted, rather than the Holy Spirit for whom the dissidents may first have introduced the word 'paraclete'. If Jesus is sponsor before God, he may also give **understanding to know him who is true** by virtue of his relation to God (statement v). At the same time the writer widens his role beyond sponsorship of community members, and at full stretch Jesus becomes the life-giver, the world saviour (statement ii), and, with a revival of apocalyptic imagery (statement iii), the community's champion against the Evil One. In some such manner the christological statements can be brought together. Reflection suggests that the writer was not drawing upon a well-articulated christology, certainly not upon a gnostic redeemer mythology, but was plugging the gap left by the dissidents with whatever came to hand. It includes elements of christology which are more comprehensively accommodated in the Gospel.

We are in him who is true moves a step forward, in characteristic Johannine manner, from 'knowing' to 'being in' (see on 2:5f.); that is to say, we are in the true God inasmuch as we are **in his Son Jesus Christ**. The deepest level of awareness of God is achieved only by intimate communion with the Son.

The question then arises whether the next sentence adds a further statement about Jesus or is simply an emphatic repetition of what was previously said: **This is the true God and eternal life. This** (*houtos*) could certainly refer to its immediate antecedent (though it need not; cf. 2:22, 2 Jn 7) and most modern commentators think it does: 'it is fitting that at the climax of the Epistle . . . . full deity should be ascribed to Jesus' (Marshall, p. 254, n. 47). But this is the rather ragged ending of the Epistle, not its climax; and it would be surprising if the writer (who has been fighting the dissidents in order to give Jesus a secure function in the awareness of God) were now to ascribe full deity to him in a throw-away line when he has not previously even called him Lord. Either this is a secondary addition (for which there is no other evidence), or it puts a final emphasis on the writer's theme, such as is present in Jn 17:3: 'this is eternal life, that they know thee the only true God, and Jesus Christ whom thou has sent'.

The **true God** is set in sharp contrast to idols. That is not a Johannine word, except for Rev. 9:20, a piece of stock Jewish polemic against the images of the gods. The communities addressed in the Apocalypse were warned against eating food sacrificed to idols (*eidōlothuta*, Rev. 2:14, 20) and were treated to spirited condemnation of idolaters and other wicked persons (Rev. 21:8; 22:15); but nothing in the Epistle suggests that the community were attracted by traditional pagan religion or had failed to shake themselves free of it. In the Community Rule of Qumran the sons of light detest all unclean idols, but the words bear a rather general meaning. The most fearsome curses are uttered against anyone 'who enters the Covenant while walking among the idols of his heart' which appears to mean someone who becomes an initiate while having reservations about or objections to the obligatory rules (1QS 2.11–17; 4.5; Vermes, pp. 73f., 76; Leaney, p. 134).

So here, **idols** may mean no more than practices and convictions which the writer dislikes; but that suggestion scarcely accounts for the unexpected introduction of the word. It was probably intended as a finally wounding blow against the dissidents' attachment to God—in the writer's view a false God—and implies that they were a group that would share the Jewish detestation of idols. Thus the closing section of the Epistle consistently sharpens the opposition between the community and the dissidents while admitting a degree of toleration for loyal members of the community which could not survive on rigorist principles.

THE SECOND EPISTLE OF
JOHN

1–3. The writer of this letter tries his hand at an elaborate introduction. But he cannot properly manage the syntax and produces something that sounds rather effusive and pretentious—perhaps the result of anxiety. Like other *NT* letter writers, he adopts the oriental letter-style in its hellenised form (Lohse, p. 5) in which A announces himself, addresses B, and expresses some appropriate good wishes for him. In this letter, A formally addresses B in the third person, adds C, changes to the first person and indicates his love for B and C, then joins D to himself, changes to the first person plural and comes to an end with a confident but awkwardly attached statement about **the truth**; and then repetitively starts again with the promise of blessings from God for **us** and finally subsides with a loosely attached reference to **truth and love**. That pair of words forms a hendiadys: **truth** (see on 1 Jn 1:6) means the proper religious way to behave, which is in fact to exercise **love** (cf. **whom I love in truth**). This initial emphasis on **truth**, taken up in v. 4, is less to do with orthodoxy than with orthopraxy. A proper Christian community comprises those **who know the truth,** for the truth resides within the tradition of the community and will be their sufficient resource **for ever,** for it brings the godly benefits of **grace, mercy and peace.** That triad became conventional in the second phase of *NT* letter writing (1 Tim. 1:2; 2 Tim. 1:2) and need not here be treated too seriously.

Grace (*charis*), a fundamental component of Pauline teaching, though scarcely of Johannine (only Jn 1:14, 16, 17; and a variant reading in 3 Jn 4), means the divine generosity to unworthy and thankless people. **Mercy** (*eleos*), fairly common in *NT* but not elsewhere in John, appears frequently in LXX to render *ḥesed* (God's faithful care of his covenant people) and in general means God's compassion for needy and sinful people. **Peace** (*eirēnē*) plays a modest role in John, both as a standard greeting (Jn 20:19, 21, 26; 3 Jn 15) and as a consequence of Jesus' conquest of the world (Jn 14:27; 16:33). Both uses refer to the thought of total well-being. Even if the triadic formula is conventional, the attribution to God the Father and Jesus Christ the Father's Son is not, for it is intended as an immediate correction of erroneous views.

Who, however, is **the elder** who addresses **the elect lady and her children,** and who is she? There are two possibilities for the **lady.** (i) She may have been a particular woman, the mother of her own

children and the aunt of her sister's children (v. 13), her name
being, improbably, Electa (for that would be her sister's name too),
but possibly Kyria, corresponding to Martha in Aramaic. If so, she
is being warned not to give house-room to a group of deceivers, and
is encouraged to expect a visit from **the elder** who sends greetings
from her sister's children. But such a reading scarcely suits the
solemnity of the opening or the anxious concern with practice and
teaching in what follows. So (ii) the two elect sisters are Christian
communities who have a common interest in **the truth** (for that
figurative use of *kyria*, see AGB, s.v., 2; cf. 1 Pet. 5:13, 'she who
is in Babylon, who is likewise chosen', *syneklektē*). **Elect** is not
otherwise a Johannine word, except for a variant reading at Jn 1:34,
and for Rev. 17:14, 'those with him are called and chosen and
faithful'. The elect lady sounds like the self-conscious language of
a pietistic in-group.

Who then is **the elder** who is also named at the beginning of 3
Jn? The word *presbyteros* does not occur elsewhere in Johannine
writings, except for the twenty-four elders in Revelation. It may
signify an elderly man, or someone of an earlier generation, or a
senior member of the community with special responsibilities and
authority (AGB, s.v.). In Judaism the lay members of the Sanhedrin
were called elders, and the word could also be used for those who
were the sources of tradition (Mk 7:3, 'the tradition of the elders').
Within the Christian movement, at least during its second stage
even if not in its first Pauline stage, people with ruling authority
were called elders (1 Tim. 5:17; Tit. 1:5; Jas 5:14; 1 Pet. 5:1), and
Luke presented the picture of the church, both in Jerusalem and
elsewhere, as guided by elders (Ac. 11:30; 14:23; 15:2–23; 16:4;
20:17; 21:18). It is therefore possible that the elder was a person of
authority in some local Christian community.

What kind of authority must be determined by indications in the
letter. (a) The elder not only sends greetings from a sister community (13), but in some sense speaks on behalf 'us Christians', and
indeed of **all who know the truth** (1, 2). (b) With some formality
he addresses another local community, and speaks to them out of
love not authority (1, 4). He has much to write to them but hopes
to see them face to face (12). Thus several possibilities are left open,
and it is possible to conclude that 2 Jn would have done for more
than one community. (c) The writer uses mild threats and warnings
(8), lays down an instruction against receiving 'deceivers' (10), and
gives a ruling that even to greet a deceiver is to share 'his wicked
work' (11). (d) He bases his understanding of **the truth** on a commandment received from the Father (4), not a new commandment

but one held from the begining (5), and he stresses the need to remain in the teaching (9).

Thus the elder, whoever he was, regarded himself as a guardian of the tradition which he passed on without question or reformulation. His duty was to prevent the spread of error by inhibiting the entry of those who taught it and by raising the confidence of those who knew the truth. He is to be distinguished from the writer of 1 Jn by the secondary and over-anxious quality of what he writes, and is scarcely to be compared to the elders who provided Papias (c. AD 60–130), at some distance, with such interesting information about the disciples of the Lord (Eusebius, *H.E.* 3.39; Bruce, pp. 135f.; Bornkamm, *TWNT* VI, pp. 670ff.). He had read 1 Jn with little imaginative grasp, and somewhat uneasily did what he could to stop the rot.

4–6. I rejoiced greatly (as 3 Jn 3, cf. Phil. 4:10), like *NEB*, 'I was delighted', is an example of over-intense translation. The phrase is common in ordinary letters (MM, s.v. *chairō*) and should be rendered conventionally as 'I was very glad'. The elder had found out (*heurēka*, perfect tense), that some members of the community (partitive use of *ek*) were walking in **the truth** (an expression confined to 2 Jn and 3 Jn; on the figurative sense of walking, which *RSV* translates as **following**, see on 1 Jn 1:6, where Christians walk in the light). **Following the truth** (v. 4) has the same meaning as **follow his commandments** in v. 6; and **truth** again means the proper way to live. Why is it said that only **some** are **following the truth**? Possibly because others, even a majority, are not; possibly because the elder had encountered some but not others (cf. the embassy of 3 Jn 3); or, much more likely, because the elder is writing an all-purpose letter and is inclined to caution. The first component of **the truth** derives from what was **commanded by the Father**, namely, **that we love one another**. The elder thus reproduces one of the leading themes of 1 Jn, even to asserting that it is not **a new commandment** but one which the community has **had from the beginning** (cf. 1 Jn 2:7; 3:11, 23), though he misses the subtle reflection in 1 Jn 2:8 that the old commandment is after all a new commandment. Even so, his presentation is clumsy: **I beg you . . . . that we love one another** has an awkward ring, disguised only by the oddness of the intervening words. Verse 6*a* reverses the statement that to perform God's command is to practise love by saying that to love is to **follow his commandments**. This latter assertion has a parallel in Jn 14:15, 'If you love me, you will keep my commandments'; but the converse statements presented together seem unhelpfully circular. Finally, v. 6*b* is an awkward repetition: **this is the commandment, as you have heard from the beginning,**

that you should walk in it. The feminine pronoun 'it' (*autē*) would
naturally refer to the antecedent **commandment**, but *RSV* rescues
the elder from tautology by referring it to love, and *NEB* substitutes
what he might reasonably have said, namely, 'to be your rule of
life'. What is meant is clear enough, but it is not well expressed.

7–9. Now he introduces (with an inconsequential **For**, *hoti*) the
second component of the truth which is phrased on the model of 1
Jn 4:1–3 (though without reference to spirit) and 2:22–23 (see the
discussion of those passages; for **deceivers**, see 2:26). The *RSV*
translation is particularly apt: **men who will not acknowledge** (representing the *mē* rather than *ou* before the participle *homologountes*)
the coming of Jesus Christ in the flesh (ingeniously rendering the
present participle *erchomenon*, 'coming', instead of the perfect *elē-
lythōs*, 'having come', of 1 Jn 4:2). The misleading views of the
deceivers had little to do with docetism: their refusal, as the elder
makes plain, consisted of abandoning the teaching of Christ (*didachē tou Christou*). *RSV* and *NEB*, but not *GNB*, *JB*, and *NIV*,
translate *didachē* by **doctrine**, which in modern usage inevitably
suggests a formulated christology and implies an objective genitive
(teaching about Christ). But the genitive could equally be subjective
(teaching given by Christ), referring to Christ's teaching about love
both by his words and his actions.

If the **deceivers** are the dissidents of 1 John, they dispensed with
the example and testimony of Jesus in favour of the spirit. The
elder has at least grasped the importance of keeping hold of Jesus
as the means of access to the Father, and not of going ahead and
leaving Jesus and his teaching behind. He formulates his concern
in an antithetical couplet reminiscent of 1 Jn 2:23f.:

> **Anyone who goes ahead**
> **and does not abide in the** teaching **of Christ**
> **does not have God;**
> **he who abides in the** teaching
> **has both the Father and the Son.**

That this is an imitation of the formula of 1 Jn is suggested by
goes ahead (the only metaphorical use of *proagō* in *NT*), and by
'abiding in teaching' (the nearest parallel is Jn 8:31, 'abide in my
word'; in 1 Jn Christians abide in light and life, in the Father and
the Son, but not in teaching).

Before writing the formula, however, the elder has uttered his
warning and mild threat in a form that perplexed the copyists.
According to *RSV* he said: **Look to yourselves** (the only Johannine
use of *blepete* to signal a warning) **that you may not lose what you**

have worked for, but may win a full reward. All the verbs following *blepete* are referred to 'you', but there is a considerable though not impressive array of evidence for referring the second verb to 'we' (Metzger, p. 721, prefers it; so also Nestle-Aland). If so, *NEB* is right to translate 'that you may not lose all that we worked for' (similarly *RV, GNB, JB*); but the decision is exegetical, not textual. If the elder is thought to be defending his missionary converts from error, the change of person is reasonable; but the first section of the Epistle does not suggest that much can be deduced from such changes. It is better to decline the 'we' reading, and at the same time to reject the Byzantine text, which put all three verbs into the first person plural and is translated in *AV*.

10–11. This at least is clear: despite the primitive Christian tradition of hospitality (as one example, 'Practise hospitality ungrudgingly to one another', 1 Pet. 4:9) no one is to be received or even given a greeting if he is not a bearer of the teaching of Christ ('a bearer of' represents *pherei*; *RSV*, **bring**: there is no close parallel in AGB 4*a* to this use of *pherei*).

In some way he is a wicked person, and even to greet him is to share **his wicked work**. This sounds like the policy which Diotrephes follows in 3 Jn 9; so is Diotrephes the author of 2 Jn (Houlden, p. 147), or is the elder retaliating against Diotrephes? Such questions cannot be decided and are not important. But two comments can be made, one on the relation between 1 Jn and 2 Jn, and one on the policy advocated by the elder.

(i) 1 Jn is an attempt to restore the confidence of members of the Johannine community who had been disturbed by the departure of the dissidents and were perhaps still in part attracted by their views. The writer displays energy and tactical subtlety in dealing with the situation, first using material presented to him by a leadership group and then engaging his mind with the theological and moral issues. But 2 Jn, even in its short length, carries signs of secondary writing: a rather clumsy and heavy-handed style, the bare repetition of slogans, and the desire to prevent discussion rather than engage in it. Together with the surprisingly frequent non-Johannine turns of phrase, this suggests that the elder was not the writer of 1 Jn. It is likely that he had read 1 Jn and was using phrases from it, in a simplistic way, in order to hinder the spread of views which the dissidents had gone out into the world to propagate.

(ii) The elder's policy was to preserve the truth by denying recognition and entry to those who held erroneous views about Christ's teaching—not, it would seem, those who gave a divergent interpretation of the teaching but those who rejected it as no longer necessary. That is something more than a stock sectarian dispute. The dissidents believed that the community could now move into a new phase of its life in which the spirit replaced the coming of Jesus Christ in the flesh. The question at issue was the primacy of Christ or the spirit. The elder's defence of the truth was therefore directed to a fundamental question and not to a permissible variation of understanding. Since, in the early days, the Christian movement spread and maintained itself by constant interchange of visits from members of one community to another (cf. the travelling preachers and prophets of the possibly contemporaneous *Didache* 11–12), a decision had to be taken about visitors who wished to make a radical change in the community's convictions and therefore in its self-awareness. Was it necessary or indeed wise to repel the visitors? The action against them would become known and would spread knowledge of their errors. Was it taken for granted that error, if allowed in, would drive out the truth? Or was error dangerous because it contained some genuine awareness of God not well represented in the truth of the community's tradition? How could the elder know what to do for the best in a difficult situation for which there was little precedent? If 2 Jn displays his predicament, it also throws into relief the boldness of the more imaginative solution finally presented in John's Gospel.

12–13. The final greetings are closely similar to those in 3 Jn 12–13, though not verbally identical. They bind the two letters together: either one letter is an imitation of the other (Bultmann, p. 115), or more probably, both are by the same author. He prefers talking to writing, and may himself have sensed the awkwardness of his efforts. He adopts a final phrase from 1 Jn 1:4, and closes with formal greetings.

THE THIRD EPISTLE OF JOHN

1–4. **The elder** (see on 2 Jn 1) writes to an unknown **Gaius** (a common name which occurs elsewhere in 1 C. 1:14 and twice in Acts). He calls him **beloved**, addresses him thus three times in vv. 2, 5 and 11, and says that he loves him **in the truth** (cf. 2 Jn 1). To **love in the truth** does not mean to love genuinely rather than in pretence (what would be the point of saying that? it would only arouse suspicion); it means to love within the circle of those who practise the truth (see on 1 Jn 1:6). Already the main purpose of the letter is in view, namely to certify **Gaius** as belonging to that circle.

The vocative use of **beloved** is not uncommon in *NT*, especially in the later writings, and is a striking feature (in the plural) of 1 Jn. It is in general a persuasive form of address, used when some feature of religious thought needs explanation (1 Jn 2:7; 3:2, 21), or some action is required (1 Jn 4:1, 7, 11). In this Epistle it is persuasive in vv. 5 and 11, but purely formal in v. 2 where it introduces a neat version of the standard good wishes (which is the meaning of **I pray**) at the beginning of a hellenistic letter (cf. 'above all I pray that you may have good health, faring prosperously unharmed by the evil eye'; MM, p. 268). *RSV* seems to miss the point: **that all may go well with you and that you may be in health** as indeed **it is well with your soul** (*RSV* substitutes **I know** for 'as indeed'). The word **soul** occurs in Jn and 1 Jn and always means physical life, except Jn 12:27, where it refers to inward life. Here, however, it refers to that function of human existence that is concerned with morals and the things of God. So Philo in *Who is the Heir* 285 says that when all goes well in our outward circumstances the results are well-being and good reputation; when all is well with our body we have health and strength, and with our soul we have delight in the virtues (Schnackenburg, pp. 321f.; Schweizer, *TWNT* IX, pp. 651f.). Hence the elder is hoping that the physical health of Gaius is as good as his moral and spiritual state; i.e., he undoubtedly belongs to the circle of those who practise **the truth**. This is explicitly stated three times in vv. 3a and 4 (cf. the repetitions of **truth** in vv. 8 and 12).

For **I greatly rejoiced**, see on 2 Jn 4; the verb is reinforced by **no greater joy** in v. 4, though there is manuscript evidence of a desperate scribal effort to introduce a more theological word into the Epistle by replacing *charan*, **joy**, with *charin*, 'grace' (Metzger, p.

723). The favourable report of some visiting or returning brethren is recorded, and the elder gives his enthusiastic support to Gaius whom he includes among **my children**. He extends a father's protection over him; indeed he acts as sponsor or paraclete (see on 1 Jn 2:1), accompanied by **the brethren** as additional supporters. It now becomes plain that this Epistle is in fact a testimonial, one of those 'letters of recommendation' to which Paul refers in 2 C. 3:1. It is in fact both a certificate of approval for Gaius and of disapproval for Diotrephes. That explains two odd features: the elder's failure to give his own name (he is writing formally not personally) and his omission of the standard greeting after v. 1 (he is writing in effect 'to whom it may concern').

5–8. The brothers already mentioned reported to the community (*ekklēsia*, a non-Johannine word except in Rev.) the helpfulness of Gaius when they had **set out for his sake** (*hyper tou onomatos*, on behalf of the Name); cf. Rom. 1:5, 'to bring about the obedience of faith for the sake of his name among the gentiles'. Gaius received the travelling missionaries and sent them forward without calling on gentile charity. The elder gives his approval even though in receiving visiting missionaries who are strangers there is always a risk, for they may be the bearers of erroneous views (2 Jn 9–11). But what Gaius decides is dependable (*pistos* in v. 5; *RSV*'s translation **it is a loyal thing** misses the point, which is: 'You are acting dependably in whatever service you render to the brethren, even if they are strangers'). He is doing what Christians ought to do, and in this way they became **fellow workers in the truth**. In other words, the elder solves the difficult problem he has created in 2 Jn by putting the decisions on to Gaius.

9–10. Now he turns on **Diotrephes** who was all too willing, it seems, to take decisions. Exactly what the elder intends, however, is not clear, for he says **I have written something to the church; but Diotrephes . . . . does not** admit us. The same verb (*epidechomai*) in v. 10 means to admit someone to the community; so in v. 9 it may indicate a refusal to accept the elder's authority (*RSV* understanding 'us' as 'me'), or to have anything to do with the elder and his friends (*NEB, NIV*). Whichever it is, there is clearly a struggle for power between the elder (represented in the church by Gaius) and Diotrephes. It has been suggested that Diotrephes suppressed the letter which the elder wrote, or that the letter has been lost; but that is to read too much logical progression into the elder's phrasing (as many scribes did, and tried to produce a smoother statement; see Metzger, p. 723). He probably intends to say that he made his wishes known in a note (*JB*), namely, 2 Jn; and that Diotrephes took it into his head to carry out the process of exclusion to the disadvantage of the elder's protégé. The elder had little love for writing letters, and must have wished that he had settled these matters by a visit. In a half-hearted way he threatens a visit when he **will bring up what he is doing**; for the moment he condemns Diotrephes for liking **to put himself first** (*philoprōteuōn*, perhaps a verb invented from the adjective; 'power-hungry', Houlden, p. 149), for his mindless outpouring (*phlyareō*, for which *RSV* uses the archaic **prating**) of wicked accusations against the elder and his group, and for excluding **the brethren** (presumably Gaius and his group) and those who support them from the church.

It is clear from the impotent strength of this language that Diotrephes held the dominant position. Since he is not denounced for abandoning or advancing beyond 'the truth', it must be concluded that he could not be faulted on that score. Perhaps indeed his fault was to be more rigorous than the elder; but it is certainly difficult to give him the role of arch-heretic (as is done by Bauer, p. 93). Nor is it easy to regard Diotrephes as the monarchical bishop upholding legitimate ecclesiastical tradition against the elder who was advancing the novelties of Christian gnosticism and so posing a threat to nascent catholicism (Käsemann (1957): the elder is a member of Diotrephes' group of presbyters, has been excommunicated though he still keeps his title, and is too much hampered by his gnostic views to mention them in 3 Jn). The suggestion that Diotrephes was the first monarchical bishop, i.e., the ruling authority in a single community, goes back to Harnack in 1897. He saw him opposed by itinerant missionaries deriving their authority from the elder who was leader of a missionary organisation. In various forms the view is still put forward (Bornkamm, *TWNT* VI, pp. 670f.; cf. Houlden, p. 153; Marshall, p. 89), though others would see in Diotrephes no more than a self-appointed demagogue (Bruce, p. 152, who refers to Dodd, p. 164: either the first 'monarchical bishop' known to history in the province of Asia, or a symptom of the disease which the quasi-apostolic ministry of monarchical bishops was intended to relieve).

It may be true that the loosely-related component communities within the Johannine orbit were beginning to assert their independence of tradition-bearing figures like the elder and were hoping to go their own way in theology and organisation; but two considerations tell against a confident recognition of Diotrephes as the leader of a successful bishops' revolt. (i) The view is plausible only if it can be shown that the Johannine Epistles were written later than the Gospel. In this commentary that view is not accepted, but the Epistles are regarded as having contributed to the composition of the Gospel which shows 'no interest in hierarchy, order or organisation in the Church' (Houlden, p. 17). (ii) The very fact that 2 Jn and 3 Jn were preserved suggests that the elder, despite his disadvantages, was in the end successful. Therefore either Diotrephes was not a prototype monarchical bishop, or the experiment failed.

11. This letter of commendation and condemnation has kept strictly to its purpose; but, since it is to be presented to a Christian community, a stock piece of moral advice is thought to be appropriate, strengthened by a moralising reference to God composed in the familiar couplet style. It underlines the religious origin of the judgments that have been recorded.

12. Demetrius, perhaps the bearer of the letter, is authenticated as a proper agent of the truth, thus reintroducing the theme with which the letter began.

13–14. See on 2 Jn 12–13.

15. 'The disciples are addressed from a peculiar esoteric aspect as "friends" in Jn 15:14f., and 3 Jn 15 shows that this address is used as the most intimate self-designation of the "brethren" among themselves' (Käsemann (1968), p. 31).

INDEX OF BIBLICAL PASSAGES, APOCRYPHA AND JEWISH WRITINGS

Old Testament and Apocrypha

Gen.	4:1–16	110
	14:18	139
Exod.	4:9	137
	33:11	103
	33:20	103
	34:6–7	53
Lev.	4:1–5	60
	8:1–10:20	60
	17:3–14	59
	17:11	60
	19:2	101
	19:17	113
	20:27	142
Num.	15:30f.	143
	20:11	137
	35:33	60
Dt.	4:12	127
	6:4	124
	13:1–5	119
	14:1	99f.
	17:6	138
	17:12	143
	19:15	138
	30:11	133
	32:4	54
1 Sam.	15:25	105
	25:28	105
1 Kg.	21:10	139
	22:19	103
	22:21–23	91
Ezr.	9:15	54
Neh.	9:33	54
Ps.	2:7	98
	7:1–17	53f.
	10:18	54
	11:7	103
	17:15	103
	31	54
	36:5–10	48, 54
	43:3	48
	71:15f.	54
	89:14–15	48
	116:5	54
	119:137f.	54, 61
	143:1	54
Prov.	21:24	75
Isa.	6:1	103
	24:13	96
	45:21–24	54
	52:7	84
	55:7	50
	59:13	91
	61:1	83
	61:2–3	84
Jer.	13:25	91
	28	119
Dan.	9:9–19	53
	9:25	84
	9:27	80
Hos.	1:10	100
Jl	2:32	101
Am.	7:2	96
	7:7	103
	9:1	103
Mic.	1:2	140
Hab.	1:13–17	72
Mal.	3:5	140
Tob.	4:3	96
	4:6	49
	6:17	96

Jewish Writings

INDEX OF ANCIENT WRITINGS

INDEX OF MODERN WRITERS

INDEX OF SUBJECTS